# Beyond the Classroom Walls

# Beyond the Classroom Walls

## Imagining the Future of Education, from Community Schools to Communiversities

Bertram C. Bruce

ROWMAN & LITTLEFIELD
*Lanham • Boulder • New York • London*

Published by Rowman & Littlefield
An imprint of The Rowman & Littlefield Publishing Group, Inc.
4501 Forbes Boulevard, Suite 200, Lanham, Maryland 20706
www.rowman.com

86-90 Paul Street, London EC2A 4NE, United Kingdom

Copyright © 2022 by Bertram C. Bruce

*All rights reserved.* No part of this book may be reproduced in any form or by any electronic or mechanical means, including information storage and retrieval systems, without written permission from the publisher, except by a reviewer who may quote passages in a review.

British Library Cataloguing in Publication Information Available

**Library of Congress Cataloging-in-Publication Data**

Names: Bruce, Bertram C., author.
Title: Beyond the classroom walls : imagining the future of education, from community schools to communiversities / Bertram C. Bruce.
Description: Lanham : Rowman & Littlefield, [2022] | Includes index. | Summary: "Provides a coherent account of how schooling can and should relate to learning beyond the classroom walls"—Provided by publisher. Identifiers: LCCN 2022023342 (print) | LCCN 2022023343 (ebook) | ISBN 9781475867114 (cloth) | ISBN 9781475867121 (paperback) | ISBN 9781475867138 (epub)
Subjects: LCSH: Community and school. | Communication in education. | Education—Aims and objectives.
Classification: LCC LC215 .B74 2022 (print) | LCC LC215 (ebook) | DDC 371.19—dc23/eng/20220623
LC record available at https://lccn.loc.gov/2022023342
LC ebook record available at https://lccn.loc.gov/2022023343

*To friends in Nepal who have shown me how
learning occurs in every aspect of life*

# Contents

| | |
|---|---|
| Foreword | ix |
| Preface | xiii |
| Acknowledgments | xix |
| Introduction | xxi |

**PART I: COMMUNICATION AND EDUCATION** — 1

1. Models of Communication — 3
2. Schooling and Society — 19

Profile: Claudia Șerbănuță — 29

3. Beyond the Walls of Formal Education — 33

**PART II: EDUCATION IN CRISIS** — 45

4. Crises in Education — 47
5. A Dreadful Crisis — 63

**PART III: LEARNING IN THE WILD** — 75

Profile: Caroline Haythornthwaite — 77

6. Learning Online — 81

Profile: Ching-Chiu Lin — 95

7. Community Engagement through Work — 99

## PART IV: THE THIRD MISSION — 107

Profile: Ebru Aktan — 109

8  Community Schools — 111

Profile: Dave Leake — 127

9  Precursors of the Communiversity — 131

## PART V: COMMUNIVERSITY — 143

Profile: Udgum Khadka — 145

10  Ruptures of Community Engagement — 147

Profile: Ann Peterson-Kemp — 159

11  Community as Curriculum — 163

Conclusion: "Walk Beside" versus "Talk To" — 175

Glossary — 183

Index — 187

About the Author — 191

# Foreword

This is a book that classroom educators and school administrators will love to read. Chip Bruce brings us new ways of thinking about education along with the stories we need to hear about experiments and programs that encourage meaningful collaboration. Together, the thinking and the stories provide a foundation for visions and vistas of what schooling may become. Bruce helps us see beyond the obstacles and inertia of educational systems that have been in place for far too long. He gives us examples and case studies that will stimulate us to work to conceive new possibilities and make them actual. This is a book that educators need to read because it gives us hope for change. It is the kind of book I needed early in my teaching career.

One of the many challenges I faced early in my high school teaching career was the problem of grading. As a teacher of writing, I wanted to help my students gain control of their meaning, and I knew that the most effective method for growth and improvement was to develop the habit of revision. I wrote comments, set priorities, named the next steps, and encouraged follow-up conversations. But I also assessed a grade, and in far too many cases, students paid attention to only that letter. Grading stood in the way of much that I wanted to accomplish with my students, yet my job description demanded that I assess grades. I tried many things to surmount the problem, but the basic contradiction remained. I was trying to draw students into writing as a process by helping them see what they had written in a new way—re*vision*. They were looking at the grade as a finality or at best an obstacle that turned them away from any further effort—*re*vision, meaning, "not again." The best I could hope for in this situation, a hope I shared with each of my classes, was that my comments and suggestions made the grade transparent: you could see through the grade the ways in which the writing achieved or struggled with the assigned task.

I knew I was in a box, but I couldn't think of any effective alternative. One of my colleagues decided to assess no grades at all on any work, but at the end of the semester, he still had to report a grade. When I asked students about their experience with this teacher, they were either bemused or frustrated by what they saw as a quirk that still ended with a grade. I knew that many of my colleagues struggled with grades, but the consensus among them was that the best a teacher can do is to develop the reputation among students of being hard but fair.

At a conference I attended in the late 1980s, Ed Yeomans introduced a story of transformation and liberation that he called "the best kept secret in American education." Yeomans was for many years the principal of the Shady Hill School in Cambridge, Massachusetts. The secret he let us know was an experiment that proved how schools could thrive in the absence of grades. The Eight-Year Study began in 1932 with thirty high schools, both public and private. The big idea was to encourage experimentation in program and pedagogy by removing all external standards of evaluation. Under the leadership of the Progressive Education Association, 200 colleges and universities agreed to release student applicants from the participating schools from reports of grades as well as all standardized tests for 4 years. The program proved so successful that after four years, the program was extended for another four years. The institution of a draft at the beginning of World War II put an end to the program, but reports of the participating schools and the success of students from those schools were impressive. Yeomans was right: the Eight-Year Study was so secret that I was surprised to discover that my own school had been one of the participating institutions.

Learning the secret opened new vistas of possibility. The way to resolve contradictions was not through accommodation but through cooperative effort, and not just cooperation among individual teachers, but institutional cooperation as well. A new Eight-Year Study was not in the cards, but learning about what schools had done during those years encouraged me to find ways to work collaboratively both within my school and with other institutions in my community. The Eight-Year Study inspired me to work on programs that engaged me and my students with community organizations and with students and teachers from other schools. The secret that Yeomans revealed was not just about the successes of a bygone era; it was also about creating institutional structures to give life and purpose to our schools.

Chip Bruce unites the broad international experience of community education with a deep understanding of educational theory. He seeks an education that calls on the fullness of the human being. He has the highest regard for what school can be, but he also knows how little schools as they are presently configured have been able to accomplish. We need to change not just one or two things about school: if we want our schools to flourish, we need to change the entire system of schooling. The imperative here is not new, nor are the forces that militate so powerfully against any effort to alter the system so long in place, a system that thrives on separation. It is not only the separations of class, race, and ethnic origin that bedevil meaningful education but also the separation of the school from daily life that is fundamental to the inertia and the failure of our schooling practices. Despite the many ballyhooed efforts at school reform and accountability that have commanded public attention and demanded great expense over the past fifty years, the emphasis on scalable models, test scores, and outcomes has not produced any meaningful improvements in the quality of school life for most of our children.

Bruce proposes new ways for us to think about and plan for meaningful change in education. The beauty of his approach is that he presents not only arguments but examples. Integrating school life with community life is the goal, but the integration responds to local and specific circumstances. Integration is both means and end, a Deweyan pragmatism for the modern age. Bruce recalls Dewey's efforts to bring the school and the community together in the concept as well as the activity of an experience. As Dewey noted a century and more ago, the failure of schooling is the failure of isolation, transmission, and preparation. When we isolate the school from community life, we erect more than walls of a building: we erect artificial barriers that make the school irrelevant to the outside world. When we consider the task of school as the transmission of the known to a rising generation, we demean learning, stifle curiosity, and reward passivity and obedience. When we tell our students that the value in what they learn lies in what school prepares them to do later on, we tell students that what they are doing in school in the present is fundamentally meaningless.

Bringing school and community together demands what Dewey called "reconstruction." Teaching and learning become dynamic and interactive as school walls become permeable membranes. To achieve that permeability, we need to rethink the ways in which communication occurs. Bruce grounds that new thinking in a brief but rigorous discussion of communication theory. His integrative model of schooling emerges from communication that he calls "transactive," a shared production of meaning that transcends any particular message or response. This is a reconstruction that responds to the actors and institutions in a particular place at a particular time. A commitment to a model of transactive schooling is a commitment to practice. And this is precisely where Bruce's work is so compelling.

Bruce illustrates the range of transactive schooling in a breathtaking variety of institutional examples and individual profiles from many countries. A new educational model is important to understand, but if we are ever to change our patterns of schooling, we need to invoke the power of narrative. Bruce does this in two ways: descriptions of institutional practices and profiles of the individual creators who have found ways to integrate school and community. This powerful combination provides the kind of encouragement that educators seeking change have always needed.

Andy Kaplan, Editor, *Schools: Studies in Education*,<br>
published by the University of Chicago Press in<br>
Association with the Francis W. Parker School

# Preface

I was fortunate to have a childhood with its occasional crises, but on the whole a protected, white, middle-class existence. The streets were safe; neighbors were friendly; and opportunities to play and learn occupied my time. The realities of poverty, racism, and strife had little impact on my young mind.

School for me was an unwelcome diversion from living. I developed literacy through reading, math through games, and science through exploring nature around me. I thought that experience through daily life was a better teacher than what I found in the classroom. The latter seemed boring to me, repetitious, and focused more on performance than real learning.

Despite being anti-school, I was a bit of a nerd about facts. As a nine-year-old, I had a chart of the orders of insects. As I recall, there were twenty-plus orders identified at that time; today there are twenty-nine.[1] I memorized all of the orders, with examples and the criteria for including a particular specimen in an order. But I would have lost interest if that were as far as it went.

What kept me going was an insect collection, which I could display and share with family and friends. I needed screening, cotton, and carbon tetrachloride from the hardware store to make a killing jar (itself obtained from our family kitchen); Homasote, cigar boxes, pins, and paint for mounting specimens; cheesecloth, wire, and a dowel to make a butterfly net; and other such items from various other places. Assembling all of that involved drawing on the kindness of family members, storekeepers, and friends.

I enrolled in classes on insects at the Children's Museum, which included collecting expeditions in the Botanical Gardens and tours of the museum collections. These activities and others kept me in close contact with a community of fellow collectors and supporters. It was clear that the insect order project was about participating in the community, not the accumulation of facts.

Over time, I came to see that I had missed a lot that the school, or later the university, offered. Direct experience was essential, but formal education offered the chance to extend that to new levels. I could learn the dinosaur orders without needing a dinosaur net to capture specimens. One might argue that I could have learned about them through fossils and geological formations, but practically speaking, my route lay through books and formal instruction.

Ironically, for someone initially so anti-school, I went as far as I could in formal learning and spent a lifetime teaching in colleges and universities, schools, workshops, and other venues. I was drawn to books such as *Teaching as a Subversive Activity*, *Deschooling Society*, *Summerhill*, *How Children Fail*, *Run School Run*, *Pedagogy of the Oppressed*, and others, which in sum reflected my own view that something was seriously lacking in formal schooling. If asked to choose the ideal of education, I would definitely have placed daily life above the classroom, but I thought that the classroom could be changed to reflect more of what I saw outside of school.

I was inspired by teachers such as Gwladys Spencer. She had taught a course in audiovisual materials in my Library Science program at the University of Illinois, but a half century earlier. She clearly saw that audiovisual materials were more than simply devices for delivering facts. More striking still is that she included "pantomimes, playlets, pageants, puppet shows, shadow plays" and "trips, journeys, tours, visits." Audiovisual materials should be conceived as opportunities for enhancing experiences, rather than simply as media for transmitting information.

I endeavored to create a learning community. When that succeeded, students seemed to learn much more and to enjoy the experience. I was happy with my teaching. Failures reminded me how important a learning community can be. The learning community perspective extends beyond the idea of learning as individual sensemaking, instead emphasizing the view that learning is constructing knowledge with others.[2] In a learning community, students learn from each other and I learned as well.

I was surprised to learn that having a classroom or school learning community was not enough. When learning in the classroom is insulated from daily life, its value is circumscribed. Students could share their life experiences, but that indirect connection meant that we missed many opportunities for learning. A description of a field trip was not a field trip. On the other hand, learning could not be only field trips, no matter how meaningful they might be.

It became clear to me that the issue was not how to choose between daily life and the classroom, but how to draw the best from each and connect them to one another. I realized that for me, and for many students, formal learning was so abstracted from life that it held little meaning. The school failed to provide handholds for importing outside experience or opportunities to apply what was being taught.

As one example of many, it is no wonder that many adults hate mathematics. Despite studying it for twelve or more years in the classroom, they find themselves flummoxed by basic calculations, incapable of making reasonable estimates, deaf to statistics, uninterested in the history of numbers, and, perhaps worst of all, unable to find pleasure in thinking mathematically and thereby losing the ability to learn.

What applies to mathematics learning holds true for any area of the curriculum. All too often, the principal learning for some students is that they don't like science, or find history boring, hate foreign language study, or don't like to read. The focus on facts and narrow assessments means that for many, schooling is something to be endured, not enjoyed.

In the early 1980s, my colleagues and I developed a project called *Quill*,[3] which was designed to teach writing to K-12 students in a way that expanded their sense of wonder, not suppressed it.[4] Although *Quill* was classroom-based, we wanted the student activities to link to daily life. At that time, there were many curricula and software to teach components of writing—vocabulary, grammar, punctuation, and so on—and even prompts and scoring rubrics for the production of full texts. But these tended to be abstracted from real life. They left out the most crucial aspects of writing, such as purpose and communication with a real audience.

As an alternative to sterile lessons, we worked with teachers to develop writing activities with a real purpose and audience in mind. For example, Sister Judy Tralnes was a middle school teacher of indigenous students in the village of Holy Cross, Alaska. She considered the village community and audience to be a source of legitimate purposes, but her ultimate goal was to help her students feel a sense of power over their lives, something that had been lost due to neocolonialism:

> One thing that struck me again and again while teaching in Holy Cross was the sense of powerlessness among the people. . . . I was determined to help the youngsters that I taught to become more aware of their own personal power, more aware of their impact on one another and their possible impact on the world. I hoped that they could come to a real sense of achievement and experience the rewards of their own accomplishments.[5]

She and the students decided to create a brochure about Holy Cross. Students researched and wrote sections on topics such as population: "Holy Cross has about 275 people; most are Athabascan Indians and Yup'ik Eskimos. There are also some white and black people. Everyone here speaks English."[6] They also discussed clothes, architecture, history, and the school itself.

The brochure became a gift to the community. It was also a "Chamber of Commerce brochure" which could be sent to classrooms in the lower forty-eight when they wrote to ask for information about the village with an interesting name in the seeming middle of nowhere. Through the Holy Cross brochure, Sister Judy started from her life's purpose to help others, particularly to help students feel empowered. Writing, with an authentic purpose and audience, was one way to do that.

I was educated through *Quill* and other such projects. I learned that the classroom and daily life could be linked. More than that, a mutually transforming relationship could develop: The Holy Cross brochure was an opportunity for the students to learn important skills, but more, to experience purpose and efficacy in their lives. At the same time, it contributed to the growth of the community, helping all residents understand more about their village and neighbors.

Over time, there were many such projects in areas such as reasoning under uncertainty (using probability and statistics), investigative science, and reading. Along the way, I became entranced by the community of Paseo Boricua in the Humboldt Park area of Chicago.[7] It is a fifty-year experiment in connecting the classroom and daily life. Chapter 11, "Community as Curriculum," presents that work in more detail.

A closely related project was Youth Community Inquiry (YCI).[8] In that, youth used digital media to address problems in their own communities. For example, in rural Illinois, students used GIS/GPS technology to map historical sites and cemetery locations in their community as they learned about local changes in relationship to national currents of change. In an urban setting, students studied the history of the community by interviewing older residents, mapped community assets, and created videos, websites, and flyers to tell their stories. YCI drew inspiration from Paseo Boricua and other ongoing community building efforts.

Over the last five or six years, I've been working with colleagues in Nepal on progressive education practices in both formal and informal education, at all age levels. This has involved several two-month-long stays in Nepal in which I advised, but even more learned from Nepali projects. During those visits, I saw how makerspaces could make learning more tangible and fun for students, while also helping to link classroom and outside community.[9] I saw how online mapping could address societal needs (e.g., for earthquake resilience) and also foster the development of civic intelligence among students.[10]

One aspect of that work is the "Integrated Course" for undergraduates in a business program. Analysis of the first iteration of that course reveals much about both the rewards of classroom and daily life learning and the challenges of making it work.[11] This is discussed more in chapter 10, "Ruptures of Community Engagement."

As I reflect on these experiences, it becomes clear to me that meaningful learning emerges not from the formal classroom alone, nor solely from lived experience in the world, but from bringing these approaches together in a productive relationship. The book shows many ways that this can be done.

## BIBLIOGRAPHIC NOTE

References to John Dewey's writing are to *The Collected Works of John Dewey, 1882–1953*, edited by Jo Ann Boydston (Carbondale and Edwardsville: Southern Illinois University Press, 1969–1991). SIU Press publishes this in three series: *The Early Works* (EW), *The Middle Works* (MW), and *The Later Works* (LW). For example, LW 13:29 refers to *The Later Works*, volume 13, page 29.

## NOTES

1. Debbie Hadley, "A Guide to the 29 Insect Orders," *ThoughtCo*, https://www.thoughtco.com/a-guide-to-the-twenty-nine-insect-orders-1968419 (accessed January 9, 2022).
2. Chris Watkins, "Classrooms as Learning Communities: A Review of Research," *London Review of Education* 3 (2005): 47–64.
3. *Quill* (1982–) comprised Apple II-based software including a word processor, an email system, planning tools for writing, and a library program. There was also an activity guide, an online community for teachers, and other components.
4. Bertram C. Bruce and Andee Rubin, *Electronic Quills A Situated Evaluation of Using Computers for Writing in Classrooms* (Hillsdale, NJ: Lawrence Erlbaum, 1993).
5. Ibid: 106.
6. Ibid: 107.
7. Chaebong Nam, "Technology as Connected and Critical Learning Practice," in *International Handbook of Progressive Education*, edited by Mustafa Yunus Eryaman and Bertram C. Bruce (New York: Peter Lang, 2015), 419–36; René Antrop-González, "This School Is My Sanctuary: The Pedro Albizu Campos Alternative High School," *Centro Journal* 15, no. 2 (January 1, 2003): 232–55.
8. Bertram C. Bruce, Ann Peterson Bishop, and Nama Raj Budhathoki, eds., *Youth Community Inquiry: New Media for Community and Personal Growth* (New York: Peter Lang, 2014); Chris Ritzo, Chaebong Nam, and Bertram C. Bruce, "Building a Strong Web: Connecting Information Spaces in Schools and Communities," *Library Trends*, September 11, 2009, 1–13.
9. https://www.karkhana.asia/.
10. Kshitiz Khanal, Nama Raj Budhathoki, and Nancy Erbstein, "Filling OpenStreetMap Data Gaps in Rural Nepal: A Digital Youth Internship and

Leadership Programme," *Open Geospatial Data, Software and Standards* 4, no. 1 (December 2019): 12.

11. Raunak Chaudhari, Smriti Karanjit Manandhar, and Bertram C. Bruce, "Realities of Implementing Community Based Learning during Lockdown: Lessons from a Troubled Journey," *Schools: Studies in Education* 19, no. 1 (Spring 2022): 109–36.

# Acknowledgments

Even a casual reading of this book should show that I am indebted to many excellent teachers both in the classroom and in communities of all sorts. My only hope is that I have been a successful student under their guidance.

I'd like to give a special thanks to Andy Kaplan for the foreword and for his comments on the manuscript. Also, to those who invested their energy and time to produce their profiles to be used in the book. They also commented on the manuscript in helpful ways: Claudia Șerbănuță, Caroline Haythornthwaite, Ching-Chiu Lin, Ebru Aktan, David Leake, Udgum Khadka, and Ann Peterson-Kemp.

The writing was greatly improved by insightful comments from other readers including Brian Drayton, Leigh Estabrook, Walter Feinberg, George Hein, Maureen Hogan, Shihkuan Hsu, Andy Kaplan, Kevin Leander, Jim Levin, Allan Luke, Wojciech Malecki, Alex Rath, and Martin Wolske.

This book could not have been written at all without the steadfast support from my immediate family, Susan, Emily, and Stephen. They each gave valuable guidance on the manuscript and more significantly kept me going through rough times.

# Introduction

> The ideal of using the present simply to get ready for the future contradicts itself. It omits, and even shuts out, the very condition by which a person can be prepared for his future. We always live at the time we live and not at some other time, and only by extracting at each present time the full meaning of each present experience are we prepared for doing the same thing in the future.
> —John Dewey, *Experience and Education*[1]

One cannot delve far into the discourse on education without hearing about preparation for the future. This may be about preparing for tomorrow's quiz, elementary school students preparing for middle school, middle school students preparing for high school, high school students preparing for college, or any student at any level preparing for work outside of school. Education is thus conceived as ephemeral, something to do simply to prepare for real life beyond the academy. Above all, the classroom is portrayed as distinct from daily life.

The epigraph from Dewey questions the very idea of learning as preparation for the future. It goes further to highlight the unhelpful dichotomy of classroom versus daily life in our discourse about education. On the one hand, we equate education with *schooling*, with fully defined learning objectives, well-tested methods, and attention to detail. This promises an inexorable accumulation of new knowledge, as long as one follows all the rules. Imagine the learning shown in figure 0.1. The boys shown there are expected to benefit from carefully chosen books, guided lessons, and learning in a social context.

On the other hand, we envision *experience* as the best teacher—the more painful the stronger the lesson. In this case, education is a by-product of

**Figure 0.1 Boys Reading in a Primary Classroom.** *Source*: US Department of Education, CC Attribution 2.0 Generic.

daily life. We get lost, find our way or not, and in the process, may or may not germinate knowledge about the world we inhabit. Figure 0.2 shows a girl encountering a novel experience in which a fish and her Peruvian-style hat interact. Whatever she may learn, it appears quite distinct from ordinary classroom learning.

These models of learning, formal schooling and everyday experience, are often seen as exclusive, or at best useful only for specific, narrow purposes. Dewey asks us to consider that extracting the full meaning of each present experience is a form of life that brings these together. Experience is vital, but formal learning helps us extract the meaning that enriches our lives.

## FORMAL INSTRUCTION VERSUS THE SCHOOL OF HARD KNOCKS

Some people have strong opinions about these modes and equally strong opinions about the obtuseness of those who advocate for the other side. Erica Stone, Doris Day's character in the 1958 romantic comedy *Teacher's Pet*, is a journalism instructor at a local university who embodies the schooling or instructionist mode (figure 0.3). She sees formal instruction as a noble calling, one necessary for the institution of journalism.[2]

Introduction

**Figure 0.2 Girl Learning from a Novel Encounter with a Fish and Her Peruvian-Style Hat.** Willamette National Forest, Trapper Creek Outdoor School. *Source*: Public domain.

**Figure 0.3 Erica Stone and James Gannon Engaging in a Lesson in *Teacher's Pet*.** *Source*: Paramount/Getty Images.

James Gannon, Clark Gable's character in the same film, is the city editor for a large metropolitan newspaper, with no education past the eighth grade. He is convinced that formal education is "a waste of time" for anyone who would like to become a journalist. Experience in the workplace is the necessary, and only, key to success. Much of the story relates to the argument between Erica and James over which is the best way to learn journalism: the classroom or daily life.

James seeks grounding in "real stuff," emphasizing practical doing and concrete reality. He values on-the-job learning, the wisdom of experience, and learning through life.[3] When James asks Erica how she could give up a "real" newspaper job for teaching, Erica retorts,

> Maybe for the same reason that occasionally a musician wants to be a conductor. He wants to hear a hundred people play music the way he hears it. If I can influence a few students who might some day become reporters and eventually editors. Well, I think it's worth a try. You see, I have my own ideas about what newspapers should be and I know they can be a great deal better than they are.

In the early part of the movie, there is more of this one-upmanship. But as the story develops, there are cracks in each facade. Neither is able to convince the other that their preferred mode of learning is best. Instead, the story shifts to the two principals seeking to find how those modes can be brought together. It is no surprise that some rapprochement occurs between the leads in a romantic comedy, but how that happens is revealing about the nature of communication, education, and how the academy and the community can be mutually supportive.

Appealing to our lived experience, James's initial approach can paradoxically result in the rejection of the experience of others, and the loss of cultural heritage. It can narrow to the development of isolated skills, which falter as soon as conditions change. It can reduce our capacity for sensemaking. But Erica Stone's approach risks ignoring the wisdom of practice that James Gannon embodies.

In *Teacher's Pet*, the contretemps between Erica and James is in essence about more than how to learn to be a journalist, how to learn to write, or even whether formal schooling or experience is the best way to learn. It reflects a deeper divide between body and mind that has pervaded our thinking at least since the time of Plato. Erica and James do argue about what journalism is and how one can learn about it. But more fundamentally, they argue about the process of learning itself and the degree to which it comes from experience in the world or through organized teaching and learning.

They, and the audience, eventually see value in the other side, suggesting that each mode is worthy. But is that what we want, or need—that one side prevails, or that we advocate a portion of disembodied learning leavened with some real-world experience? As the movie unfolds, Erica and James learn, and show us, that the question should not be "Do we value the classroom or daily life," but "How can we connect those two realms?"

## SEPARATION OF BODY AND MIND

Community schools in action ultimately reveal the falseness of the dichotomy between Erica Stone's formal schooling (Mind) and James Gannon's school of hard knocks (Body). When disciplinary knowledge drifts away from the lived experience that nurtured it, it soon becomes brittle; the knowledge is ungrounded and subject to easy refutation. Mind cannot exist outside of the complex nexus of bodies, work, materiality, daily practices, culture, and social relations.[4] Paraphrasing John Muir from his unpublished journals, we need to go *out* from the cloister to discover what is really *within* it.[5]

In a similar way, what we learn from experience is inherently limited when we fail to connect it with our own prior experiences and the experiences of others. Academic study can enable that. Learning may continue when isolated from others, but the human significance of that learning depends on its connection to the nexus of ideas, theories, disciplines, and inquiries by others through the ages.

The best learning occurs when these nexuses themselves are connected. Community schools and community-engaged higher education (communiversities) show us how to do that. We can learn from the many kinds of community schools, the diverse challenges to implementing them, and the many surprising implementations.

Plato's theory of forms held that ideas encapsulate the true and essential nature of things, in a way that physical forms cannot. Descartes extended this dualism as he attempts to reconcile a role for religion in a world of scientific materialism. He reified *mind* as an entity that exists independent of the neurons, electrical impulses, ions, hormones, and other material elements that might otherwise be thought to constitute mind.

Dewey writes of this divide as manifested in

> a so-called cultural education which tends to be academic and pedantic, in any case aloof from the concerns of life, and an industrial and manual education which at best gives command of tools and means without intelligent grasp of purposes and ends.[6]

He could have been writing about Erica Stone and James Gannon. He goes on to decry "the separation of mind and body which is incarnated in religion, morals and business as well as in science and philosophy."

A decade later, Arthur Bentley elaborates this argument. He says that most philosophers view knowledge as "a capacity, attribute, possession, or other mysterious inner quality of a 'knower.'" They are willing to acknowledge that this knower resides in or at a body. But they reestablish the separation by viewing the body as cut off from the rest of the universe by a skin. Thus, the human skin becomes "philosophy's last line of defense."

Rather than simply separating mind from body, the view of Bentley's contemporaries was to admit the mind into the body, but then to separate that body from the rest of reality:

> If there is a "knower" and if there is a "known," if one of these lies apart from the other and if there is a process of "knowing" which involves both, then skin lies somewhere along the line of march, and must be taken into account.[7]

The attempt to separate mind and body also reflects and perpetuates social class divides in society, some of which are evident in *Teacher's Pet*. A small percentage of people are invited to devote their energies to knowledge work disconnected from daily life, whereas most people find their lives ever more decontextualized, removed from connections to history, culture, emotions, or personal meaning. As some develop their creative capacities and capitalize on knowledge as a new natural resource, others see work that is now bereft of the meaning that many had found in earlier times in traditional trades or farming.[8] Any one of us may feel that life is neither relevant to the world in front of us nor possessing any sense beyond immediate drudgery.

Following this analysis, Dewey argues that the relation of mind and body is not an abstract philosophical question, but "the most practical of all questions we can ask of our civilization." It is a demand, a call to action. We needed to find ways that

> the labor of multitudes now too predominantly physical in character be inspirited by purpose and emotion and informed by knowledge and understanding . . . that what now pass for highly intellectual and spiritual functions shall be integrated . . . the physical, and thereby accomplish something beyond themselves.

Dewey wanted education, especially what has been called general education, to speak to this divide. Every student should have opportunities to learn liberal arts (history, literature, science, arts, etc.), without a priori limits. At the same time, those in the academic track should learn through their hands as well as their minds. Manual learning (including making and building, use of the body, and more) should draw rich examples for study from daily work.

In the process, learners would develop a greater understanding and empathy for others.

It is a stretch to equate the classroom with mind and daily life with body. After all, the classroom is an embodied space with physical activities of all sorts, and daily life includes reading, meditation, the internet, and other activities associated with mind as well as body. Nevertheless, as any child can tell you at recess time, getting out of the classroom is a physical release and an escape from a focus on the mental.

How often do any of us fail to turn dreams into action? Or, conversely, how often do we act without a clear sense of why, even after the fact? Dreaming without action becomes a habit, which leaves us unfulfilled, but doing without a sense of purpose or meaning can lead to fruitless activity, bereft from even our unrecognized dreams. Could we escape this dichotomy? Is it possible to reflect on our lives, experience the world as embodied selves, and carry out sensible actions at the same time?

This question relates directly to the concept of *eudaimonia*, usually translated as human flourishing.[9] In his *Nichomachean Ethics*, Aristotle presents one view of eudaimonia. He asks what it takes to achieve happiness. Just as "the function of a lyre-player is to play the lyre, and that of a good lyre-player is to do so well," the primary human function, one that leads to a deep sense of happiness, is to fulfill the function of being human. He deduces that for a complete life "human good turns out to be activity of soul in accordance with virtue."[10]

The virtuous life that Aristotle envisions calls on us to aim for self-fulfillment by recognizing our potential and to cultivate love and friendship. This requires engaging in life: "as in the Olympic Games it is not the most beautiful and the strongest that are crowned but those who compete . . . so those who act win, and rightly win, the noble and good things in life."[11]

When we separate abstract learning from lived experience we cannot follow the eudaimonia path. Instead, eudaimonia grows out of action in the world: "We learn by doing, e.g., men become builders by building and lyre-players by playing the lyre; so too we become just by doing just acts, temperate by doing temperate acts, brave by doing brave acts."[12]

In *Healing Psychiatry*, David Brendel argues that repairing mental health requires attention to both body and mind.[13] But psychiatry as a field is split between those who favor bodily interventions (medications, electromagnetic stimulation, etc.) and those who emphasize talk therapy, focusing on improving the patient's cognitive functioning. The inability of the field to integrate its own divisions limits its ability to help individual patients. Outside of the field, approaches like yoga or even just walking more directly blend body and mind to improve mental health.

There is an analogous situation in education: The separation of the classroom and daily life limits both as sites for learning. Until we can integrate the two we will find that individual learning and eudaimonia are compromised.

## COMMUNITY SCHOOLS AND COMMUNIVERSITIES

Could we devise an education that integrates mind and body through action? How can we know what the balance should be? A formidable problem derives from our language for talking about education. We tend to describe it as a closed system, separate from daily life. Seymour Sarason questions this inside/outside problem: "Why is it that when we use the phrase 'school system' we think in terms of pupils, teachers, principals, school buildings, Board of Education, superintendents, etc., and we automatically relegate other groups and agencies (e.g., parents, finance board, politicians, schools of education, state and federal department of education) to an 'outside' role?"[14] Notice that he might have included many other stakeholders, such as local community groups and industry.

But the "outside" is crucial for our learning. When asked about meaningful learning experiences, those that changed life directions or resonated many years afterward and upon which we have built our foundation for further learning, many of us recall experiences such as being advised by a caring supervisor, getting to interact with an exotic animal close up, going on a rare field trip to the beach, or being introduced to a book excluded from the school curriculum, in short, engaging with the "outsiders."

Reflection on outside experiences can hold a value unmatched by hours of classroom lessons. When classroom lessons or units are recalled, it is often for the culminating experience beyond the walls—a walk in the rain, building a large-scale model, and interacting with those from another community. Learning beyond the walls means connecting education from the textbook, lecture, and predigested knowledge to those kinds of experiences, to the unpredictable world of life outside. It expands opportunities for self-directed, holistic, and meaningful learning.

Any of us, young or old, experienced or new to the world, can learn through both formal instruction and experience in the world. We learn the most when we can draw from both of these realms of knowledge.

Our educational systems are organized in ways that make this integration difficult. We have elaborate systems of formal instruction—academies, schools, universities, and training institutes—all to facilitate learning within the walls. At the same time, we have ample opportunities for learning in the wild. Unfortunately, these systems diverge to the point that they do little to support learning that allows us to draw from both the realms of knowledge.

Transactive communication, or transactive pedagogy, is a way to reconnect mind and body.

Moreover, it is vital to make these connections in the world of today. To bring together the classroom and daily life, we need an educational system that does that as well. Doing so requires us to look at the nature of communication itself, whether that be within the classroom or between the academy and the community.

Much of that communication is *transmissive* in the sense that it presumes a one-way transfer of knowledge, either from the teacher to the student or from the academy to the community. It would work better to be *interactive*, in which the recipient of the communication can provide feedback, ask questions, or suggest new lines of inquiry. Better still would be *transactive* communication, in which the parties assume an equal relationship in the dialogue and construct meaning together, often meaning that neither could develop alone.

In other contexts, "transactive" or "transaction" means an exchange or transfer of goods, services, or funds. A transactional act is then one in which the actor benefits from doing something in a business-like event, regardless of the consequences for the other. It reduces to "I'll do something if you give me something." Any benefit to the other is incidental.

In contrast, the use of *transactive* in this book refers to a communicative action or activity involving two parties. They are reciprocally affected or influenced through their co-construction of meaning. This implies listening and open collaboration, a meaning almost opposite to that of the business-like transaction.

## ETHICAL KNOWING

Connecting the classroom and daily life through action clearly holds the potential for mutually transforming relationships: Both the classroom (school, university, etc.) and the communities we live in can change. This is what is meant by *transactive communication*. There is no guarantee or even high probability that such communication can erase the racism, violence, or polarization we see in society today. But the notion of dialogue for democracy is all the more important when times seem the bleakest.

That dialogue must be based on a shared sense of the common good. Jane Addams writes that "the identification with the common lot which is the essential idea of democracy becomes the source and expression of social ethics."[15] That identification comes from a mutually transformative relationship involving both the academy and the community. It relies on the realization that "we can only discover truth by a rational and democratic interest in life."[16]

An implementation of this idea in formal education can be seen in Harold Rugg's social studies curriculum from the 1930s. It asked students to discuss questions such as "How do you think the Native people thought about all the Europeans coming?" The point was not to arrive at a predetermined answer but to learn how to take the perspective of another. This is what it means for our knowledge to be sound ethically as well as logically. Knowing is then an attitude and a way of being rather than an accumulation of facts or procedures.[17]

But we can see social ethics operating in every area of life. Consider, for example, anthropogenic climate disruption (ACD). A recent report from the UN's Intergovernmental Panel on Climate Change concludes that ACD is fully upon us and will dramatically worsen unless something is done immediately. The report recognizes the interdependence of climate, ecosystems, and biodiversity. We are witnessing "biodiversity loss, overall unsustainable consumption of natural resources, land and ecosystem degradation, rapid urbanisation, human demographic shifts, social and economic inequalities and a pandemic."[18] It also says that there is substantial evidence that changing the politics and norms around who participates in climate action enables connecting climate change mitigation, climate change adaptation, and sustainable development. Working at the local level can produce solutions that can aggregate to global impact.[19]

The report serves several useful functions, such as focusing public attention on climate disruption and galvanizing nation-level support. But its findings of disruption, interdependence, and the role of fossil fuel use have been well known for decades. The existence of the greenhouse effect, while not named as such, was proposed by Joseph Fourier nearly two centuries ago. Students of science learned about the processes of climate change through textbooks and lectures. Even popular science, represented in publications such as *Popular Mechanics*, talked a century ago about the effects of carbon burning. Most of the atmosphere is transparent to infrared radiation, but greenhouse gases make it nearly opaque to wavelengths emitted by the surface. Positive feedback cycles already underway lead to the evaporation of all greenhouse gases into the atmosphere, as happened with Venus.

This rather academic understanding of climate disruption has been accompanied by on-the-ground reality for every person on the planet. People living near the ocean have seen their coastlines erode and houses fall into the sea; those living on permafrost have observed it melting and emitting methane, a potent greenhouse gas; the ocean itself is heating up and acidifying, endangering life at all levels; others have experienced thousand-year flooding and wildfires; and everyone has seen rising temperatures, which have been damaging to health, crops, and wildlife. Our daily life has been disrupted along with the climate, and the effects are amplified every year.

But the academic understanding of climate change is difficult to link with the daily experience of its effects. One can study the physics of radiation and absorption without fully grasping how it impacts daily life. At the same time, someone might complain about an unusually hot summer day but feel little impetus to understand how that relates to the extinction of whales, much less to the established science that might explain these problems and their connections. The connection between different ways of knowing is too weak to support concerted action to do anything about the problem.

Moreover, this ignorance conveniently supports those who profit from doing nothing in terms of there being little resistance to say, fossil fuel burning. At an individual level, there is minimal pressure to act morally and ethically, or even to understand how that applies to ordinary actions in the context of climate disruption. If we do not connect the classroom and daily life, we miss an opportunity for enhancing education; we may also find ourselves destroying human life.

## ORGANIZATION OF THE BOOK

The practice of dialogue, or even simple conversation, is explored in Part I of the book. A key idea is that different modes of communication are associated with different pedagogical styles, ranging from formal lectures to collaboration in action in the world. *Transactive communication* is needed to build a link between the classroom and daily life.

Part II shows that the integration of formal learning with daily life is vital for the future of education; it is not simply about another instructional method or curriculum reform. Education is in crisis, both in terms of long-standing problems emanating from society at large and new problems related to demographic changes, emerging technologies, and economic forces.

Part III looks at various ways that education can be more engaged in the world around, including through online learning and learning through work. Many of these ways are currently disconnected from formal education.

Part IV considers how community schools have evolved as attempts to bridge the classroom and daily life divide. These bridges have been built for education from early childhood through graduate study and lifelong learning.

Part V extends the descriptions of existing programs in Part IV to emerging and experimental ideas about communiversity (applied here to education at all age and grade levels). There are both resounding successes and failures to guide future work.

## NOTES

1. Dewey, LW 13:29–30.
2. The quotes in this and the following chapter are from the Oscar nominated screenplay by Fay Kanin and Michael Kanin, "Teacher's Pet (1958)" (December 29, 2021), https://www.scripts.com/writer/fay_kanin/11453.
3. Bertram C. Bruce, *Education's Ecosystems: Learning through Life* (Lanham, MD: Rowman & Littlefield, 2020).
4. The argument that the AI mind cannot exist when devoid of cultural and physical embedding is developed more fully in the author's "Intelligence, Artificial and Natural, for a Sustainable Future" (Global Institute for Interdisciplinary Studies, Nepal, February 18, 2021), https://vimeopro.com/chipbruce/presentations-projects/video/516771632.
5. "I only went out for a walk and finally concluded to stay out till sundown, for going out, I found, was really going in." from John Muir, *John of the Mountains: The Unpublished Journals of John Muir* (Boston, MA: Houghton Mifflin, 1938), 471.
6. John Dewey, "Body and Mind," in *The Collected Works of John Dewey, 1882–1953*, ed. Jo Ann Boydston (Carbondale & Edwardsville, IL: Southern Illinois University Press, 1967), LW 3:25–40. Original version delivered before The New York Academy of Medicine, November 17, 1927.
7. Arthur F. Bentley, "The Human Skin: Philosophy's Last Line of Defense," *Philosophy of Science* 8 (1941): 1–19.
8. Samuel Bowles and Herbert Gintis, *Schooling in Capitalist America: Educational Reform and the Contradictions of Economic Life* (Chicago, IL: Haymarket Books, 2014).
9. Aristotle's original use of "man" for "person" remains here, but his analysis clearly applies to all people.
10. Aristotle, "Nicomachean Ethics," in *The Complete Works of Aristotle. Bollingen Series LXXI 2 Volume II*, trans. W. D. Ross: 1098b30-1099a4, p. 1736.
11. Ibid.
12. Aristotle, 1103a26-1103b2, p. 1743.
13. David H. Brendel, *Healing Psychiatry: Bridging the Science/Humanism Divide* (Cambridge, MA: MIT Press, 2006).
14. *Revisiting "The Culture of the School and the Problem of Change,"* The Series on School Reform (New York: Teachers College Press, 1996), 10.
15. Jane Addams, *Democracy and Social Ethics*, ed. Anne Firor Scott (Cambridge, MA: Harvard University Press, 1964), 11.
16. Ibid.
17. F. James Rutherford and Andrew Ahlgren, *Science for All Americans* (New York: Oxford University Press, 1990).
18. Intergovernmental panel on climate change, "Climate Change 2022: Impacts, Adaptation and Vulnerability" (New York, NY: United Nations, February 27, 2022), https://report.ipcc.ch/ar6wg2/pdf/IPCC_AR6_WGII_FinalDraft_FullReport.pdf.
19. Edward R. Carr, "We Are Not Doomed to Climate Chaos," *Boston Globe*, March 16, 2022.

*Part I*

# COMMUNICATION AND EDUCATION

When we truly communicate, we also educate; we convey new ideas from one mind to another or construct new thoughts collaboratively through our interactions. Similarly, when we teach and learn, we do so through communicating thoughts, questions, feelings, and beliefs. Communication is relevant to every aspect of education: when one student talks with another or with the teacher; when we build curriculum to communicate across generations; and when we connect formal schooling and learning outside of the school.

Much of that communication is *transmissive* in the sense that it presumes a one-way transfer of knowledge, either from the teacher to the student or from the academy to the community. It would work better to be *interactive*, in which the recipient of the communication can provide feedback, ask questions, or suggest new lines of inquiry. Better still would be *transactive* communication, in which meaning is not simply shared but cocreated.

In the last case, parties assume an equal relationship in the dialogue and construct meaning together, often a meaning that neither could develop on their own. They can both change in the process. This richer communication is the key to revitalizing education and to integrating learning within the classroom with that from experience in the outside world.

## Chapter 1

# Models of Communication

> There is more than a verbal tie between the words common, community, and communication. Men live in a community in virtue of the things which they have in common; and communication is the way in which they come to possess things in common. What they must have in common in order to form a community or society are aims, beliefs, aspirations, knowledge—a common understanding.... Such things cannot be passed physically from one to another, like bricks.
> —John Dewey, *Democracy and Education*[1]

The opening chapter of *Democracy and Education* is titled "Education as a Necessity of Life." Dewey means here "human life." We need education in some form to develop as humans, and the varieties of education that we experience shape who we become. Education, formal or otherwise, is what happens when we have that genuine communication.

The importance of communication for ordinary social life is undeniable. But this also applies to teaching. How we teach and what that means for students and teachers depend on the forms of communication. Moreover, how schools and other organizations for learning—universities, libraries, museums, and informal learning programs—connect with the local community or the larger society shapes what they mean for learning. The meaning of education for individuals and society, as well as the future of the educational enterprise per se, is vitally dependent on the forms that these communications take. They shape the ongoing construction of our culture.

Take an extreme case: In his study of Marcos Rodríguez Pantoja, an abandoned child raised by wolves, Gabriel Janer Manila concludes that the stories of abandoned children above all highlight the role of culture in developing human personality:

The rigorous study of those cases of children who have grown up alone, isolated from any human contact, sometimes breastfed by animals, sometimes abandoned to the rigor of the jungle in which they have been able to subsisting on their own means leads us to consider the need for culture in the process of building human personality.[2]

Pantoja's story highlights how communication is integral to human life in even the most extreme circumstances. Communication in some form—with animals, with other people, with nature, or with oneself—is essential for human development. Conversely, the lack of human culture during his formative years led to lifelong difficulties for Pantoja.

## THE TRANSMISSION MODEL

There are many models of the process of communication and the ways that it builds or maintains culture. These help us to see aspects of communication and to compare various ways to communicate, whether among students, between teacher and student, or between the academy and the surrounding community.[3]

The starting point for discussions of communication is often the *transmission model*. This model views communication as the movement of a thing, like an information packet, from one place to another. It is essentially talking to the other. A schematic of the transmission model is shown in figure 1.1.

Good examples of transmission can be seen in the first part of the movie *Teacher's Pet*. Erica Stone and James Gannon are adversaries. Their strong commitment to their own mode of pedagogy outweighs even the obvious attraction they feel for the other. Early in their encounters, James writes a letter to Stone to decline her invitation to speak to her class. He writes,

> Thank you for the flattery implied in your request that I appear as guest lecturer in your journalism class. Thank you, but no, thanks. . . . If I came, I might get carried away by the spirit of academic integrity and tell your unsuspecting students the truth that the only way to learn about the fourth estate is with first-hand experience.
>
> In the school I graduated from there were no lectures without four letter words in them. No books except those thrown at you to wake you up. No degrees besides the third. Information was gotten by keeping your eyes and ears open and your nose clean.

Erica gives a strong response to the letter, saying among other things that James is "one of the few relics of antiquity on display outside the Museum of Natural History." There is little real listening or collaboration in these early

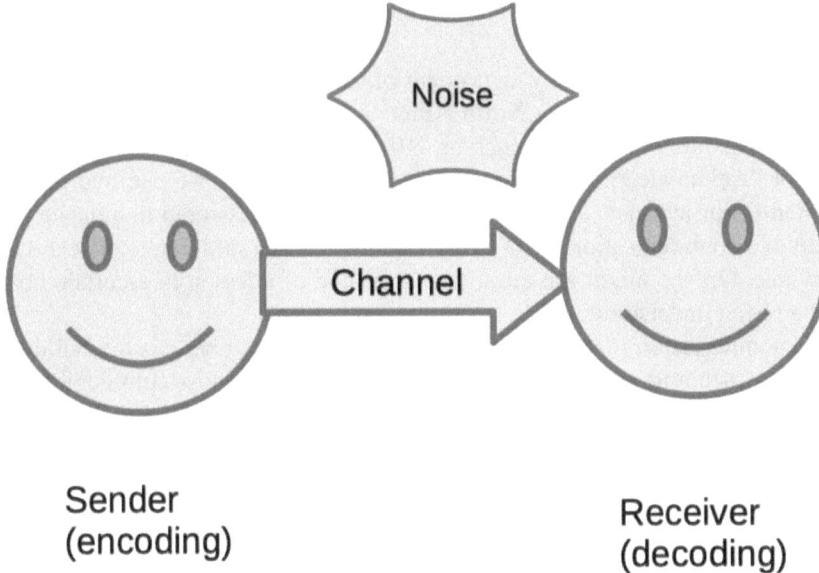

Figure 1.1  The Transmission Model of Communication. *Source*: Author created.

encounters. Each party transmits their own prejudices with little attempt to understand that of the other.

Notice that the examples (and the model) highlight the sending of a single message through a communication *channel*, such as a conversation or a letter. For basic communication theory, this is a complex enough process. The *sender* must formulate a message and *encode* it into an appropriate language for efficient transmission.

One cannot assume that the message will be delivered totally intact. In general, there is noise in the system so any message can be lost or distorted. To combat the noise, the sender may need to repeat some or all of the message (*redundancy*). In computer systems, an *error-detecting code* can alert communicators to a problem. For example, the message could contain a number indicating how many characters are in the original message. If that does not correspond to the message as received, then there may be a need to resend it.

This happens in human communication as well, as when we ask for repetition of a phrase or for the speaker to speak louder. Good teachers anticipate noise in the system when they use multiple channels to communicate—notes on a whiteboard, speech with appropriate emphasis on key points, audiovisual aids, and so on.

In the transmission model, the receiver gets the message and *decodes* it to obtain the meaning. Note that the model implies that both sender and receiver know the language for codifying the message. They must also agree on a mutually acceptable time for the communication, on which channel to use, and on the order of speaking.

Different systems employ meta codes of various types to facilitate this. For example, two-way radio in North America, especially among law enforcement, uses numerical codes such as "10-1" for "Receiving Poorly" or "10-4" for "Acknowledgment." In ordinary communication, we use many such systems. For instance, a teacher may flip lights in a classroom to indicate the start of a communication, most likely with the teacher speaking to the class as a whole. Or, she might ask questions at the end of a lesson to ascertain how it had been understood.

Communication in the transmission model is defined here as the building block of sending and receiving a single message. In most communication this would be followed by another message, most likely from the original receiver, leading to a reversal of the arrows and the roles. This model is widely useful for computer-to-computer communication, such as on the internet. It also provides a first-level description of what is happening in some human communication.

Note that it also accounts for much of ordinary language use, such as one person telling another specifics of a simple procedure or communicating the time of day. It finds success when there is a careful construction of the message, so that meaning can be transferred from one to another. It gives a poor account when feedback is needed to clarify the meaning or when the meaning is dependent on the context.

Just imagine the case of someone trying to tell the time of day or the date, but doing so over a phone line, where concepts of "here" and "there" are ambiguous. The idea of sending one clear message captures only a small part of the process of making that communication successful.

The transmission model has severe limitations when proposed as an account of human communication in general.[4] Notably, it omits feedback, a crucial part of any human communication. The model also ignores the context of the communication, treating each transmission as a process that occurs independently of physiological, psychological, social, cultural, or other factors that we know influence communication.

## THE INTERACTION MODEL

The back and forth of transmission entails a clean send-message process with rigid roles for participants. In actual conversations, interlocutors speak using partial messages, with ambiguities, metaphors, and other linguistic clues to help them co-construct meaning. They also respond to both the social and physical contexts. The transmission model is ultimately limited because it oddly isolates a solitary act from a fundamentally collaborative process. The message receiver exists, but only as a recipient for the action of the sender.

An alternative is the *interaction model*, as shown in figure 1.2. This model emphasizes communication as an interaction in which a message is sent and then followed by a reaction (feedback), which can be followed by another reaction. Communication is not simply the transmission of one message, but a process producing a conversation, which is necessary for full communication. In addition, the model portrays these interactions occurring within physical and psychological contexts. We could describe it as talking with the other.

As the movie *Teacher's Pet* progresses, the communication becomes more inter*active*. Erica and James begin to collaborate around specific texts and their theories of pedagogy. One such text is a news story about a crime. Given the basic facts of the case, James's version of it starts as follows:

A trigger-happy teenager bent on robbery shot Jerome Heffner, 62, at 5:30 p. m. yesterday and left him bleeding to death on the sidewalk in front of his grocery

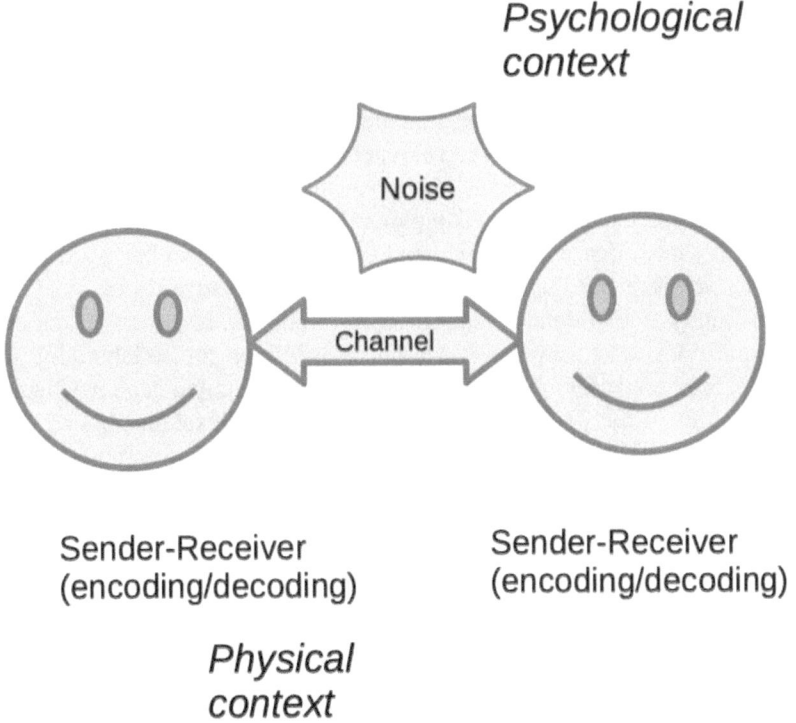

Figure 1.2 The Interaction Model of Communication. *Source*: Author created.

store at 286 East 110 Street. Within minutes after the shooting, Rosario Salas, 17, was captured in an alley behind the store and brought to Heffner's side. "'That's the one,' cried Heffner," pointing at Salas.

Erica praises James's story, but later talks about how it could be improved. She says that "trigger-happy" is a cliché. But more importantly, she asks James to do an "interpretive follow-up." James retorts that "nobody's interested in a rehash. . . . Doing another story on it would be like trying to make a salad out of old lettuce."

Erica says that the kind of reporting that relates only to the facts went out with Prohibition. She advocates "talking about the big why behind the story." She argues that "this is the function of a newspaper in today's world. TV and radio announce spot news minutes after it happens. Newspapers can't compete in reporting what happened anymore. But they can and should tell the public why it happened."

This calls for a story to explore Salas's reason for firing the gun. He had said, "people been throwing things in my face all my life. I guess I couldn't take it no more." The story should tell why he said that, and why he committed the crime. Continuing this kind of discussion, Erica and James begin to listen to each other and to find common ground through a common project.

Late in the movie, James recognizes what could go into a longer interpretive piece: "Salas was alone when he killed the old man. He had four partners always with him. Poverty, prejudice, bitterness, and despair. Salas pulled the trigger but they loaded the gun." He responds to Erica's ideas about interpretive writing and even proposes doing more of that at the city newspaper. But he also reminds Erica about the economics of the newspaper business. A long interpretive piece takes up space that could be sold to advertisers.

This interactive communication involves feedback, responses to the content, questions, and answers. It creates possibilities for collaboration and meaningful connection. An important aspect is the simple acknowledgment of the hearer. After all, in everyday behavior, can we examine talking without a hearing?[5] The interaction model insists on viewing communication as mutual, reciprocal, and impossible to reduce to a one-step process.

Each participant is then both a sender and a receiver, a *sender-receiver*. The channel is two-way. This is important because feedback is seen as an essential feature. Something like "10-4 Acknowledgment" can mark the difference between a lot of talk with noise and successful communication. Moreover, the interaction model recognizes that communication never occurs in an abstract space but is subject to both the physical context and the psychological context.

A (somewhat degenerate form of) the interaction model can be seen in the initiation-response-feedback, or IRF, pattern of discussion in conventional classroom discourse. In this pattern, the teacher initiates, the learner responds, and the teacher gives feedback. Each step is a form of interactive feedback that furthers the communication.

- T: What are the three branches of government?
- S: Judicial, and I don't know.
- T: You got one part right, but you need to re-read the selection.

This approach to the exchange of information in the classroom has been criticized as being more about the learner saying what the teacher wants to hear than really communicating. But with a minor modification it can provide a starting point for meaningful communication:

- T: What are the three branches of government?
- S: Judicial, and I don't know.
- T: That's one part right. How come that one stuck in your mind?

The interaction model serves better than the transmission model at showing how several people might set the agenda for a meeting, taking into account the physical and psychological contexts, and allowing for rich feedback to clarify and amplify meanings. It includes context and feedback loops. It represents dialogue as a game for two, not just a game of solitaire. But like the transmission model, it assumes that communication is a process of delivering messages. Meaning exists prior to the communication; it just needs to be shared with another. This assumption breaks down when there is no a priori meaning to communicate, but that meaning instead is constructed through dialogue.

## THE TRANSACTION MODEL

The *transaction model*[6] views communication as integrated into our social realities in such a way that it helps us not only understand them but also create and change them. It describes communication as a process in which communicators generate social realities within social, relational, and cultural contexts. In this model, communication is neither a transmission of established meaning through the production of a message nor an interaction with something but a *transaction* in which we coinvent and co-attribute meanings to realize life purposes. It can be glossed as walking beside the other. See figure 1.3.[7]

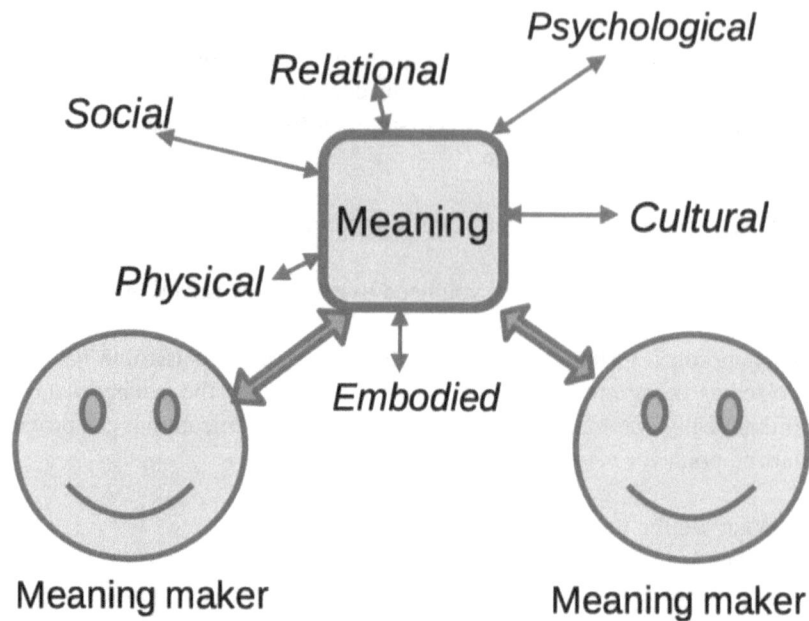

**Figure 1.3** The Transaction Model of Communication. *Source:* Author created.

In *Teacher's Pet*, Erica shares that she is writing a book about her father, who ran a country newspaper called *The Eureka Bulletin*. It was a small town paper read around the world. One editorial he wrote won the Pulitzer Prize. James is impressed that she has real newspaper work in her background.

Their interactions continue; their communication changes. Initially it is *transmissive*, with each simply declaring what they believe to be true. This could be glossed as "talk to" the other. As they listen to the other, if only to rebut what the other says, their communication gradually shifts to being more *interactive*. They could be said to "talk with" the other.

As the plot unfolds, Erica and James share personal stories, then they begin to truly listen, and finally they work together toward a common goal. Their communication becomes *transactive*. They continue to talk, but also to act together and to begin to share each others' worlds. They change one another through a mutually transforming relationship. Drawing on a phrase proposed by Jane Addams, they "walk beside" one another.[8] The spectrum from "talk to" through "talk with" to "walk beside" offers a framework for examining communication situations, but also for collaborative experiences in general.

Erica recognizes how much James knows:

> If you look it up, you'll find that the definition of knowledge is "knowing, familiarity gained by experience." You'll also find that wisdom is defined as "the

possession of experience and knowledge." Being experienced, you therefore have education, you have knowledge and you have wisdom. You're brilliant.

At one point, James says,

> To me, journalism is like a hangover. You can read about it for years but until you've actually experienced it you have no conception of what it's really like. That's what I felt, but I've got to admit I'm beginning to think there's something to this education bit, too.

Near the end of the movie, Erica renews her invitation to the person she now knows as Jim Gannon (he had earlier used a false name):

> Mr. Gannon, I was wondering if I could prevail upon you to give a series of guest lectures to my classes? You know, the practical touch added to the academic approach? The wedding of the old pros and the eggheads. Weren't those your words?

We do not see the usual romantic comedy wedding, but it is clear that Erica and James are engaging in transactive communication and have come to a wedding of ideas. The co-construction of meaning through talk bodes well for their continuing collaboration, and possibly more. This is the kind of dialogue that is too often lacking between the academy and the community.

In addition to simply being more equitable, the transaction can lead to greater learning all around. Jack Easley and Russ Zwoyer showed in their research that even in mathematics class, simply listening to students and respecting their (alternate- or mis-)conceptions can result in deeper learning.[9]

Both listening and talking are important in transactional communication. Dewey argues that both of these involve getting outside of our own experiences and understanding "the life of another":

> To be a recipient of a communication is to have an enlarged and changed experience. One shares in what another has thought and felt and in so far, meagerly or amply, has his own attitude modified. Nor is the one who communicates left unaffected. Try the experiment of communicating, with fullness and accuracy, some experience to another . . . and you will find your own attitude toward your experience changing. . . . The experience has to be formulated in order to be communicated . . . getting outside of it, seeing it as another would see it, considering what points of contact it has with the life of another.[10]

Walt Whitman's opening to "Song of Myself" prefigures this kind of collaboration:[11]

I celebrate myself, and sing myself,
And what I assume you shall assume,
For every atom belonging to me as good belongs to you.

Although he is not a formal communication theorist, Whitman nevertheless captures another key aspect of the transaction in the line, "My tongue, every atom of my blood, form'd from this soil, this air." The atoms of meaning are shared with others, but also with the very soil we walk on and the air we breathe. The construction of meaning is thus embodied, and it is embedded in the world.

This concept of shared meaning, even shared bodies, is also evident in Bakhtin's analysis of *dialogism*. He shows how a novel (or any utterance) is constructed from a diversity of styles and voices, assembled into a structured artistic system. This challenges the idea of linguistic creativity as a unique use of language. Even within a single perspective, there are always multiple voices and perspectives, because the language which is used has been borrowed from others. The originality is in the combination, not the elements.[12]

Dean Barnlund calls for *transaction* as an entirely new model of communication, applicable to ordinary communication as well as formal genres. Transaction fundamentally alters the very way we talk about or examine communication:

> Meanings may be generated while a man stands alone on a mountain trail or sits in the privacy of his study speculating about some internal doubt. Meanings are invented also in countless social situations in which men talk with those who share or dispute their purposes. But no matter what the context, it is the production of meaning, rather than the production of messages that identifies communication.[13]

Barnlund's insights are belied to some extent by his implicit assumption, as Mary Louise Pratt would say, that "community is male."[14] But adopting a broader perspective, as she does, provides even more support for his basic point. Pratt identifies a set of verbal practices which are commonly associated with women, for example, "planting suggestions in the minds of other people so that they think they thought of it themselves."

Because of their identification with women, whether actually employed more or less by women, these practices are often omitted from communication theories, or from the set of classic examples. But none of them are explicable in terms of a transmission model. "Planting suggestions" sounds vaguely transmission-like. But the point is not the suggestion as message, but the practice of talking in such a way that the listener thinks that he or she thought it up by themselves. Even an interaction model, which incorporates context and allows for question-answer interchanges, fails to explain why these practices occur or how they work.

We communicate to further relationships, to form alliances, to influence others, to shape our self-concepts, to win arguments, and to create communities. Even the other is unnecessary: As both Barnlund and Pratt point out, we sometimes communicate with ourselves.

Dewey and Bentley lay out a similar notion of transaction in *Knowing and the Known*. In that work, they seek to develop an entirely new epistemology. Their analysis is surprisingly close to the communication model distinctions here. They write of three views of things and actions,

- *Self-action*: where things are viewed as acting under their own powers.
- *Inter-action*: where thing is balanced against thing in causal interconnection.
- *Trans-action*: where systems of description and naming are employed to deal with aspects and phases of action, without final attribution to "elements" or other presumptively detachable or independent "entities," "essences," or "realities," and without isolation of presumptively detachable "relations" from such detachable "elements."[15]

In their scheme, self-action is remarkably similar to the transmission model of communication in which one party composes and sends a message. Interaction, like the interaction model of communication, recognizes the causal connection between interlocutors. Trans-action is described in quite different terms from the transaction model of communication, but its insistence on not reducing the process to "detachable 'elements'" makes a similar point.

In contrast with the transmission and interaction models, the transaction model does not assume that we even have a message to communicate, or that one party could hold such a message. Utterances are not just shared but co-constructed, and out of that meaning is constructed. The work of Charles and Marjorie Goodwin shows this co-construction process operating in diverse ways for actual human conversations.[16] More recently, Deborah Tannen has examples of how "cooperative overlapping" can be a way to show enthusiastic engagement with what the speaker is saying. Rather than interrupting or silencing the speaker, it encourages them to keep going.[17]

It is the norm for human conversation that an utterance initiated by one person can be completed by another. Speaking overlaps so that it is unclear even what each individual has heard. The initial speaker may alter meaning by stopping mid-sentence, shifting their gaze, or changing intonations. Other participants show their assent, interest, or disagreement only partly through words, using also facial expressions, gestures, or eye glances. The content, such as it is, emerges only as the talk proceeds; it does not exist a priori.

In an influential book, Paul Grice proposes that participants in (transactive) conversations adhere to the *cooperative principle*:

> Our talk exchanges do not normally consist of a succession of disconnected remarks, and would not be rational if they did. They are characteristically, to some degree at least, cooperative efforts; and each participant recognizes in them, to some extent, a common purpose or set of purposes, or at least a mutually accepted direction.[18]

Jeffrey Stout reminds us that ultimately transactive communication (conversation) is all we have. His comments are especially pertinent in today's polarized political environment:

> Conversation is a good name for what is needed at those points where people employing different final vocabularies reach a momentary impasse. . . . The political discourse of a pluralistic democracy, as it turns out, needs to be a mixture of normal discourse and conversational improvisation.[19]

## USING THE MODELS

The three models of communication can be used to analyze general communication patterns, to analyze the special communication found in teaching, or to analyze the relations between the school or college and the world beyond the walls of the academy. They can also be used strategically, to foster particular modes of learning.

As analytical tools, the models help to explain what is going on in conversational interaction. One analyst might employ the transaction model to account for the collaborative construction of meaning in a conversation. Another might choose the transmission model as being sufficient for the first-level analysis of an encounter, or perhaps to apply to human-machine or machine-machine communication.

Both the transmission and interaction models assume that the purpose of communication is to transmit information about our realities. The transaction model sees its purpose as to construct and make sense of our realities. A schematic of the models applied to ordinary language, pedagogy, and community engagement is shown in table 1.1.

Some teaching involves efficient delivery of information; the expert transmits what he or she knows in the most efficient and error-free way possible. This might be useful, for example, when someone is explaining the safety

Table 1.1 Application of the Models to Ordinary Language

| Communication Model | Effective Use | Process | Meaning | Model Breakdown |
|---|---|---|---|---|
| Transmission | Things to know and do before the flight takes off | Careful construction of clear message | Sent from one party to the other | When detailed feedback and clarification are needed, or when the second party is not listening |
| Interaction | Agenda for our next meeting | Feedback to ascertain and clarify the message | Sent but with feedback, clarification, and amplification expected | When no a priori meaning exists |
| Transaction | Making sense of a shared experience | Collaborative construction of meaning | Constructed through dialogue | |

Source: Author created.

Table 1.2  Application of the Models to Education

| Communication Model | Ordinary Language | Pedagogy | Community Engagement |
|---|---|---|---|
| Null | - | - | Isolation |
| Transmission | Telling some useful items of information | Lecture | Outreach |
| Interaction | Setting up a meeting | Discussion with Q/A | Work/study program |
| Transaction | Making sense together of the movie with an obscure plot or message | Collaborative knowledge building | Community as curriculum |

*Source*: Author created.

procedures to use a power tool. In the beginning, the learner might do best to listen intently, accepting a one-way communication.

Other forms of teaching become more interactive, with the learner seeking clarification, asking questions, signaling comprehension, or otherwise providing feedback and two-way communication. Finally, education can move into a transactive mode of communication, in which the teacher learns alongside the student.

A schematic of the models applied as analytical tools for education is shown in table 1.2.

We can also employ the communication modes as strategic tools. This implies different relations between the academy and the community. In the null communication case, the academy exists in isolation from the surrounding communities. This might apply to the medieval cloister, but also to many schools and corporate training centers today. They may have literal walls, even barbed wire, to separate them from ordinary life, which is seen as dangerous or at best distracting from the primary educational mission. More importantly, they have symbolic walls separating their activities from daily life.

## NOTES

1. John Dewey, MW 9: 7.
2. Gabriel Janer Manila, "La Problematica Educativa De Los Ninos Selvaticos: El Caso De 'Marcos,'" *Anuario de psicología. Universitat de Barcelona* 20 (1979): 81.
3. *Communication in the Real World: An Introduction to Communication Studies* (Minneapolis, MN: University of Minnesota Libraries Publishing, 2013), https://open.lib.umn.edu/communication.

4. Claude Elwood Shannon and Warren Weaver, *The Mathematical Theory of Communication*, 21. print (Urbana: University of Illinois Press, 1998).

5. John Dewey and Arthur F. Bentley, "Knowing and the Known," MLW 16: 126.

6. "Transaction" has another meaning which is not intended here, namely an exchange or transfer of goods, services, or funds. A transactional act is then one in which the actor benefits from doing something in a business-like exchange. The use in this book refers to a communicative action or activity involving two parties that reciprocally affect or influence each other.

7. Barnlund, Dean C., "A Transactional Model of Communication," in *Foundations of Communication Theory*, by Kenneth K. Sereno and C. David Mortensen (New York, NY: Harper and Row, 1970), 83–92.

8. Jane Addams, *Democracy and Social Ethics*, ed. Anne Firor Scott (Cambridge, MA: Harvard University Press, 1964), 70.

9. Jack A. Easley Jr. and Russell E. Zwoyer, "Teaching by Listening—toward a New Day in Math Classes," *Contemporary Education* 47, no. 1 (September 1, 1975): 19–25. See also the review in Arthur Bakker, Jantien Smit, and Rupert Wegerif, "Scaffolding and Dialogic Teaching in Mathematics Education: Introduction and Review," *ZDM* 47, no. 7 (November 2015): 1047–65.

10. John Dewey, "Democracy and Education," MW 9: 8.

11. Walt Whitman, "Song of Myself," In *Leaves of Grass* (Norton, 1973).

12. M. M. Bakhtin, *The Dialogic Imagination: Four Essays*, edited by Michael Holquist, University of Texas Press Slavic Series, no. 1 (Austin: University of Texas Press, 1981).

13. Barnlund, 47–48.

14. Mary Louise Pratt, "Linguistic Utopias," in *The Linguistics of Writing: Arguments between Language and Literature*, edited by Nigel Fabb et al. (New York: Methuen, 1987), 54–55. See also her "Arts of the Contact Zone," in *Ways of Reading*, edited by David Bartholomae and Anthony Petrosky (New York: Bedford/ St. Martin's, 1999), 581–600.

15. Dewey and Bentley, MLW 16: 101–102.

16. Charles Goodwin, *Conversational Organization: Interaction between Speakers and Hearers*, Language, Thought, and Culture (New York: Academic Press, 1981); "Sentence Construction within Interaction," in *Aspects of Oral Communication*, edited by U. M. Quasthoff (Berlin/New York: Walter de Gruyter, 1995), 198–219; "The Interactive Construction of a Sentence in Natural Conversation," in *Everyday Language: Studies in Ethnomethodology*, edited by G. Psathas (New York, NY: Irvington, 1979), 97–121; with Marjorie Harness Goodwin, "Concurrent Operations on Talk: Notes on the Interactive Organization of Assessments," *IPrA Papers in Pragmatics* 1, no. 1 (January 1, 1987): 1–54.

17. "Would You Please Let Me Finish," *The New York Times*, October 17, 2012.

18. Herbert Paul Grice, *Studies in the Way of Words* (Cambridge, MA: Harvard University Press, 1995), 26.

19. Jeffrey L. Stout, "What's Beyond Politics," *First Things* 148 (December 2004): 8–9.

*Chapter 2*

# Schooling and Society

> Citizens of a community are "engaged" when they play an effective role in decision-making . . . defining the issues, identifying solutions, and developing priorities for action and resources.
> —Alan Bassler et al., *Effective Citizen Engagement*[1]

The Bassler et al. definition applies to citizen engagement in general but is very relevant to the kinds of engagement we find too rarely in education. All too often, citizens are not involved in defining issues, identifying solutions, or developing priorities for action and resources relevant to education. Or, their involvement can be narrow and counter-productive.[2] The relation between the academy and the community is too much like the early encounters of Erica Stone and James Gannon in *Teacher's Pet*—cordial on the surface, but with very little real communication or acknowledgment of the other's value, much less collaboration and common purpose.

A modern challenge is to find ways of connecting citizens with their vital function of shaping the next generation. This brings us back to the issue of modes of communication. Is it the role of the academy to transmit its privileged understanding of knowledge to the masses? To interact with the public to define issues and priorities? Could it instead engage in true, transactive dialogue? We can consider these questions in the light of a brief history of schooling and society.

## CLOISTERS AND ENGAGEMENT

A review of formal education, at least in the West, shows an on- and off-again relationship between cloistered study removed from the everyday world and full engagement with that world. The dichotomy shown in *Teacher's Pet* needs to be played out in each generation.

During the time of the Sophists in Greece, from around 450 BCE, there was education through tutors, but no state-provision of schools. Only the rich could afford tutors. There were open-air exercise facilities (gymnasia) for daily workouts promoting the integration of mind and body. Oral communication was used for political conversations in the Assembly and the spread of news at the symposium. Activities included meeting friends, assisting to fulfill public office duties, and attending the gymnasium together. An older male would choose an adolescent boy as his favorite to educate. The sexual bond between mentor and protégé was accepted as long as the mentor did not exploit the protégé physically and neglect their education.

The Sophists were considered to be wise men—skilled at public speaking and philosophical debates. They had many students (all male) who wanted to excel at public speaking in the democratic and oral-centered polis. The Sophists would also compose speeches for use at the Assembly or in the law courts for a price. Thought was tied to action in the Agora or the Assembly. Many Athenians were skeptical of their opinions due to their persuasive skills.

The Sophists concentrated their thought on human beings and human society. They asked questions about the language in relation to things and about general theories of knowledge. Their work emphasized the subjective element. There was an integration of mind and body in action which Dewey recapitulated two millennia later.[3]

This emphasis helps to explain the philosophical hostility of Plato and Aristotle. Plato, especially, thought that anyone who looks for the truth in phenomena alone cannot hope to find it there. Phenomena obscured the search for truth and represented a rejection of philosophy. Many subsequent thinkers agreed with Plato that the Sophists did not rank as philosophers. Rejection of the Sophist position led to the idea of education as removed from daily life, a view that was only amplified later on in Europe.

Roman education largely followed the Greek model of tutors for the wealthy; in fact, many of the tutors were Greeks themselves. Following the decline of the Roman empire, education in Europe, such as it was, came under the purview of the Western church. Medieval church-based education was even more sequestered from daily life than it had been under Plato and Aristotle (see figure 2.1). Only the wealthiest were able to receive an education at all. Those who had the highest level of education would often work within the church; those based in monasteries took an isolation vow, which meant their scholarship was also isolated.

Figure 2.1 Teaching in Paris, Tonsured Students on the Floor, from a Late Fourteenth-Century Grandes Chroniques de France. *Source*: Unknown author, Castres, bibliothèque municipale, ms. 3, f. 277r, public domain.

As the mercantile era began to develop, the merchant trade required a population that was better educated. This increasing demand for education drove some trading towns to start their own grammar schools, which were often funded by wealthy local merchants. Latin grammar was still heavily featured in lessons as it was the lingua franca for merchants who traded across Europe. Dutch and Spanish merchants, for example, did not understand English, but they could converse in Latin. As such, many traders sent their sons to grammar schools to ensure they could continue the business.

The teaching centered around ensuring the boys were able to recite new information from memory, regardless of whether or not they had understood that information. Each school was small; many provided only a single room for all of the boys attending and their teachers. This teacher would come from a religious background and would focus on teaching the older boys, who would then be tasked with teaching the younger.

If boys succeeded in grammar school, they could then be sent to the university. Oxford and Cambridge Universities were both founded during medieval times and were renowned for their teaching, so they were common choices in England for those who could afford further education. The ability of peasant sons to gain an education depended on permission from the lord of the manor.

Without that, they would face a large fine. This may well have been one way of ensuring that peasants were no threat to the Feudal System.

In contrast, education has played a central role in Islam since ancient times, owing in part to the centrality of scripture and its study in the Islamic tradition. This education was more engaged with the worlds of science, technology, mathematics, medicine, and exploration than that in Europe. Education would begin at a young age with the study of Arabic and the Quran. Beginning in the eleventh and twelfth centuries, the ruling elites began to establish institutions of higher religious learning known as madrasas. These soon multiplied throughout the Islamic world, which helped to spread Islamic learning beyond urban centers and to unite diverse Islamic communities in a shared cultural project. Madrasas were devoted principally to study of Islamic law, but they also offered other subjects such as theology, medicine, and mathematics. They were engaged with daily life.

The importance of learning in the Islamic tradition is reflected in a number of hadiths[4] attributed to Muhammad, including one that instructs the faithful to "seek knowledge." This injunction was seen to apply particularly to scholars, but also to some extent to the wider Muslim public, as exemplified by the dictum "learning is prescribed for us all."[5] Literacy rates were relatively high, at least in comparison to their European counterparts (figure 2.2).

**Figure 2.2 A Madrasa of the Jamia Masjid Mosque in Srirangapatna, India.** *Source*: Prakash Subbarao, June 23, 2007, public domain.

Back in the West, prior to the Enlightenment, European educational systems were principally geared for teaching religious orders, physicians, lawyers, and scribes. Merchants learned through the guild apprenticeship system. As the scientific revolution and religious upheaval broke traditional views and ways of thinking, reasoning and scientific facts came to play a bigger role. By the late Enlightenment, there was a rising demand for a more universal approach to education. The literacy rate in Europe grew significantly.[6] Education was gradually opened up to ordinary people, but as we see today, formal education was never provided equitably.

The explosion of print culture, which started in the fifteenth century with Gutenberg's printing press, was both a result of and a cause of the increase in literacy. A system of public cultural institutions, such as libraries and museums, developed. Social gathering places such as coffeehouses, clubs, academies, and Masonic Lodges provided alternative places where people could read, learn, and exchange ideas. Partly under the influence of Islamic culture and education, which had maintained the classical tradition, European education reengaged with the world.

Recent histories of Western education emphasize the industrial era and the automation that took over factories and schools. But much of what we see today derives from broad lines of schooling reaching back two thousand years. This can be seen in the hierarchy and cultural symbolism, especially of university-level schooling, but also in the emphasis on obedience and following directions throughout all of schooling.

Writing in 2020, Graham Oliver asserts that

> the 19th century implementation of the universal, compulsory state schooling ... [was] made possible because of the European schooling that was already in existence and was so easily adopted by the much later factory interests, and the military and managerial interests of modern statehood.[7]

He cites Eton, as a schooling factory. Its heritage derives from medieval structures but is now modified for the industrial age: "My own secondary schooling was at a state institution deliberately modeled on those medieval public schools, with its brick, the carved sandstone, the wood panelling, the teachers' gowns—and the caning." The schooling factories and the industrial factories both grew out of medieval and earlier workshops. He concludes that "compared to schooling ... industrial factories are belated affairs."

Postsecondary education in the American colonies had been available to a limited segment of society and focused on a few subject areas. Colonial colleges established in association with Christian denominations enrolled predominantly white men in classical and professional disciplines. New colleges created following the independence of the United States from Great Britain broadened enrollment and fields of study. However, lack of reliable funding meant that many were closed. In the early to mid-nineteenth century, demand grew for postsecondary education in agricultural and technical disciplines, as did interest in expanding educational opportunities more broadly.[8]

Starting in 1862, there was a major shift in how colleges and universities conceived their role in public engagement. This was largely due to the Morrill Acts of 1862 and 1890, which created land-grant institutions, colleges, and universities focused on the agricultural and mechanical arts. These institutions now address many academic fields in addition to those of their foundational colleges of agriculture.

Federal legislation defined three functional pillars of land-grant institutions. First was the teaching function established through the Morrill Acts of 1862 and 1890. Later legislation added research and extension, establishing the roles of land-grant institutions in producing original agricultural research and in bringing that research to the nonuniversity public through agricultural extension. To this day, land-grant institutions maintain these three pillars (or missions), typically following a mandate of 40 percent teaching, 40 percent research, and 20 percent extension, or public service.

The original funding for the land-grant system deserves serious scrutiny. Their creation involved a massive transfer of wealth. Land was expropriated from tribal nations not only for campuses but also to provide seed money for higher education. The act redistributed nearly 11 million acres across 80,000 parcels of land. This role of the act in the violent history of colonization has remained little known.[9] Many who have learned about it would insist on at least a full apology to tribal nations and free tuition and fees at land-grant institutions for indigenous people.

## TRANSMISSION PEDAGOGY

Despite moments of community or societal engagement, this cursory review of Western education reveals an emphasis on the transmission mode of pedagogy. The assumption is that the academy possesses vital knowledge that should be passed on, at least to an elite portion of the populace. One can imagine bricks being passed from expert to novice to fill an empty bucket.

It also shows ambivalence about the walls of schooling. On the one hand, education serves to sequester learners apart from the mundane events of the day. On the other, there are periodic attempts to link learning with daily issues. This can be seen from the Sophists through the land-grant colleges.

A simple approximation suggests that early education sought to construct venues, procedures, titles, and other apparatus designed to separate students from mundane life. We may have succeeded too well. Education is now often so removed from practical experience that it seems irrelevant, counterintuitive, if not incomprehensible. We need to undo some of the successes of the early academies and reestablish a connection between the classroom and lived experience.

On the whole, we still assess students, teachers, schools, and entire curricula in terms of transmitting information little connected to lived experience, marking success by achievement of learning objectives or report card grades that represent little of what some would consider to be the real goals of education. Unfortunately, this transmission is always partial; the students absorb only part of what the teacher (or syllabus, text, curriculum, etc.) knows.

Furthermore, this transmission occurs within a fixed and constricted environment. It is not the communication of the master bricklayer on the job, helping the apprentice with a novel situation that requires creative action. Instead, it is the discourse around imagined bricklaying within a box. Even then, that communication reifies divisions across gender, race, and class, leaving out most learners.

The passing bricks model of education is the default mode, the point from which most discussions of education begin. One reason is that it accords well with the structural model in which the place-based academy encompasses and controls various activities—classroom learning, online learning, and clinical training. Of course, the school always exists in an environment with other activities—libraries, museums, agriculture, health care, business, city life, transportation, factories, and more—but it often operates autonomously.

## ALTERNATIVES TO THE TRANSMISSION MODEL

Alternatives to the transmission model exist. One is to encourage true *interaction*, in which participants provide feedback, ask questions, and help direct the engagement in ways that meet the current situation and the backgrounds of participants. Where a student might gain, say, 10 percent of the knowledge offered through transmission, they might garner several times as much, 20 percent, 30 percent, or more with sufficient interaction.

Going further, one can seek *transaction*, in which meaning is co-constructed by participants through action. Recall what happens in *Teacher's Pet* when Erica and James share personal stories, work together on complex tasks, and make the effort to understand the perspective and experiences of the other. With transaction it makes little sense to talk about what percentage of the knowledge is transferred, since new knowledge is created through the transaction. But the potential for learning is unlimited.

John and his daughter Evelyn Dewey discuss various transactive approaches, including the Gary Plan, an educational system instituted in Gary, Indiana, in 1907. The plan called for changes across the curriculum, even on the use of the school building after school hours. In the areas of civics education, students learned by doing:

> Pupils learn civics by helping to take care of their own school building, by making the rules for their own conduct in the halls and on the playgrounds, by going into the public library, and by listening to the stories of what Gary is doing as told by the people who are doing it. They learn by a mock campaign, with parties, primaries, booths and ballots for the election of their own student council. Pupils who have made the furniture and the cement walks with their own hands, and who know how much it cost, are slow to destroy walks or furniture, nor are they going to be very easily fooled as to the value they get in service and improvements when they themselves become taxpayers.[10]

During a period of greater immigration to the United States than we see today, this civics education was especially important. The parents of a large number of children were foreign-born and knew little about the government or organization of the city, nor its possibilities and limitations. The Deweys go on to say about the Gary schools that they

> not only teach the theory of good citizenship and social conditions, they give the children actual facts and conditions, so that they can see what is wrong and how it can be bettered . . . [this results in] the larger return in alert and intelligent citizens.[11]

Transactive communication between the academy and the community does not guarantee good education nor does it ensure equitable participation by all, but it does set up the framework for "the larger return in alert and intelligent citizens."

## NOTES

1. Allan Bassler, Kathy Brasier, Neal Fogle, and Ron Taverno, "Effective Citizen Engagement: A How-To Guide for Community Leaders," Manual (Harrisburg, PA: Center for Rural Pennsylvania, April 2008), 3.

2. A recent example is the movement to eliminate critical race theory from the curriculum, where it scarcely existed to begin with. Another is the move to add Holocaust denial literature to create so-called "balance."

3. Debra Hawhee, *Bodily Arts: Rhetoric and Athletics in Ancient Greece* (Austin, TX: University of Texas Press, 2004).

4. Ḥadīth or Athar in Islam refers to a record of the words, actions, and the silent approval of the Prophet Muhammad.

5. "All" excluded women in Islamic education of this period as was true of Christian education in Europe at the time.

6. Emily C. Bruce, *Revolutions at Home: The Origin of Modern Childhood and the German Middle Class*, Childhoods: Interdisciplinary Perspectives on Children and Youth (Amherst: University of Massachusetts Press, 2021).

7. This and subsequent quotes in this section are from R. Graham Oliver, "The Medieval in Our Schools: How Our Schools Owe so Much Less to the Nineteenth Century Factory," *The Educational Mentor* (blog), 2020.

8. Genevieve K. Croft, "The U.S. Land-Grant University System: An Overview," R45897 (Washington, DC: Congressional Research Service, 2019).

9. Robert Lee and Tristan Ahtone, "Land-Grab Universities," *High Country News*, March 30, 2020.

10. John Dewey and Evelyn Dewey, "Schools of Tomorrow," MW 8: 335–336.

11. Ibid., MW 8: 336.

# Profile
## *Claudia Șerbănuță*

The relation between formal learning and learning through daily experience has taken many forms across cultures and times. In recent years, this has meant incorporating a transaction model of pedagogy. Community leaders, including teachers, need to adopt roles as facilitators, supporters, and collaborators with community members. This entails trusting citizens to engage in the issues.[1]

There are many examples of leaders who have undergone that letting go, despite the fact that it often conflicts with their nominal professional duties. Introducing the various chapters are profiles of individuals who have worked on healthy partnerships between formal learning and the community. Their accounts show us what it takes to become that kind of leader and the diversity of life experiences that led them to see beyond the walls.[2]

People who become engaged with learning beyond the walls follow diverse paths to get there. The reasons for their interest and their own experiences shed light on what it takes to devote a career to learning in diverse ways. Their profiles tell us more than any organization chart would about how such learning comes about. The key questions for the seven profiles were "How did you become involved in this kind of boundary crossing work? What sustains your involvement, especially when the institutional supports are often lacking?"

The first profile, of Claudia Șerbănuță, shows how one educator became a leader in learning beyond the walls of the classroom. She did this in the context of a history of severe information control, where open-ended learning and the promotion of it was a political act.[3]

Claudia says,

At the age when I had to make decisions about my professional path I realized a number of things. Firstly, the paths known by my parents shifted as Romania exited the totalitarian regime and entered the new territories of free market and democracy building. So, given the fact that I was the first in my family to go to college, I had no guidance, other than my curiosity, in identifying a direction I wanted to take.

Secondly, given the structure of formal education, the decisions that we had to make at a very early age were set to put us in professional directions that moved away from each other and seldom intersected with topics from other fields.

I chose Computer Science because of my affinity for the topics but I focused on using technology to model or structure solutions that addressed the needs of people and communities. It was not until I gathered the courage to sit in a Community Informatics roundtable at the Graduate School of Library and Information Science of University of Illinois that I understood where curiosity was guiding me and discovered my path.

I realized that there are professionals out there whose thoughts about technology advancements are motivated by bettering the lives of people from struggling communities. Moreover, the efforts they were making towards the advancement of technology were founded on building trust, strengthening communities, and empowering the silenced.

Upon returning to Romania, my work followed the same path. I started with volunteering in projects and initiatives. Slowly, but naturally, the institution of public library became a permanent partner in my endeavors. In a struggling society where democracy is still more of a theoretical concept than a lived practice, public libraries offer a great opportunity for supporting individual and community efforts of development and growth.

I focused on initiatives that complement the formal education and focus on STEM education and on developing democratic practices in Romania. These projects help existing local institutions and partners ensure sustainability and future development. This is especially true with public libraries in rural communities.

The youth living in rural communities have few opportunities and chances to build a better future for themselves. Bringing more opportunities for them to learn STEM is a focus of my work. As part of the team of Progress Foundation, we developed two national programs that are having an impact at the local level: Ora să TIM (Time to KNOW/STEM) and CODEKids.

Ora să TIM[4] focuses on encouraging public librarians to read to children, while also planning for and offering fun interactive STEM experiments inspired from the stories read. Learning to enjoy books and encouraging exploration and inquiry were practiced together using age appropriate techniques and support materials. This transformed libraries from spaces that are storing books to real discovery spaces.

More than 250 libraries from Romania and Republic of Moldova received packages of illustrated books and training to implement the project activities for children ages 3 to 10. The resources created in the project were openly shared and are still used to this day.

What was stunning about this approach was that many of these librarians used local resources to help illustrate science and technology topics. They complemented reading books with visiting local farmers, beehive keepers, pottering or crafting workshops. Locals were happy to present their work to children, allowing them to explore and experiment. This way children connected stories from books with real life experiences.

Since 2017, together with the Progress Foundation team, I worked in Code Kids,[5] a national program helping middle schoolers to learn how to code in a safe environment, at the public library. The program is free for anyone and provides content and guidance for children who, in two years of participating in coding clubs at the library, are not only learning their first steps in coding but also think about and implement Arduino & Scratch projects.

The curricula for the program was revised annually based on the analysis of the results and impact, and new activities were added. This proved a challenge for some librarians, as they had to permanently adapt their approach in keeping club members engaged and curious in their learning. As more librarians decided to offer this new service for their young public, they also started to look for support in their communities.

The diversity of the help received by libraries who had coding clubs was amazing: Parents of children in the club who had technical backgrounds volunteered to explain the components of a desktop computer; local businesses sponsored activities of the club; local authorities made the young coders ambassadors of their communities; and local community members living abroad donated computers.

When I look back at the road that brought me here I see a connection and a common purpose to empower librarians to offer new services that address local needs. In almost 10 years since my return to Romania I learned that public libraries are key institutions in providing access, especially for underserved communities. The information ecology of the country limits the available options for lifelong learning for people with low income. The process of learning for community development is still very much unguided exploration, but the determination of young people and the commitment of librarians makes the effort worthwhile.

## NOTES

1. Allan Bassler et al., "Effective Citizen Engagement," 3.
2. *The profiles have been edited for length and clarity.*
3. An early example of her work was a two-day workshop, called "Information spaces in the Community." The audience was thirty international librarians, including participants from Vietnam, Japan, China, Palestine, Kenya, Nigeria, and Colombia. In small work groups, they visited various information spaces in the surrounding community. These included libraries, health or art centers, a movie rental shop, the student union, and a bus stop. Using various analogue and digital information tools, each group gathered data about the information space and created a multimedia presentation. A project such as this shows not only how learning occurs outside of the classroom walls but also how that learning can be connected with formal education.

Between 2014 and 2016, Claudia was the interim director of the National Library of Romania. She then worked at Progress Foundation Romania as a Community Development Manager on projects promoting democratic access to education and new library services. She is now a library specialist with EduCaB (Educational Capacity Building in Local Libraries) initiative. She is also one of the main organizers of Occupy Library international conference and was recognized as a Change Agent in the *Library Journal*'s 2021 Movers & Shakers class.

Her main research interest is understanding how information cultures are transformed by prolonged and severe information control and censorship practices. See, for example, Claudia Serbanuta, Tiffany C. Chao, and Aiko Takazawa, "Bridging the Digital Divide: Libraries Providing Access for All? 'Access for All and for How Long?'" (BOBCATSSS 2010, Parma, Italy, 2010).

4. http://www.progressfoundation.ro/ora-sa-stim/.
5. http://www.codekids.ro/about/?lang=en.

*Chapter 3*

# Beyond the Walls of Formal Education

> Human beings are unique among all living organisms in that their primary adaptive specialization lies not in some particular physical form or skill or fit in an ecological niche, but rather in identification with the process of adaptation itself—the process of learning. We are thus the learning species, and our survival depends on our ability to adapt not only in the reactive sense of fitting into physical and social worlds, but in the proactive sense of creating and shaping those worlds.
> —David Kolb, *Experiential Learning*[1]

When we see learning as an evolutionary adaptation, we cannot locate it solely within the bounds of formal schooling. Plutarch recognized this over two millennia ago. He asked how we might think about ourselves as a learning species: Is pedagogy the transmission of facts and training in specific skills? If so, then it is like filling an earthen vessel with stones (figure 3.1). Consequently, pedagogy would be a bit like masonry.

He argued instead for a view of learning as a growth process. Pedagogy is then more like cultivating a garden.[2] It was enhancing a fire: "The mind requires not like an earthen vessel to be filled up; convenient fuel and aliment only will inflame it with a desire of knowledge and ardent love of truth" (figure 3.2).[3] Thus, real learning is about fueling wonder.

Conceiving of pedagogy as adding kindling to fire moves it to the transaction mode of communication. The teacher becomes "a guide on the side" rather than "a sage on the stage."[4]

The cover photo on this book provides one image of the contrast between these two modes of pedagogy. The student is in the classroom physically, but her mind seems to focus on the land beyond its walls. All the while, she holds a tablet that she can connect to the internet. Depending on how it is used, it

**Figure 3.1 Pedagogy as Filling an Earthen Vessel.** *Source*: Susan Bruce, September 25, 2021.

can be a tool to support the metaphors of either kindling a fire or filling an earthen vessel.

## THE GRAND INQUISITOR

The dichotomy between filling vessels and fueling fires is expressed in a different way in chapter 5 of *The Brothers Karamazov*.[5] It is a classic statement of an educational dilemma: We desire the freedom to pursue our own interests and are frustrated in the end when we are not able to do so. Yet we are all too ready to give up that freedom and just be told what to do.

In one chapter Ivan Karamazov relates a story he composed of an encounter between the Grand Inquisitor and his Prisoner, Jesus.[6] It appears nominally as a dialogue, but the Grand Inquisitor does all of the talking, mostly criticizing Jesus for failing to understand people. He notes that religion has led to greed, killing, idol worship, and other ungodly acts: "In the cause of universal worship, they have destroyed each other with the sword. They have made gods and called upon each other: 'Abandon your gods and come and worship ours, otherwise death to you and your gods!'"

The Inquisitor says that people claim to want freedom but are all too ready to relinquish that and bow down for earthly bread. He goes on to say that

**Figure 3.2 Pedagogy as Adding Kindling to Fire.** *Source*: Jon Sullivan, July 27, 2006, public domain.

he and his church have at last vanquished freedom. Although people are certain that they are completely free, they "have brought us their freedom and obediently laid it at our feet." A modern parallel is Morpheus in the film *The Matrix*. He offers a choice between a blue pill and a red pill. The former means rejecting freedom and choosing a life of ignorance.

The Inquisitor points to the time of Jesus in the wilderness and his "failures" on the three questions he was posed. Among those, Jesus was invited to turn stones into bread:

> Turn them into bread and mankind will run after you like sheep, grateful and obedient.... But you did not want to deprive man of freedom and rejected the offer, for what sort of freedom is it, you reasoned, if obedience is bought with loaves of bread? You objected that man does not live by bread alone.

The discussion continues, with the Inquisitor essentially saying that people are happy to abandon freedom if someone will give them bread and tell them the answers or, in our terms here, to fill their buckets but not to light their fire. Jesus says nothing, but when the Inquisitor says *Dixi* (I have spoken), Jesus "approaches the old man in silence and gently kisses him on his bloodless, ninety-year-old lips."

Although not intended as such, the Grand Inquisitor story is an extreme example of transmission communication, even to the point that there is literally no communicative interaction until the last gesture by Jesus. Notably, Ivan is also lecturing Alyosha, with only brief interruptions for questions. One could offer more mundane examples, such as the way that the lecture format dominates much of academic teaching, even to the point of having lectures about the ineffectiveness of lectures. Or, the all-too-common implementation of online learning as a series of video lectures.

But Ivan's story is more than just an instance of a lecture gone awry. One thing it makes clear is how the recipient of the lecture is complicit in both its form and function. The Inquisitor implies that people want to have the truth transmitted to them without any need or opportunity to question it. They are willing to abandon their freedom for "the banner of earthly bread." Indeed, they judge that they are successful as they follow that banner and abandon any pretense of freedom.

Anyone who has taught has observed moments when the student says essentially, "just tell me what to do." There is a comfort in relinquishing responsibility for learning, to assume that the lecturer's words coalesce the essence of a phenomenon. Even the Inquisitor recognizes that the people will "fall down before idols." They seek to be handed simple answers, rather than struggle with freedom and the uncertainty it entails.

The Inquisitor says in effect that in order to bring about universal religion, the church must employ the methods of the devil. It needs to control people, offering instead simple rules to follow, which take away their freedom. This relies on denigrating people, seeing them as incapable of independent thought and action. It is akin to what we do in formal education when we posit narrow learning objectives and define educational success as mastery of these limited goals.

The story also shows the power of listening.[7] We remember the patience of Jesus and his kiss in the end, more than any specifics of the Inquisitor's monologue. His response turns the otherwise one-way transmission into a transaction that calls for reflection on the meaning of human nature, religion, dogma, truth, freedom, and pedagogy. The interaction as a whole also leaves one with the nagging conviction that the sixteenth-century struggle to reconcile freedom and bread is far from over.

## DEWEY'S ADVOCACY OF THE SOCIAL PROCESS

Many teachers, current and future, turn to John Dewey, having heard that he has important things to say about education. Parents, administrators, policy makers, and engaged citizens have done the same. Many are disappointed with what they find. Even the relatively accessible *Democracy and Education* appears to many as a dusty tome; the modern reader knows that some social capital may accrue if one claims familiarity with it, but they would never imagine reading it for pleasure nor consulting it to solve a practical problem.

Part of the difficulty here is that Dewey's language can seem convoluted, and at best suited to a time long ago. This is compounded by there being few examples, images, fleshed out stories, diagrams, tables, charts, or formulas. Above all, one can read many of Dewey's books and still come away with little idea of what specific action to take; there are no prescriptions for how one should teach or test learning. One searches in vain for answers to contemporary questions about how to expand STEM for all, how to improve test scores, whether online teaching is a good idea, or what middle schools should be doing.

Dewey's oft-cited, but equally often ignored, insights about education do have a bearing on the issues of today, but not by favoring this method or that. Instead, they cause us to reflect on the very nature of education, and what that has to do with community, shared understanding, democratic life, and personal growth. That reflection can lead us to radically reconceptualize everything we do, both in formal education and in life in society beyond. This can mean major changes in what any teacher or parent would do on a daily basis.

Thinking perhaps that the job of a teacher is to transmit important knowledge to students so that they can get good jobs, the modern reader may encounter Dewey saying,

> Not only is social life identical with communication, but all communication (and hence all genuine social life) is educative. . . . One shares in what another has thought and felt and in so far, meagerly or amply, has his own attitude modified. Nor is the one who communicates left unaffected . . . one has to assimilate, imaginatively, something of another's experience in order to tell him intelligently of one's own experience.[8]

Dewey goes on to emphasize the social nature of learning. Social relations are necessary for learning, and their very existence means that some learning occurs for participants. Communication is thus "like art. Any social arrangement that remains vitally social, or vitally shared, is educative to those who participate in it." It is only when communication becomes cast "in a mold" and runs in a routine way that it loses its "educative power."[9]

There is nothing here about what knowledge to impart, how to present it, nor how to check whether students have absorbed it. There is definitely no assertion about job skills, much less an explanation of how education develops those skills, even for the needs of a century ago.

Instead, Dewey adopts an explicit transaction model for communication. He argues that communication is an art, one in which we imaginatively take part in the experience of another. Sharing in what another has thought and felt causes us to learn, to modify our own attitudes. This "vitally social process" is the core of education. When we reduce it to the routine transmission of facts, no matter how well they may be conceived or presented, we "lose its educative power."

Educators have long recognized the value of going beyond the walls of formal education. But it is not a simple matter to do so. The potential loss of control is a problem encountered at every level. The individual teacher can be uncomfortable; the parents wonder what is going on; the principal feels on the spot; and the district policy makers are apoplectic.

This can be seen in an example from one Grade 4 class. There was a discussion of the planets, presumably a safe topic for transmission pedagogy. A student asked, "Why are the planets round?" Another jumped in to say, "I went to the Children's Museum this weekend. It was fun to make bubbles." The teacher, not to any great surprise, brought the class back to the topic, "We're discussing planets today, not bubbles."

During his museum visit, the student had observed that giant soap bubbles tend toward a spherical form, as do the planets. One could imagine a discussion to follow that would at least pose whether the roundness of planets and the roundness of bubbles were related. If the teacher were to lead such a discussion that would violate the transmission assumptions of the mandated lesson, assumptions no doubt reinforced by the fact of being observed by another.

Within the current system, the teacher's job was to efficiently explain certain facts about the planets, not to make new meanings together. This would ensure that the students would perform well on district and state exams. From that perspective, the student's report of his museum visit was noise in the communication channel, a signal of loss of control, which needed to be eliminated.

The constructivist approach to knowledge that Dewey advocates recognizes the necessity of learning from our cultural heritage as well as from ordinary experience, but it does not reduce education to transmitting social knowledge and cultural tools per se, nor does it define education as serving narrow functional goals, such as job preparation.

Going beyond the walls means that real-life experiences beyond the classroom are part of the conditions that permit students to pursue essentially independent objectives based on their own experiences, interests, and concerns. But the idea that social conditions should determine educational objectives is a fallacy: "Education is autonomous and should be free to determine its own ends, its own objectives. To go outside the educational function and to borrow objectives from an external source is to surrender the educational cause."[10] External conditions should enrich education but not define it.

## EXPERIENTIAL EDUCATION

New directions in learning beyond the walls draw from multiple sources: *progressive education, community as curriculum, self-directed learning,* the *lab studio model,* and more. *Experiential learning* emphasizes how we learn from primary experience, especially sense experiences.[11] This learning is part of the human toolkit for evolution. Recognition of experiential learning leads to the *experiential learning cycle* in which students actively engage in a concrete experience, reflect on that experience, relate it to their prior knowledge, generate new understandings that modify their existing conceptualizations, and test their conclusions/hypotheses by applying their knowledge to new experiences.

One version is *expeditionary learning.* Students engage in fieldwork involving the active collection of data. They might create trail signage celebrating aspects of their community, including the flora and fauna of a local creek, or local history. They learn through doing, become comfortable taking risks, making mistakes, and getting dirty, all in the pursuit of greater knowledge and understanding.[12]

Models such as expeditionary learning might invite the idea that there are two kinds of learning, the experiential kind that furthers our unique human adaptive specialization and all that other learning in which we just accumulate facts by being told. That can be useful as a rhetorical device, but in fact all learning is experiential.

When the student sits in a lecture hall or reads a textbook, they are having experiences. It may be thoughts about the cute classmate three rows down or about the professor's attire. It could be connecting some diagram in the chemistry textbook to an emerging understanding of what the formula for a chemical reaction means. All too often these experiences are constrained and limited in scope. They are weakly connected to the student's other experiences, much less to their motivations and desires. But they are still experiences, and learning is still going on.

But experiences of whatever kind taken alone are not enough. As Dewey points out,

> Experiences in order to be educative must lead out into an expanding world of subject-matter, a subject-matter of facts or information and of ideas. This condition is satisfied only as the educator views teaching and learning as a continuous process of reconstruction of experience.[13]

An earlier argument for this comes from John Keats. He describes how he had much "travell'd in the realms of gold, And many goodly states and kingdoms seen." But it was only in connecting that travel with his reading from Chapman's translation of *Homer* that he can say,

Yet did I never breathe its pure serene
Till I heard Chapman speak out loud and bold:
Then felt I like some watcher of the skies
When a new planet swims into his ken;[14]

The questions are then: What kind of experiences do we have? Are they rich and varied enough to provide grist for reflection and the possibility for expanded opportunities for learning and life in the future? How are they connected to our learning through reading, discussion, analysis, and reflection?

## SCHOOL AS SOCIAL CENTER

Is the community the center or is the school the center? Writing in 1902, Dewey argued that the school should be the social center of the community. His analysis seems prescient more than a century later:

> We find that our political problems involve race questions, questions of the assimilation of diverse types of language and custom; we find that most serious political questions grow out of underlying industrial and commercial changes and adjustments; we find that most of our pressing political problems cannot be solved by special measures of legislation or executive activity, but only by the promotion of common sympathies and a common understanding.[15]

Following an analysis of then-contemporary changes in modes of transportation and communication, of demographic changes, of global communication, knowledge work, and the need for lifelong learning, again reminiscent of today, Dewey calls for the idea of the school as a social center of the community. It grows out of the idea of the larger democratic movement. The community owes each one of its members the fullest opportunity for development. This is not a matter of charity, but one of justice. He says that it is even "higher and better than justice—a necessary phase of developing and growing life."[16]

The idea of the school as center is another facet of the community as curriculum, which places the beginning of learning in the community. Sharing the intellectual and spiritual resources of the community is its very meaning. The school as a social center means its active promotion of this sharing of art, science, and other modes of social intercourse.

## EDUCATING THE WHOLE PERSON

Adopting a societal, cultural, and political perspective on education in South Africa and India, Mahatma Gandhi worked toward a conception of education radically different from that of the existing colonial system. He saw that system as part of a colonial project of subjugating people. He not only rejected that aim; he also developed specific alternatives.

For example, Gandhi agreed that it was important to develop the mind, but when that effort was divorced from the development of the body and the spirit, education was at best incomplete and more often oppressive. He considered the British system to be overly focused on cognitive goals and then only as they enabled job performance:

> The real difficulty is that people have no idea of what education truly is. We assess the value of education in the same manner as we assess the value of land or of shares in the stock-exchange market. We want to provide only such education as would enable the student to earn more. We hardly give any thought to the improvement of the character of the educated. The girls, we say, do not have to earn; so why should they be educated? As long as such ideas persist there is no hope of our ever knowing the true value of education.[17]

Gandhi recognized the value of career preparation, but he saw the necessity of integrating it with moral development and cultural relevance. It must also be done with the aim of political empowerment toward developing a just society. In particular, he was shocked by the conditions of women working as virtual slaves in the mills of Bombay. As an alternative to preparing them for that work, or other similar roles in the colonial system, he promoted traditional hand weaving in schools, which could lead to economic self-determination.

He describes education as the development of the whole person. True education requires a proper exercise and training of the bodily organs (hands, feet, eyes, ears, nose, etc.): "A proper and all-round development of the mind, therefore, can take place only when it proceeds *pari passu* with the education of the physical and spiritual faculties of the child. They constitute an indivisible whole."[18]

The connection to traditional work naturally complemented Gandhi's emphasis on *learning by doing*. Through meaningful work with dignity, the individual would learn to think creatively, independently, and critically. Furthermore, the emphasis on work culture would accord with his view of service to society as a higher goal. He essentially supplanted the three Rs of the British system with a focus on head, heart, and hand, mirrored in the United States as 4-H.[19]

Despite his insistence on service, work, cultural relevance, and other connections to the human ecosystem, Gandhi by no means rejected learning from books. In his *Autobiography*, he describes his own encounter with John Ruskin's book *Unto This Last* "that brought about an instantaneous and practical transformation in my life." There, he discovered some of his deepest convictions, especially about the good of the individual being contained in the good of all, the value of all work, and that the life of labor is the one worth living.[20]

Gandhi shows that, whatever aims we adopt, they cannot be considered in isolation from the society in which education is embedded. Equipping a young person to play a part as the citizen of a democracy has very different demands for one in an already functioning democracy or in a colonial position. It also has quite different meanings according to economic class, race, and gender.[21]

## NOTES

1. David Kolb, *Experiential Learning: Experience as the Source of Learning and Development* (Englewood Cliffs, NJ: Prentice Hall, 1984), 1. This idea was discussed earlier by Dewey in various works, notably *Democracy and Education* and *Experience and Education*.

2. Shihkuan Hsu and Yuh-Yin Wu, eds., *Education as Cultivation in Chinese Culture*, Education in the Asia-Pacific Region: Issues, Concerns and Prospects (Singapore: Springer, 2015).

3. William Watson Goodwin, ed., *Plutarch's Morals, Vol. 1* (Little, Brown, and Co., 1874), 463. Many people have attributed the saying to W. B. Yeats, quoting and misquoting it. But there is little evidence that he ever said it, or would have said it. See Robert Strong, "'Education Is Not the Filling of a Pail, but the Lighting of a Fire': It's an Inspiring Quote, but Did WB Yeats Say It?" *The Irish Times*, October 15, 2013.

4. Alison King, "From Sage on the Stage to Guide on the Side," *College Teaching* 41, no. 1 (1993): 30–35.

5. Fyodor Dostoyevsky, *The Brothers Karamazov*, trans. Richard Pevear and Larissa Volokhonsky, Everyman's Library 70 (New York: Knopf : Distributed by Random House, 1992). The quotes to follow are on pp. 251–262.

6. There are varied sources for the legend that Ivan "composes."

7. An application of this principle to teaching, even for math class, is shown in Jack A. Easley Jr. and Russell E. Zwoyer, "Teaching by Listening—toward a New Day in Math Classes," *Contemporary Education* 47, no. 1 (September 1, 1975): 19–25.

8. John Dewey, "Democracy and Education," MW 9: 8.

9. Dewey, MW 9: 9.

10. John Dewey, "The Sources of a Science of Education," LW 5: 38.

11. David Boud, ed., *Reflection: Turning Experience into Learning* (London: Kogan Page [u.a.], 1985); Morris T. Keeton, *Experiential Learning*, 1st ed., The Jossey-Bass Series in Higher Education (San Francisco: Jossey-Bass Publishers, 1976); M. K. Smith, "'David A. Kolb on Experiential Learning'," in *The Encyclopedia of Pedagogy and Informal Education*, 2010/2001, https://infed.org/mobi/david-a-kolb-on-experiential-learning/.

12. Andrew Withers, "Leader in Expeditionary Learning," *The Union*, November 17, 2021.

13. John Dewey, "Experience and Education," 1938; LW 13: 59.

14. John Keats, "On first looking into Chapman's Homer." Contrary to Keats, it was Vasco Núñez de Balboa, not Cortez, who helped establish the first stable European settlement in South America at Darién, on the Isthmus of Panama. It was he who claimed the Pacific Ocean and all of its shores for Spain.

15. John Dewey, "The School as Social Centre," MW 2: 75.

16. Dewey, MW 2: 93.

17. M. K. Gandhi, *Gandhi on Education*, edited by J. S. Rajput (Urbana, IL: National Council of Teachers of English, 1998), 3.

18. Ibid: 73.

19. 4-H programs were established around the turn of the twentieth century, about the same time as the first junior colleges. They are grounded in the belief that children (ages 5–18) learn best by doing. They complete hands-on projects in areas such as science, health, agriculture, and civic engagement, in a positive environment where they receive guidance from adult mentors and are encouraged to take on proactive leadership roles. Echoing Gandhi, all 4-H programs include mentoring and career readiness as core element. As the nation's largest youth development organization, the programs are now available in every county in the United States.

20. M. K. Gandhi, *An Autobiography or The Story of My Experiments with Truth*, translated by Mahadev Desai (Ahmedabad, India: Navajivan Publishing House, 1927); John Wooding, *The Power of Non-Violence—The Enduring Legacy of Richard Gregg* (Lowell & Amesbury, MA: Loom Press, 2020).

21. Samuel Bowles and Herbert Gintis, *Schooling in Capitalist America: Educational Reform and the Contradictions of Economic Life* (Chicago, IL: Haymarket Books, 2014).

*Part II*

# Education in Crisis

The work of Horace Mann pioneered universal public education, which would be free, nonsectarian, and devoted to creating critical, socially engaged citizens. That tradition has led to Massachusetts having arguably one of the best public education systems in the United States, if not the world.[1] A jewel in that system is the Boston Latin School, established in 1635 as what is now the oldest existing school in the United States.

And yet, the school system in its capital and the largest city faces challenges on diverse levels. There has been chronic leadership turmoil, and the teachers' union voted no confidence in the superintendent. Many schools have failed to provide adequate reading and math instruction. They often lack basic necessities such as light bulbs and potable water. Excluding exam schools, few have a fully functioning school library with regular hours, expert staff, and an up-to-date collection.

During the pandemic, many students have struggled to learn at home. State receivership looms. Many parents fear for their children's future; some have abandoned the school system.[2] It would be a small comfort to learn that problems such as these are unique to Boston. But many school systems face similar problems of leadership, funding, racial tensions, and declining public confidence.

Well-intentioned reforms, such as pre-K education, often fail to have the desired effects. This may be due to the retention of outmoded ideas, for example, that poor children need only drills on basic skills or practice tracing letters and numbers. Meanwhile, families of means gravitate to play-based preschool programs with opportunities for art, movement, music, and nature. Children are asked open-ended questions; they are listened to; they engage in transactive communication.[3]

To a large extent, the "chronic state of crisis" of the school system is not limited to the education sector; it reflects dysfunctions in society in general, which are often just the most visible in the schools. But some of the crisis portends more dramatic changes in our entire education system, including for higher education and formal training.

We are faced with a rapidly growing online delivery system, digital credentialing, major demographic changes, racism, and financial pressures due to a society ever more divided by race, language, and class. These forces could signal the end of place-based education as we have known it for over two centuries and pose a serious threat to the very idea of democratic education. This would be a perfect exemplar of an existential crisis.

Such a moment can engender surprise, anger, despair, or resignation. It can also be a moment of opportunity. Disruptive moments offer the possibility for reexamining basic assumptions, in this case about what education is, how formal education relates to life in the community and to lived experience.

The education system at its best is notoriously complacent and tradition-bound. This is especially the case for the organizations deemed most successful. Change will most likely come not from the elite institutions but from the margins. Brian Rosenberg argues,

> It will not be Princeton but some small college in the Midwest that pioneers a new, less siloed organizational structure; it will not be Stanford but a struggling college in New England that rethinks the reward system for scholarship and teaching; and it will not be Harvard but a new university in Africa that designs a curriculum around missions and not majors.[4]

Change will come not from unchallenged success but from recognizing the problems that beset education today and understanding the opportunities for a fundamental rethinking of what the education system is and ought to be. This requires understanding the nature of communication within the classroom and between the school and the larger society.

## NOTES

1. "History and Evolution of Public Education in the US" (Center on Education Policy The George Washington University, 2020), https://files.eric.ed.gov/fulltext/ED606970.pdf.

2. James Vaznis, "With Boston Public Schools in Crisis Problems Are Mounting. Can the System Save Itself ?," *The Boston Globe*, October 16, 2021.

3. Kelley Durkin et al., "Effects of a Statewide Pre-Kindergarten Program on Children's Achievement and Behavior through Sixth Grade," *Developmental Psychology*, January 2022.

4. Brian Rosenberg, "Is Harvard Complacent? Considering Fundamental Change in the Wake of the Pandemic," *Harvard Magazine*, October 2021.

*Chapter 4*

# Crises in Education

We cannot have a decent democracy unless we begin with the supposition that every human life is of equal value. Our society already has far too much inequality of wealth and income. We should do nothing to stigmatize those who already get the least of society's advantages. We should bend our efforts to change our society so that each and every one of us has the opportunity to learn, the resources needed to learn, and the chance to have a good and decent life, regardless of one's test scores.
—Diane Ravitch[1]

John Dewey had little patience for "nimble or severe intellectual exercise—as something said by philosophers and concerning them alone." In fact, "[if] a theory makes no difference in educational endeavor, it must be artificial" and of little value beyond an intellectual game. This led him to the radical definition of philosophy *as the general theory of education*. More broadly, all of our intellectual endeavors find their fullest realization in "the process of forming fundamental dispositions, intellectual and emotional, toward nature and [others]." Our public discourse is inextricable from our talk about education.[2]

Taken thusly, education becomes the arena in which philosophical problems arise and where their solutions make a difference in practice.[3] It should come as no surprise then that education can be credited, or more often blamed, for every disturbance in daily life as it arises and for all of the chronic problems we face.

It will seem counterintuitive to some to describe education as being in crisis. From a purely economic perspective, it appears to be doing quite well. The educational services sector provides education across a broad spectrum of subjects and at diverse levels. Services offered by this sector include elementary and secondary schools, colleges and universities, technical and trade schools, fine art schools and language schools. Its US market size is $1.35T and growing rapidly. Within the overall industry, online learning is the fastest growing segment.

One reason for this robust economic picture is that virtually every sector of the economy is becoming more highly specialized and more dependent on advanced technical skills. As professions and aspects of daily life (e.g., shopping online) become more complex and demanding, we need better tools for navigating them.

Despite its ubiquity in our discourse, its hold on the core of our economy, and our need for what it promises, there are reasons to see education as being in crisis. In particular, it is not just the quantity of education but the quality of education that is in question. Crisis narratives drive educational change against the background of capitalist structures in both universities and K-12 education.[4]

## EDUCATION AS THE ALL-PURPOSE SOLUTION

Is climate disruption a problem, one exacerbated by general ignorance about how the climate works, and even more fundamentally, about the nature of science? Then we need better education to fix that problem. How about racism, and the lack of understanding of its historical, systemic, and institutional roots? Clearly, we need critical race theory and other approaches to promote students' ability to question existing systems and assumptions. The same could be said of income inequality, authoritarian and anti-democratic movements, pollution, and international tensions.

Given the many social ills that can be attributed to education, the lack of it, or misapplication, it should not be surprising to learn that the literature on education is filled with descriptions of crisis. This is the case for schooling at K-12 levels, in wealthy nations, schooling in developing countries,[5] higher education,[6] specific disciplines (e.g., humanities),[7] and other sectors. Robert Birnbaum and Frank Shushok describe a "crisis," offering quotes from the past to exemplify this:

1865: Within the past twenty or thirty years, our long-tested and successful system of collegiate instruction has . . . been so persistently decried and so seriously menaced as to fill the friends of sound education throughout the country with alarm.

1972: Higher education in the United States and elsewhere is beset by . . . crises of public confidence, questions of continuing relevance, doubts about continuing the emphasis on doctoral instruction, and a very real financial crisis.

1996: The present crisis has both deeper and broader implications for the future than the repeated periods of stress facing colleges and universities since about 1970.[8]

It is clear that the very idea of a crisis in education serves rhetorical purposes beyond the simple reporting of a problem. Because all of us are affected by education, we are naturally alarmed when it does not proceed as we expect or wish. The word "crisis" implies a call for immediate and forceful action. But the various crises can also be used to make us reflect on what formal education has been and what it could be. They should lead us to question the special role that formal education can play in today's world. For example, the growth in online courses for specific purposes need not be considered solely as either a threat or a utopia, but instead as a call to understand what in-person schooling can alone do well.

## STUDENT CRISES

Over three millennia ago an apprentice scribe was weary of his schoolwork and daydreaming of the big city. He prays to Ptah, the god of Memphis, Egypt, to help him concentrate on his lesson.[9]

**Longing for Memphis**

Farewell, my thoughts! Absconded, they race toward a place they know well,
Upriver bound to see Memphis, House of Lord Ptah. (And I wish I were with them!)
But I idle here absent-minded, wanting my thoughts back to whisper me news of the City.
No task at all now prospers by this hand—heart, torn from its perch, just not in it.
(Come to me, Ptah! carry me captive to Memphis, let me gaze all around . . . and fly free!)
I would spend my workday wakeful and dutiful, but the will drowses, heart
Veers away, will not stay in my body; all other parts of me sickened to ennui—
The eye heavy with staring and studying, ear, it will not be filled with good counsel,
Voice cracks, and words of the recitation tumble and slur.
O Lord of the City friendly to young scribes, be at peace with me!
Grant me to rise above this day's infirmities!

Complaints from and about students have continued ever since.

When the original *West Side Story* came out in 1957, there was widespread public concern about disaffected youth, dropouts, and gang-related behavior. While some saw the need for better social services and education, others blamed the students or their parents. This dichotomy can be seen in the song, "Gee, Officer Krupke!," which mostly blames the families:

Dear kindly Sergeant Krupke
You gotta understand
It's just our bringin' up-ke
That gets us out of hand
Our mothers all are junkies
Our fathers all are drunks
Golly Moses, naturally we're punks!
Later, in the song it suggests the need for social service:
In my opinion, this child don't need to have his head shrunk at all. Juvenile
  delinquency is purely a social disease!
Hey, I got a social disease!
So take him to a social worker!

In the 1990s and following, there was the crisis derived from the myth of the "juvenile superpredator."[10] Following Columbine in 1999, many academics wrote about "moral panic theory." Debates around youth and popular culture, including dropouts, alienation, gangs, and other dysfunctions, reflect the sense of an enduring and recurring crisis for education.[11]

In recent years, there has been a growing recognition of the anxiety produced by the focus on high-stakes testing. Alfie Kohn identified the problem thirty years ago: Students are punished by rewards—"the gold stars, incentive plans, A's, praise, and other bribes" that drive educational practice.[12] Opening up educational opportunities has caused students to be even more aware of the costs of not achieving those "rewards."[13] This is not the only source of anxiety, but academic rigor defined in terms of external measures of success, such as a high grade-point average, leads to mental health problems for many.[14]

The demise of many small liberal arts colleges reminds us of the difficulty of combining the values of free, holistic, self-directed learning with education's role as a gatekeeper in market economies. These issues percolate through discussions of education at all levels. Some of the enthusiasm for STEM for youngsters is about its potential to make education more expansive, more meaningful, and more tangible, but even for five-year-olds, much of that is driven by anxiety about finding work with dignity in today's economy.

The future of both traditional place-based education and of learning beyond the walls depends on the answers to three questions: To what ends should education be accountable? How do we finance it? How do racist and classist practices shape what happens?

## ACCOUNTABILITY

Reform movements in education are always with us. For example, in the late 1920s there was a concern about too many courses, too little focus, and too little intellectual coherence in college education. In response, the University of Chicago developed its core, which would synthesize broad fields of knowledge, including in natural sciences, humanities, and social sciences, and offer an interdisciplinary framework of general education for the first two years of study. The proponents believed that the modern university should educate flexible minds who would welcome intellectual exploration and see through the temptations of rigid doctrinal systems. The founding principle was to teach students how, not what, to think.

In contrast, in the 1960s in the United States there was a sense among many that our systems were outmoded and unable to deal with the turbulent social movements of the times, due to a curriculum out of touch with current realities. There were calls for "relevance" and political "consciousness raising" in education.[15] Courses that connected to specific topical issues became prevalent, for example, those on women's rights, civil rights, or the Vietnam War. There have been many such swings over the years at all levels of education.

In 1955, Rudolph Flesch published *Why Johnny Can't Read: And What You Can Do about It*.[16] The book was influential and became an instant classic on phonics for teaching beginning reading. Reaching far afield, attention was drawn to Flesch's book when the USSR launched the first artificial Earth satellite on October 4, 1957. For many people in the United States, this was a disaster. The Soviets had demonstrated a technological superiority, one which could not be tolerated.

An argument developed as follows: If the United States employs a defective method for teaching beginning reading (the so-called look-say method), then how can Johnny learn to read, or at least to read as well as Ivan does, when Ivan uses a better method? If Johnny cannot read, then how can we expect him to keep up with Ivan in technical areas? It is no wonder that the USSR launched a satellite that now threatens our future.

What might have been a blip in the ongoing military race between the United States and the USSR became an indicator of a national failing. And that failing was directly attributable to education. This led to the "great debate" in reading education.[17] Some sided with Flesch. They saw the lack of a phonics approach as no arcane issue in pedagogy, but as a national crisis. Members of the John Birch Society claimed that it was evidence of a Communist plot, if not actual Communists in the teaching profession and in government. Note that this debate occurred shortly after the end of the McCarthy era.

Others thought that forcing a phonics approach (which one? for which students? in what ways?) could be a real detriment to education. They did not so much defend the look-say approach versus phonics as to argue for an overall education that was holistic and meaning-centered.

All of this occurred against a background in which most parents would have had difficulty explaining what the debate was about. Among those who cared about the curriculum, some just believed that their children were suffering from an inadequate teaching method. Meanwhile, most teachers employed an eclectic approach seeking what worked for their particular students.

The general theme of how we were in danger of losing to the Russians because of faulty education continued in other arenas. In response to the Soviet acceleration of the space race with the launch of the *Sputnik*, the National Defense Education Act (NDEA) was passed in 1958. The law provided federal funding to "insure trained manpower [sic] of sufficient quality and quantity to meet the national defense needs of the United States."[18]

The legislation provided for fellowships and student loans and bolstered education in the areas of science, mathematics, and modern foreign languages. The House report recommending passage of the bill stated:

> It is no exaggeration to say that America's progress in many fields of endeavor in the years ahead—in fact, the very survival of our free country—may depend in large part upon the education we provide for our young people now.

Note the hyperbole: "the very survival of our free country." The NDEA led the way for numerous education reforms in the 1960s. Many of the ideas, especially in science education, are standard teaching practices today. Again, education became the recipient, for better or worse, of concerns in other sectors of society.

Specific economic crises have also been attributed to education. Consider poverty and unemployment: When the economy falters and when people are out of work, education is to blame. Clearly, we are training too many humanists and not enough engineers. Or, we do not demand enough of students today, unlike what we demanded of previous generations. Perhaps we had poor material to work with. The argument quickly slides from blaming the education system to blaming the teachers, the parents, and ultimately the students.

This pattern reinforces Michael Katz's argument that social reformers spend much of their energy in attempts to "improve the character of poor people rather than attack the material sources of their misery." As they attempt to determine who is most deserving of their services, to sort out the worthy poor or the truly needy from a feckless underclass: "As a strategy, improving poor people consistently has awarded education a starring role." Public schools have long been assigned the impossible task of redressing the injuries of urban poverty by improving the character and discipline of its victims, turning them into better material for universities and corporations.[19]

Joseph Harris concurs:

> There is no cheaper brand of social reform than schooling, as it allows us to recast social ills as individual failings, to see the real problem as not unemployment but the unemployed, not poverty but the poor, not welfare but those made dependent on it.[20]

There are great oscillations in educational practice and theory. Some emphasize "what works." They want education directly keyed to practical concerns and job preparation. Others, worried about actions taken without planning or reflection, seek the cure through principles, guidelines, grand theories, abstractions, and generalities. Action in the world is nonexistent or reduced to an opportunity to apply what has been learned.

To what should education be accountable? For some, a key problem in education is that we have poor measures of success, whether that applies to the individual student, teacher, the school, the school district, the curriculum, or other aspects of the system. Accordingly, they say, we must have better measures, most often, tests that are standardized to create a level playing field that slices through vagaries of school location or materials.

For others, a narrow approach to accountability is precisely the major problem in education today. By focusing on scores in, say, reading or math, schools are prevented from devoting resources to character development, social responsibility, aesthetic appreciation, democratic living, understanding of diversity, physical development, or the many other goals of education. Even in an area such as reading, many suggest that the tests fail to measure advanced comprehension, alternate interpretations, or development of a love for reading.

Nel Noddings questions the obsession with a particular notion of accountability. She argues that "*accountability* forces us to answer to authorities for what we have accomplished or failed to accomplish; it points upward in the chain of power, and it encourages compliance or the appearance of compliance." In contrast, "*responsibility* points downward in the power chain; it asks us to respond to the legitimate needs of those placed in our care. It is not satisfied by meeting one narrow goal."[21]

Accountability too often reduces to a transmission mode of pedagogy in which authorities send information from the power center to the recipients. Responsibility, on the other hand, is a transactive mode of pedagogy in which teachers and students work together to create new meanings.

## FINANCE

Students and parents naturally seek the purportedly best schools. For higher education, some may choose none of the above, opt for a lesser school, or go deeply into debt. This is one of many reasons for the decline of support for liberal arts colleges and programs in recent years, and indeed support for general education in any venue.

Despite the comforting story of opening up higher education to all, we have a tiered system in terms of access and resources. Andrew Delbanco points to a shift from promoting equal opportunity to denying it:

> If higher education once helped to reduce inequities in American life, it now too often sustains and fortifies them. Like our health care system, it delivers concierge services to the affluent while consigning low- and modest-income Americans to overcrowded or underfunded facilities. And the disparities are getting worse.[22]

The finance issue operates even more insidiously for K-12, where, in the United States at least, we continue to rely on local property taxes to fund education. It is no surprise that students from wealthy families get to attend the best schools, even though they need that the least. Good schools in turn enhance the desirability of neighborhoods, raising property values, which in turn make it easier to fund schools. That results in being able to hire the best teachers and administrators, building the best facilities, obtaining the best materials, including books, information technology, and lab equipment, and being able to rely on a population of parents with the time and resources to support education for their children.

As less endowed schools decline, they predominately serve low-income students of color. That leads to further abandonment by the portion of the general public with financial and political power. The consequent destruction of equitable public schooling is a major mechanism by which class warfare operates today in the United States, and many other countries.

The schools are permeated by other injustices and expected to provide solutions they are not equipped to provide. This applies to issues of poverty in general, but also specifically to mental health, substance abuse, nutrition, and decent employment. Among these issues is housing: Wealthy US cities have too little affordable housing and offer inadequate shelters. They now turn to schools as last resort homeless shelters for their students. San Francisco City Supervisor Hillary Ronen says that "a community school mentality" is required.[23] But as valuable as that program has been, it is a far cry from the ideas of community school as simply making the classroom activities more relevant to community life.

There is a shift to corporate managerialism in public institutions. Educators are implicated in the system with their pay and retirement plans tied to loyalty. Debt financing has become the norm for both the schools and in the case of higher education, the students themselves. When school districts need financing, whether for ordinary expenses, such as salaries or equipment upgrades, or for special expenses, such as asbestos cleanup or Covid-19 mitigation, they can no longer count on regular school budgets. So, they turn to the municipal bond market. This may solve the immediate problem, but it saddles the district with extra expenses for years to come.

Wealthy investors benefit from the tax-free status of that municipal bond interest. The public essentially uses scarce tax revenues to fund those investors rather than to support the schools directly. Investment rating services base a school district's credit score on the district's existing property value and residential income. Poorer school districts are considered "riskier," so they pay more in interest and fees. Funding schools by way of credit scores thus reifies a system of prejudices benefiting the haves and punishing the have-nots.[24]

For some, we have a major disaster brewing as the majority of the population receives sub-standard schooling and is denied opportunities for continuing education. They maintain that there must be a major, renewed commitment to public education or we will all suffer. In reaction, others believe that there is too much attention to the public and particularly to a portion of the public that deserves blame. This leads to further abandonment of the public schools and neglect of its clients in favor of the private sector.

As one example of many, the former US Secretary of Education, billionaire Betsy DeVos, did not have neighborhood public schools as part of her life experience. This undoubtedly reinforced her staunch support of privately run, publicly funded charter schools.[25] These, and voucher programs, allow families to take tax dollars from the public education system to private schools. Is it a surprise that many Congressmen support privatization when the majority are millionaires?[26]

Many of DeVos's policies had a long tail. More importantly, she is part of a much larger movement to defund public education. She once proclaimed that her education advocacy would "advance God's kingdom." Although her policies did not specifically prescribe religious schooling, the practical effect of the charter/voucher movement has been to shift funding from secular to religious education, as well as to defund general, public education.

Closely related to the issue of validation is that of financial sustainability. Most people are drawn to the idea of no-cost avenues for learning across non-traditional domains. Think of the *Whole Earth Catalog*.[27] It was an American counterculture magazine and product catalog published by Stewart Brand from 1968 off and on until 1998.

The magazine featured essays and articles but was primarily focused on product reviews. The editorial focus was on self-sufficiency, ecology, alternative education, "do it yourself," and holism, The slogan was "access to tools." Steve Jobs recalled it in a commencement speech:

> When I was young, there was an amazing publication called *The Whole Earth Catalog*, which was one of the bibles of my generation. . . . It was sort of like Google in paperback form, 35 years before Google came along. It was idealistic and overflowing with neat tools and great notions.[28]

People saw *The Whole Earth Catalog* as a place where anyone could be a teacher or a learner. But those same participants might also seek marketable degrees or certificates. Issues of financing, certification, and technological change meant that the model was not sustainable over the long term.

The same kinds of issues arise with public education. Do we have the will to support it, especially when we look at who controls the purse strings? Can a historically unjust society create the conditions to promote greater diversity, equity, and inclusion?

As is so often the case, money and who controls that may determine the fate of public education as we have known it. The outlook is gloomy. Money is deeply implicated with class and race issues to the point that support for public education is not only weakening but also seen by those in power as an unnecessary expense to be purged.

## CLASS WARFARE

The class warfare aspect of education is another endemic crisis. To point to just one example from a long history, James Anderson shows how education for blacks in America was primarily used, not to reduce inequity or provide opportunities but to emphasize Bible study and obedience training. In that context, Booker T. Washington's support for vocational education appears somewhat progressive, while W. E. B. Du Bois's more liberatory visions of schooling seem utopian.[29]

The forces of certification and financing may seem dry topics in the world of accounting. But they interact in insidious ways with race and class biases.

Certification can become a way to diminish educational opportunities while appearing to be instituting a clean, mathematically neutral system for categorizing people. Financing can be organized so as to disadvantage people who have already been treated inequitably.

For example, public schools are increasingly becoming schools for people of color.[30] In addition to changing demographics, white students have more options for religious schools, suburban charter schools, homeschooling, private tutoring, private, nonsectarian education, and other "escapes" from the public system. Government policies increasingly favor using public funds to support these alternatives, while starving the public system. Digital certification will only hasten the process.

Even within the public system, white students tend to live in communities with higher tax bases. In a model that funds schools on the basis of local property taxes, wealthy students find that their schools are better funded even though their parents pay a lower percentage of their home property value or income for schooling. Racist and classist perspectives on schooling tend to normalize these practices and to assign any problems with the schools to the failures of the students or their families.

Those who resist full funding of public education, working assiduously to undermine and eliminate it, are even less receptive to the idea of funding learning beyond the walls. Think of the opposition to Midnight Basketball. This was an initiative developed in the United States in the late 1980s using late-night basketball leagues designed for social intervention, risk reduction, and crime prevention targeted at African American youth and young men. Participants could play basketball during the peak crime hours of 10:00 p.m. to 2:00 a.m. and then attend programs that gave them helpful skills for everyday life.

The program was a way for young men to form a sense of community, to escape dangerous environments, and to build hope for a better life. Midnight Basketball helped decrease crime in the neighborhoods where it was run, and it was a positive outlet for many young men. It helped many stay out of trouble, off the streets, and participate in education.[31]

Despite the positive outcomes, Midnight Basketball came under fierce attack. It was seen as social engineering, as a boondoggle for minority groups, and as a frivolous liberal expenditure. Head Start and Home Start were also attacked, despite their impact on the lives of young people and their families and the hard-nosed economic evidence that they have had a higher return on investment than almost any other government-funded program. Similar programs, most of which cost relatively little, have received comparable scathing attacks.

In 1966, the Boston area's Metropolitan Council for Educational Opportunity program, known as Metco, became one of the first voluntary desegregation efforts in the country. It expanded educational opportunities, increased diversity, and reduced racial isolation, by permitting students in underfunded schools to attend public schools in wealthier communities. Currently, there are about 3,300 students participating in 38 school districts in the Boston area and 4 more next to Springfield.

The Metco program has been successful. Participants outperform students with similar demographic profiles in the Boston Public Schools. High school graduation and college enrollment rates are about 30 percentage points higher. For example, a student from Roxbury, a lower-income community with more people of color, is provided transportation to attend a wealthy, suburban, mostly white high school in Belmont. He is able to study with mostly college-bound students in a safe and stable environment that he might not have in his neighborhood school.

But there are problems. That same student may feel isolated with interests different from those of his peers. In a class on statistics, students used a large dataset, which had been published in *Boston Magazine*. The white students in the class focused on comparisons among wealthy Boston suburbs: Which one had the highest college admission rate? Which one had the most cars per family? Which one had the most valuable houses? The student from Roxbury noticed instead that people in his community did not live as long, and asked why.

Given time, one can imagine how this culture/knowledge clash is not a problem at all but instead a stimulus for enhanced learning for all, including the teacher. It could open up discussions about wealth distribution, the relation between wealth and health, and much more. This would be yet another demonstration of how connecting classroom learning with lived experience outside can enrich education.

But with one student per class, and only a small percentage eligible overall, the impact of Metco is limited. The number of intensely segregated schools (in which 90 percent or more of the student population are students of color) has increased significantly in recent years.[32] Educational quality and funding follow the patterns of segregation. Dramatic action is needed.

The state could in principle significantly expand Metco and promote actual school integration. There could be regional magnet schools with programs in performing arts, artificial intelligence, or social entrepreneurship. There could be partnerships with area universities, museums, and hospitals, improving educational opportunities for all students, regardless of race or zip code.

Doing anything like this will probably require a lawsuit, such as what happened in Hartford, Connecticut, in 1996.[33] That led eventually to a system of "Open Choice," which allows students in the Hartford metropolitan area to attend schools across the usual barriers of district lines and wealth. A second program is built around a specially created network of forty magnet schools with free pre-kindergarten. The network draws 19,000 students from across the region.

It is necessary to note here some people dispute the use of educational resources in a way that they interpret as favoring undeserving recipients. Some even resent the mixing of students, which they thought the segregated suburbs would prevent. It is depressing to see how quickly programs such as Metco are attacked almost as soon as they are announced.

The recurring crises of education provide a backdrop that constrains and shapes reform efforts. They define the discourse of education, since it is difficult to talk about any aspect of pedagogy without addressing the societal frame of distress attributed to schooling. But the background crises may pale against some major technological, demographic, and financial forces creating an existential crisis for public education today.

## NOTES

1. Valerie Strauss, "Everything You Need to Know about Common Core—Ravitch," *Washington Post*, January 18, 2014.

2. All of the John Dewey quotes in this paragraph are from *Democracy and Education*, MW 9: 338.

3. Despite this, many teacher education programs have stopped teaching educational foundations or philosophy of education. Some teacher educators don't want to teach theory of any sort. See M. K. Naseerali, "Relationship between Philosophy and Education," *Dreamhosters* (blog), November 22, 2016, https://naseerali.in/relationship-between-philosophy-and-education/.

4. *Beyond Education: Radical Studying for Another World* (Minneapolis, MN: University of Minnesota Press, 2019), 27–28.

5. Dor Bahudur Bista, *Fatalism and Development: Nepal's Struggle for Modernization* (New York: Orient Blackswan, 1991).

6. Nicholas Carr, "The Crisis in Higher Education," *Technology Review*, April 10, 2013, 1–10.

7. Paul Jay, "The Humanities 'Crisis' and the Future of Literary Studies," n.d.

8. "The Crisis in Higher Education: Is That a Wolf or a Pussycat at the Academy's Door?" (23rd Annual Conference of the Association for the Study of Higher Education, Miami, Florida, 1998), 2.

9. John L. Foster, ed., *Ancient Egyptian Literature: An Anthology*, 1st ed. (Austin, TX: University of Texas Press, 2001). The text is from a student's "miscellany" of New Kingdom date (ca. 1550–1070 BCE).

10. John L. DiIulio, "Super Predators," *The Weekly Standard*, November 27, 1995, http://www.weeklystandard.com/article/8160.

11. Christopher M. Mosqueda, "Columbine and the Myth of the Juvenile Superpredator," Educational Specialist (Salt Lake City, UT: Brigham Young University, 2020).

12. Alfie Kohn, *Punished by Rewards: The Trouble with Gold Stars, Incentive Plans, A's, Praise, and Other Bribes* (Boston: Houghton Mifflin Co, 1993).

13. David Marchese, "Laurie Santos on Why Her Yale Students Have so Much Anxiety," *The New York Times*, February 18, 2022.

14. Wendy Fischman and Howard Gardner, "No, College Students Aren't Obsessed with Free Speech. Here's What They Do Worry about," *Boston Globe*, February 17, 2022.

15. Notable examples include John Caldwell Holt, *How Children Fail*, Rev. ed., Classics in Child Development (Reading, MA: Addison-Wesley Pub. Co, 1995); Ivan Illich, *Deschooling Society* (New York: Harper & Row, 1971); Neil Postman and Charles Weingartner, *Teaching as a Subversive Activity* (New York: Dell, 1969).

16. Rudolph Flesch, *Why Johnny Can't Read: And What You Can Do about It* (New York: Harper & Row, 1986).

17. Jeanne S. Chall, *Learning to Read: The Great Debate*, Updated ed. (New York: McGraw-Hill, 1983).

18. "National Defense Education Act" (US House of Representatives, August 21, 1958), https://history.house.gov/HouseRecord/Detail/15032436195.

19. Michael B. Katz, *Improving Poor People: The Welfare State, the "Underclass," and Urban Schools as History* (Princeton, NJ: Princeton University Press, 1997).

20. Joseph Harris, "Reclaiming the Public Sphere," *College English* 59, no. 3 (March 1997): 325.

21. Nel Noddings, "Commentary: Responsibility," *LEARNing Landscapes* 2, no. 2 (2009): 17 (emphasis in original).

22. Andrew Delbanco, "The University Crisis," *The Nation*, February 21, 2022: 33.

23. Gail Cornwall, "A School Created a Homeless Shelter in the Gym and It Paid off in the Classroom," *The Hechinger Report*, March 17, 2022, sec. Solutions.

24. Eleni Schirmer, "We're Burying Our Kids in Debt (Just Not the Way You Think)," *The New York Times*, August 27, 2021.

25. Erica L. Green, "To Understand Betsy DeVos's Educational Views, View Her Education," *The New York Times*, June 10, 2017.

26. Karl Evers-Hillstrom, "Majority of Lawmakers in 116th Congress Are Millionaires," *Open Secrets*, April 23, 2020.

27. Henrik Bennetsen, *From Counterculture to Cyberculture: The Legacy of the Whole Earth Catalog* (2011, April 22), https://youtu.be/B5kQYWLtW3Y.

28. *Steve Jobs, Stanford Commencement Speech* (Palo Alto, CA: YouTube, 2005).

29. James D. Anderson, *The Education of Blacks in the South, 1860–1935* (Chapel Hill, NC: University of North Carolina Press, 1988).

30. Between fall 2009 and fall 2018, the percentage of public school students who were white decreased from 54 to 47 percent. "Racial/Ethnic Enrollment in Public Schools" (National Center for Education Statistics, May 2021), https://nces.ed.gov/programs/coe/indicator/cge.

31. Douglas Hartmann, *Midnight Basketball: Race, Sports, and Neoliberal Social Policy* (Chicago; London: University of Chicago Press, 2016).

32. Jack Schneider et al., "School Integration in Massachusetts: Racial Diversity and State Accountability" (Beyond Test Scores Project and Center for Education and Civil Rights, Summer 2020).

33. David Scharfenberg, "The Only Way to Fix Boston Schools Once and for All," *The Boston Globe*, March 18, 2022.

*Chapter 5*

# A Dreadful Crisis

> In one of *Grimm's Fairy Tales* there is the story of a youth who went out in search of adventures for the sake of learning what it is to fear or be in dread.
> —Søren Kierkegaard, *The Concept of Dread*[1]

Many of the so-called crises in education are one-time affairs, often perversely manufactured to serve political purposes beyond the schools per se. A rise in unemployment may lead to lamentation over inadequate schooling, whose purported deficiencies would be ignored in ordinary times. The periodic kerfuffles around meaningless college rankings, which do little more than encode white privilege, are another example.[2]

Others crises are endemic; they are just reminders of the challenges that educators face every day. But there is also a brewing crisis that threatens not to end education but to end the central role of the place-based academy (brick and mortar facility) familiar to most of us through schooling, college, or industrial training, and more importantly to threaten the very concept of democratic, general education.

## FALLING SUPPORT FOR TRADITIONAL GENERAL EDUCATION

Evidence of the existential crisis for general education can be seen in the demise of liberal arts colleges. On January 23, 2019, Green Mountain College president Robert W. Allen announced that after 185 years, his college would be closing: "Despite our noteworthy accomplishments related to social and environmental sustainability, we have not been able to assure the economic sustainability of the College."[3] About half of accredited, four-year, not-for-profit, liberal arts colleges have vanished over the last three decades. Some, like Green Mountain, simply closed. Others merged with other institutions, others lost accreditation, and some converted to public, for-profit, or two-year status. In a few cases, there were creative solutions making the best of the financial crisis, such as the creation of the Green Mountain Center for Sustainability at Prescott College.[4]

Larger institutions have not fared much better. So-called optional programs are being shut down, such as master's programs for teachers that do not directly lead to teacher certification. Branch campuses of major state universities are being closed or scaled back. On June 5, 2020, Regents of the University of Alaska system voted to discontinue, merge, reduce, or rename more than forty academic programs around the state. Among the discontinued programs were those in Sociology, Geography, and a master's program in People, Place, and Pedagogy. Some programs were targeted for elimination because of union activist faculty.

It can take years to develop each of these programs, in part because there are so many stakeholders. A student seeking to develop expertise in earth and atmospheric sciences may be basing their career and career decisions on the program. Community groups and industry partners may have invested heavily. Staff and faculty often devoted years of their lives to these programs. Few of them are autonomous; they link with other programs; a master's degree may be the needed culmination of a bachelor's program, one that moves from general education to skills of service to a profession or larger community.

College enrollment has been trending downward for a decade, driven by demographic changes and the pandemic. The greatest declines are among students seeking associate degrees. Support for public universities is dropping to the point that some are considering a change of status to private.

Even at the most successful private universities, such as those in the Ivy League, or at large land-grant universities, there are dramatic changes. Once a general education emphasis has been replaced by a professionalization approach, the university appears to become more and more an adjunct to industry, sort of a minor league training ground. Good arguments can be made for connecting higher education with industry, but as we discuss below, it sets the stage for the ultimate elimination of the place-based university entirely, and with it democratic, general education.

At the K-12 level, a significant number of parents are taking their children out of public school and sending them to religious schools, other private schools, or homeschooling and tutoring programs. Support for the existing public schools then drops. This is happening more with the Covid-19 pandemic, especially as schools implement inconsistent rules about masks and vaccines, most often driven by political forces outside the school system.

The fall in support for public education is exacerbated by the fact that for the first time in recent history, a majority of students in US public schools are from low-income families. By 2013, 51 percent of public school students qualified for free and reduced-price meals, a common indicator of poverty in education. Moreover, many school systems are now majority-minority. For many citizens, this makes the public school appear to be a welfare program, one that deserves little support and should ideally be eliminated in favor of private, for-profit education. As one example among many, a district in Wisconsin opted out of the federal free-meal program on the grounds that free lunches would spoil parents.[5]

To understand this crisis, we need to look at how formal schooling and the academy define gateways to further education and jobs, and why that could be changing in a significant way, enough to upend the current system.

## THE CURRENT SYSTEM

In broad strokes, our existing system of education consists of place-based academies, such as schools, colleges, universities, technical institutes, corporate training centers, and more, which manage classroom learning, online learning, and supervise clinical experiences, such as field trips, fieldwork, internships, and practica.

There are a few generally accepted postulates of this system:

- The place-based academy (school, college, university, institute, professional school, and corporate training center) organizes and regulates the system, usually with the support and guidance of accrediting bodies and professional organizations.
- All pedagogical activities are conducted within the four walls of the place-based academy, or at least controlled and managed from within.
- A key product is the production of credentialed graduates, for example, a middle school graduate ready for high school or a doctor ready for internship.
- Teaching occurs primarily through classroom learning, supplemented by clinical experiences. For primary school students, the latter might include clubs, the playground, or perhaps a field trip. For an engineer, it might be an internship at a company in the chosen field.

See figure 5.1 for a simple schematic of this system. It highlights the solid four walls of our current educational system. Note that online learning is becoming a key player but is still shown in dashed lines because it is not yet fully integrated into this system.

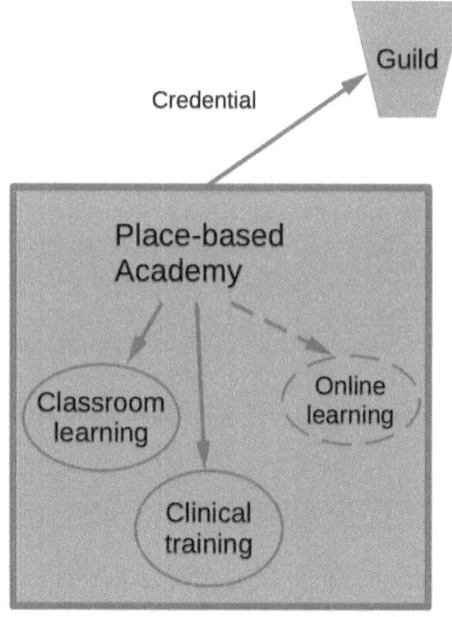

**Figure 5.1  Structure of the Current Education System.** *Source*: Author created.

This system is so familiar that it operates as the *doxa* for educational discourse.⁶ People debate how much online education is good to have, or what the balance between classroom learning and clinical training ought to be. They may question or consider the order of different elements. But in general they do not question the core idea of a centralized credential process run by the academy to produce credentialed graduates for the guild.

That core idea is thus part of what Pierre Bourdieu sees as the unquestioned beliefs that form the foundation on which our epistemic knowledge rests. As one example, he notes,

> When you ask a sample of individuals what are the main factors of achievement at school, the further you go down the social scale the more they believe in natural talent or gifts—the more they believe that those who are successful are naturally endowed with intellectual capacities. And the more they accept their own exclusion, the more they believe they are stupid, the more they say "Yes, I was no good at English, I was no good at French, I was no good at mathematics." . . . It is a formidable mechanism, like the imperial system—a wonderful instrument of ideology, much bigger and more powerful than television or propaganda.⁷

This hegemonic process is more powerful because it is internalized and consensual. In addition, the doxa of all of the participants accepts that the place-based academy is the appropriate arbiter of achievement, in English, French, or mathematics. The academy relies upon these beliefs about achievement and is its sorcerer, managing experiences to produce a hierarchy of achievement, then translating that achievement into credentials that regulate further participation in the social system.

## CERTIFICATION

Online education appears to be on a similar path, implementing more and more of the process of education and along the way gobbling up more and more of the education sector's resources. As one example, on September 7, 2021, the University of Massachusetts system announced a major expansion of its online education footprint in an attempt to reach more adult learners.

Brandman University, which currently serves 22,000 students as an independent part of the Chapman University System in California, is now UMass Global. Based in Irvine, California, Brandman operates twenty-five physical campuses in California and Washington as well as hybrid and online models. The school currently provides services for employers offering low-cost college as a worker benefit, including Chipotle Mexican Grill, Target, Walmart, Disney, and Discover Financial Services.[8]

Corporate moves such as this are widespread and primarily quantitative. But there is a qualitative change underway as well. This qualitative change comes in part because online learning inherently incorporates digital certificates to indicate and validate progress. For example, many teaching positions, government jobs, corporate, and not-for-profit work now demand ethics training. Online ethics courses lead to an ethics course completion certificate. This becomes a necessary requirement to do the work.

No one asks whether we are now producing more virtuous workers, and it is unclear how much external validation of the ethics courses has been done: What is the evidence that ethics violations have been reduced due to their implementation? Nevertheless, the system now has an apparently objective way to verify that staff have learned ethics.

Certificates of this type are common now in health care (e.g., vaccination cards), daily life (driver's licenses), education (to show prerequisites or certification to advance to the next level), foreign language learning, and much more. Some began as paper only, but nearly all now have a digital representation. These certificates are not just for isolated activities. Just as a university might declare that 120 credit hours of appropriate types are needed for a bachelor's degree, it could declare that some accumulation of digital certificates would be equivalent to some number of credit hours, or even the entire degree.

Over twenty-five years ago, an online master's program in technology and education at the University of Illinois introduced the Technology Competencies Database (TCD). It used an online portfolio approach to document students' mastery of specific standards. The TCD gave learners the opportunity to describe how they met particular competencies and allowed their instructors to verify that. "Exemplary" projects emerged to represent both the student's personal achievements and those of the course or the program.[9] At that time, the portfolio system was an adjunct to the ordinary course evaluation. But it was just a short step away from *being* the marker for the course evaluation.

Today, the place-based academies can choose how much to employ digital certificates. At one extreme, they simply issue a certificate to indicate judgment of achievement, for example, a high school issuing a diploma. At the other, they could use an automatic system to mark degree completion once the proper number of appropriate certificates had been entered. In between, there are many other options. For example, some degree programs store certificates online and can call up automatic assessments to indicate additional courses, projects, or clinical experiences that might be needed.

The convenience of these certificate systems is a Faustian bargain for the academy. Today, we look to the academy to tell us whether a student has completed elementary school, or done her engineering practicum. Regardless of how automatic the system may be, only the academy has the ultimate authority. But if the academy does nothing more than nod assent to a digital representation, how necessary is its function?

Some communiversities are associated with traditional universities, often seeking to change them from within; others are associated with a community group or may be fully independent. As hybrids, communiversities benefit from diverse perspectives but also face unique challenges. Participants often need traditional validation, or certification, through degrees, academic ranking, and other conventional measures of "academic excellence," exactly the values which communiversities often question. Whether and how does the learning experience "count" in the market economy? We cannot ignore the fact that students seek validation for their work, in a way that is recognized in the marketplace.

Digital certificates are a rapidly growing technique for verifying identity and appropriately allocating information, resources, and communication channels. They are a generalization of the idea of digital or identity certificates in cryptography.[10] They are already used for credit card transactions, vaccine and Covid-19 test status, e-signatures, compliance workshops for employment, and many other purposes.

In education, digital certificates can represent degree completion or the status of degrees in progress. They can be used for individual courses, or modules as small as a workshop or training session. Although far from universal, digital certificates are already having a large impact, some bad and some good.

On one front, digital certificates are both being propelled by and propelling the movement toward online education. As students complete learning experiences online, there must be a way to compare those to the traditional certifications offered by place-based academies. Are four short, online computer programming courses equivalent to a semester-long course in a high school or community college? If not four, would five be enough? Could there be an alignment of content to project scope to assess equivalency? How about hybrid experiences, with some work done online and some in person?

Other questions arise: Could digital certificates for either online or place-based education help with the alignment of learning across state or national boundaries? Could prerequisites for study be defined in terms of digital certificates? As the system of certificates expands, will we determine an equivalency between say a four-year, bachelor's program and some number of online modules appropriately digitally certified? Questions such as these seem unavoidable as online education becomes more the norm.

At the same time, digital certificates further the online course movement. The more that we can specify learning objectives, the easier it becomes to develop an online approach to deliver those. And this is exactly where one of the negatives emerges. Both digital certificates and online courses work best when learning is atomized into discrete bits. An ethics course can fit the framework if ethics considerations can be broken down into manageable chunks but not if the goal is to learn how to approach problems with an ethical mindset. Similarly, history fits well if it means learning specific facts and surface-level principles but not if it entails developing a working understanding of historiography or the ability to wrestle with multiple perspectives.

Digital certificates could spell the end of place-based education as we know it. If there are multiple ways to acquire a certificate, there will be unremitting pressure to find the lowest cost alternatives. This process has occurred in nearly every other industry in recent years. Just think of the impact that Amazon has had on the retailing industry.

When the online master's program in Library Science at the University of Illinois (LEEP) started in 1997, it achieved early and unexpected success. Students and faculty began to seek it out; employers rated graduates as high or higher than those from the regular on-campus program.

One reason for the success was that it is a high-touch, high-tech, and high-impact educational experience, combining asynchronous and synchronous sessions online with on-campus experiences. Welcome Weekend is a three-day required orientation on campus. This experience is structured as a mini-conference, offering small group activities and workshops that allow students to get to know their peers, faculty, and advisers. They can visit local libraries, academic, public, and community. The orientation helps build a community from the very beginning of the program and leads to stronger connections and collaborations with peers.

The program's high quality has preserved it for twenty-five years, but there is always financial pressure. Prospective students ask why they should pay for travel to Urbana-Champaign as LEEP requires, when a similar program is fully online. LEEP has since dropped the on-campus sessions.

It is worth noting that LEEP began in part because it could attract out-of-state students who would pay higher tuition. This focus on those who can pay the highest rate, such as out of district or even international students, is a common factor in education decision-making in the current climate. LEEP is a special case, but most education policy makers are forced to fund only the lowest cost programs and to facilitate enrollment by students who can pay the most. Families with the fewest resources will find that their options are poorly funded if they exist at all.

## THE COMING SYSTEM

The current system is ingrained in our beliefs as well as in a panoply of practices. So, what might change such a system? One seemingly inexorable force, as indicated by its larger presence in figure 5.2, is online learning. At first glance, this seems to suggest merely an intramural dispute: How much of learning should go on face-to-face and how much online? Granted, the percentage of online learning is growing rapidly, aided at times by budget considerations, academic competitions, pandemics, and other exogenous events, but the basic idea of a balance of different modes of learning seems unassailable.

More recently, formal educational organizations have faced the issue of online competition. If a student can complete courses at no cost from Khan Academy or the online offerings of elite universities, why should they enroll in the local college? If they do enroll in the place-based academy, why should they pay the full rates that they would for on-campus courses? Covid-19 has accelerated this shift into online environments. Mid-career professionals going back to school but still working full time have eased the way for asynchronous distance learning which can be done on their own time.

Online learning comes with two important weapons. These go far beyond the debates among educators about details, such as how well do online science simulations compare to physical demonstrations as a way to teach particular science concepts. The first of these is cost. In the early days of technology-enhanced learning, there was a flush of enthusiasm for a mode of

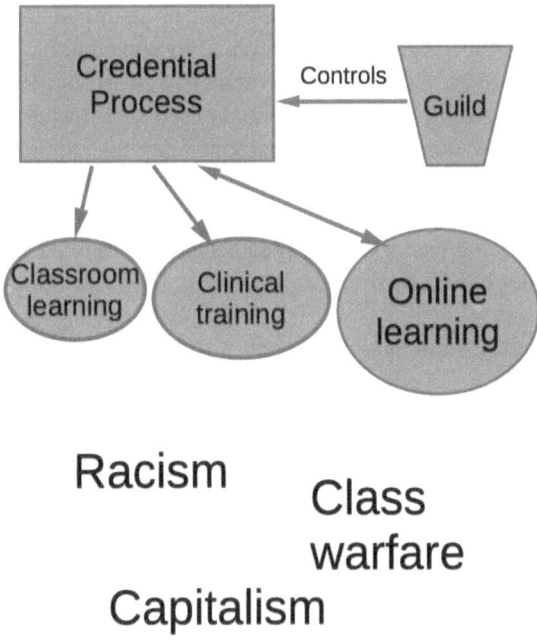

Figure 5.2 Structure of the Coming Education System. *Source*: Author created.

learning that would be significantly cheaper than current modes of education. The industry soon learned that high-quality online learning could be far more expensive. In addition to expenses for equipment, including hardware, software, maintenance, and frequent upgrades, there was training for teachers, the complex process of integrating online and physical learning, new curricular needs, and much more.

But costs are coming down. Online learning is part of an ecology of information and communication technologies. Educators do not need to purchase equipment that students already bring with them to school. Educational applications can draw from standard productivity software, such as the ability to read, annotate, or make pdf files. The process is accelerated as standards are lowered to accommodate often lesser educational experiences.

The power of capitalist enterprise seems unstoppable. In July 1995, Amazon opened as an online bookseller. Many people at that time marveled at this new way to buy books. They wondered how long it would last, but feared that like many technological innovations, it was unsustainable. Since then, Amazon has grown to become one of the largest companies in the world, with a 50 percent share of online retail spending and a 10 percent share of total US retail spending. Those who fret about Amazon no longer ask whether it will survive, but whether it will take over too much. Already, many small businesses have been eliminated or absorbed within Amazon's orbit. The Post Office seems to have become its subsidiary.

Currently, the place-based academy manages classroom learning, clinical training, online learning, and the credential process. But what if other entities could offer various packages for classroom learning, clinical training, and online learning, and there was an agreed-upon system for digital learning certificates, a currency, so to speak. We then no longer need the place-based academy. Its enticing use of the certificate system would be its downfall.

The new order has its own set of postulates:

- The education system is self-regulated through the currency of digital certificates.
- Guilds, which are organizations of workers in different fields, direct the certification process.
- As in the current system, teaching occurs through a combination of online and classroom learning, plus supervised clinical experiences, but these are now offered by a wide variety of agents.
- Capitalist modes of production push toward the lowest cost for each component of the teaching.
- Rhetoric about equal opportunity leads the larger public to reject policies that appear to favor people of color, even when those policies just seek to level the playing field.[11] As demographics change and as white parents reject public schooling, schools become increasingly institutions for low-income families, immigrants, and people of color. Large segments of the population with power further exaggerate the effects so that the schools are seen and defined in racist and classist terms.

## DYSTOPIA IN ACADEMIA

Like smartphones, digital certificates are one of those technological innovations that are generally annoying, but indispensable. This may have both positive and negative consequences for education.

Meanwhile, financial pressures and racial and class discrimination are equally likely to grow, rather than diminish. Disparities in wealth, income, housing, food security, and other measures are becoming more extreme.[12] The rise of overt white supremacy movements creates an environment in which education becomes a site for class and race warfare. The changes we perceive today in education are also likely to accelerate in the years to come. For anyone interested in democratic education, opportunities for the disenfranchised, holistic approaches to pedagogy, some preservation of what we have called the liberal arts tradition, or other aspects of general education, this is a dismaying vision.

Forces of economics, racism, classism, and technology are already burning down the walls of traditional, place-based education. The privatization movement to defund public education draws attention as it fuels an already raging fire.[13] This burning is literal as historically black colleges face bomb threats, in the year 2022![14] Even without the concerted, well-funded assault of privatization, it is unlikely that mitigation measures such as simply closing a school or two, merging others, changing accreditation, or conversion to for-profit status would forestall the existential crisis. The walls are coming down.

What will remain? It could be that we will have independent, mostly for-profit entities offering disconnected bits of education—basic literacy, an accounting course, instruction in Java programming, and a course on music appreciation. Most of these will be online, but some place-based learning will survive, especially for privileged classes. Supervised clinical experiences will be offered in a similar way. These bits will sustain themselves through participation in an economy whose primary currency is digital certificates, aggregated at key points to validate certification for particular jobs.

Issues such as integrating knowledge across disciplines, learning how to understand life in a diverse society, appreciating the perspectives of others, learning how to work together, or becoming a critical-socially engaged citizen will be relegated to bullet points in some courses such as "team management," if they are acknowledged at all.

The question becomes whether to accept that historical process as we see it proceeding or to ask about alternatives. Are we compelled to witness the end of liberal education, general education for all, or democratic education in our lifetimes?

## NOTES

1. Søren Kierkegaard, *The Concept of Dread*, trans. Walter Lowrie (Princeton: Princeton University Press, 1973), 139.

2. Malcolm Gladwell, "Lord of the Rankings / Project Dillard (Two-Part Series)," Pushkin Industries, July 1, 2021, https://www.pushkin.fm/episode/lord-of-the-rankings/.

3. Scott Jaschik, "Another Small College Will Close," *Inside Higher Ed*, January 24, 2019.

4. Melissa Tarrant, Nathaniel Bray, and Stephen Katsinas, "The Invisible Colleges Revisited: An Empirical Review," *The Journal of Higher Education* 89, no. 3 (May 4, 2018): 341–67.

5. That policy was later reversed.

6. Richard Nordquist, "What Does the Term 'Doxa' Mean?," *ThoughtCo.* (blog), https://www.thoughtco.com/doxa-rhetoric-term-1690480 (accessed March 19, 2022).

7. Terry Eagleton and Pierre Bourdieu, "Doxa and Common Life," *New Left Review*, no. 191 (February 1992): 114.

8. Chris Lisinski, "UMass Eyes Bigger Online Education Footprint With New Brand," *State House News Service*, September 3, 2021.

9. The software system to support the competencies database is described in Sandra R. Levin, James G. Buell, and James A. Levin, "The TEbase Initiative_Research, Development and Evaluation for Educational Reform," *Journal of Computing in Teacher Education* 16, no. 3 (2000): 6–11. The use of the system to identify and share exemplary work is discussed in James A. Levin, Nicholas C. Burbules, and Bertram C. Bruce, "From Student Work to Exemplary Educational Resources: The Case of the CTER White Papers," *E-Learning* 2, no. 1 (February 10, 2016): 39–49.

10. A public key certificate is an electronic document used to prove its ownership. The certificate includes information about the key, information about the identity of its owner, and the digital signature of the issuer. If the signature is valid and the software examining the certificate trusts the issuer, then it can use that key to communicate securely with the certificate's subject. In email encryption, code signing, and e-signature systems, a certificate's subject is typically a person or organization. However, a certificate's subject can be a computer or other device, as with HTTPS, a protocol for securely browsing the web.

11. This phenomenon occurs across the board—in education, health care, job opportunities, and disaster relief. See Dick Startz, "Equal Opportunity in American Education," *Brown Center Chalkboard* (blog), January 15, 2019, https://www.brookings.edu/blog/brown-center-chalkboard/2019/01/15/equal-opportunity-in-american-education/; James R. Elliott, Phylicia Lee Brown, and Kevin Loughran, "Racial Inequities in the Federal Buyout of Flood-Prone Homes: A Nationwide Assessment of Environmental Adaptation," *Socius: Sociological Research for a Dynamic World* 6 (January 2020).

12. The Gini index represents the income or wealth inequality within a nation or a social group. The World Bank data <https://data.worldbank.org/> shows that the index for the United States has been higher (greater inequality) than that of other developed economies. It has been steadily rising in recent decades.

13. Diane Ravitch, *Reign of Error: The Hoax of the Privatization Movement and the Danger to America's Public Schools* (New York: Vintage, 2013).

14. Margaret Renkl, "Bomb Threats Are Roiling Historically Black Colleges and Universities," *The New York Times*, February 21, 2022.

*Part III*

# Learning in the Wild

We tend to think of cognition as a property of the mind, and even of abstract reasoning, not emotions or physical sensations. But our physical embodiment means that we are also part of the world of objects and living things around us. Our hands are an instrument of thought as much as our brains.

Moreover, we always operate within a social world, constructing meaning out of both personal experiences and the experiences that others share. Susan Sontag expresses this well when she describes her "crusade . . . against the distinction between thought and feeling." She argues that the purported split between mind and body is the basis of all anti-intellectual views:

> We think much more with the instruments provided by our culture than we do with our bodies, and hence the much greater diversity of thought in the world. Thinking is a form of feeling; feeling is a form of thinking.[1]

This perspective is confirmed by anthropological studies: Ed Hutchins studied how people reasoned as they navigated a ship. He found that cognition extends beyond the individual mind to include the computational basis of navigation, its historical roots, and its social organization. Culturally constituted activities manifested in daily norms and practices, physical objects, cultural memories, computations, and more revealed cognition as significantly different from that seen in artificial laboratory settings.

Moreover, this cognition arose from the cultural situations and practices that individuals participated in. It was *cognition in the wild*.[2] That phrase has now come to signify studies of thinking as it occurs outside of formal communication situations and where cultural activity systems reveal cognitive properties different from those of the individuals who participate in them.

Caroline Haythornthwaite et al. extend Hutchins's concept to *learning in the wild*, meaning the learning that occurs outside classroom settings.[3] Learning in the wild can appear strikingly in online communities. This implies a transactional mode of pedagogy. Mike Sharples argues that understanding it better can help us reimagine education in general:

> Rather than seeing mobile communication and online communities as a threat to formal education, we need to explore how education could be transformed for the mobile age, through a dialogue between two worlds of education: one in which knowledge is given authority through the curriculum, the other in which it emerges through negotiation and a process of coming to mutual agreement.[4]

*Learning in the wild* can apply not only to online learning but also to learning through work or any engagement with life. It also applies to allowing the wild to redefine formal learning, as in conceiving of the *community as curriculum*. More generally, it calls us to ask: How should learning in the wild inform the creative response we so desperately need to the crises in education today?

## NOTES

1. Jonathan Cott, "Susan Sontag: The Rolling Stone Interview," *Rolling Stone*, October 4, 1979, https://www.rollingstone.com/culture/culture-news/susan-sontag-the-rolling-stone-interview-41717/.
2. Edwin Hutchins, *Cognition in the Wild* (Cambridge, MA: MIT Press, 1995).
3. Caroline Haythornthwaite et al., "Learning in the Wild: Coding for Learning and Practice on Reddit," *Learning, Media and Technology* 43, no. 3 (July 3, 2018): 221.
4. Mike Sharples, "Learning As Conversation: Transforming Education in the Mobile Age," March 23, 2017: 2.

# Profile
## Caroline Haythornthwaite

Using a social network analysis perspective, Caroline Haythornthwaite's research explores how interaction via computer media supports and affects work, learning, and social relations.[1] She is especially interested in full two-way communication—a transaction among participants, in which the distinction between teacher and students blurs. She says,

> I worked for a company that had one of the earliest email systems. Being immersed in that, I had a feel for the real life aspect of online communication. It was an essential channel of communication. We maintained collegial and friendly relationships with people who were distributed around the world. We also used online chatting. It wasn't just the transformation of a memo into the online environment. It was a new way of working.
>
> One of the first things I looked at was a video conferencing system. People weren't adopting it. I set out to find out what people were doing, how much were they maintaining friendships through these different media—asking who talked to whom about what and via which media. Can you keep friendships there? Can you keep working relationships there?
>
> When I left that company—to a world without online communication—I suddenly felt, where had it gone, where were my colleagues, where was my universe? Stepping out of that was like suddenly going backwards and finding nobody understood the online world, at all—nobody understood how different it was.
>
> When I joined the University of Illinois in 1996, they didn't automatically give students an email account. It was all very strange for me to encounter a world where it's not available to everybody. It's only available to the elites. It's only available to those who know about it and ask about it.

When we went into online learning it just seemed natural to think of exploring this new environment, as I had known at the company, not simply replicating the classroom online. But it was new for each student and they were all alone. There was no one they could turn to and say, "Hey, you've done this before." So I was asking what makes it possible for people to work in these environments, to be able to get their work done, to form a community? How do they learn to do that? It was about the support structures around learning.

We know it's just not about delivering content; it's about creating community. People are seriously struggling. The instructors are struggling, which is probably a reflection of how the students are struggling and the parents of students who are struggling. What do you need to do beyond pushing content?

We found out that for maintaining relations online extra work was being done by auxiliary people—for example, the Associate Dean was constantly answering questions online—giving quick feedback on things, answering questions. But most important, the students were talking to each other. You've got a supportive administration and students who were able to start talking to each other and make the community. They were learning from each other.

This is what's happening in Reddit and YouTube communities. People are putting up their own content. When someone posts on Wikipedia, it is for an imagined community—one that isn't there yet for this topic that they really care about. We are seeing how people learn outside the classroom, in the wild. There are emotional and social issues. Life is hard and you have this on top of your life. Online students are balancing online learning with other challenges in their lives.

When we started, we would select readings and make them available online. Now many more pieces are available online. You want to encourage people to learn from what's out there and not just from what's in the curriculum.

Our early online environment worked because students could talk to each other (synchronous lecture, week long asynchronous). In contrast, the last online learning environment I worked on depended on pre-recorded videos, which meant there was little or no interaction during the lecture [transmission pedagogy]. There were asynchronous exercises, but students weren't hearing each other's questions. As we really move out of the classroom—open, online resources, discussion groups, lists, videos, etc.—there is much work to be done to understand how online learning occurs, and how it can connect to classroom education.

## NOTE

1. Caroline Haythornthwaite is professor emerita at both Syracuse University and the University of Illinois. She has taught and directed graduate programs at

Syracuse and the University of British Columbia. See Caroline Haythornthwaite et al., "Learning in the Wild: Coding for Learning and Practice on Reddit," *Learning, Media and Technology* 43, no. 3 (July 3, 2018): 219–35; Caroline Haythornthwaite, "Rethinking Learning Spaces: Networks, Structures and Possibilities for Learning in the 21st Century," *Communication, Research and Practice* 1, no. 4 (2015): 292–306.

*Chapter 6*

# Learning Online

> The pandemic disrupted life as we knew it and forced us into new relationships with technology. Technology helped us connect remotely to work, to school, to each other. Virtual communities don't replace real time ones, but together they offer a level of flexibility and access either alone cannot.
>
> —Teresa Martin, "Thinking Outside the Classroom"[1]

Online learning has meant many different things over the years. It was once computer-assisted instruction, in which the computer substituted for a human tutor in a transmission mode of communication. Later, it meant the computer as a tool through the use of spreadsheets, graphing devices, probe controls and monitors, word processors, messaging services, and planning tools.[2] It has also meant the computer as *tutee* through the use of programming, as with Logo. The latter highlights the fact that the computer can be a tool for writing as well as for reading and may be an even more powerful resource in that role.[3]

More recently, online learning has been equated with learning management systems that present information, facilitate instructor presentation, offer discussion boards for communication among students and faculty, and assess student learning. We should call these *online replicants*. They are intended to mimic classroom learning and be almost as good, although without the social interaction or hands-on learning.

But the field is much wider than any of these formulations suggest. It now includes an unending variety of devices, tools, and procedures for direct instruction, facilitated activity, communication between human and machine or human to human, stand-alone electronics, and much more. These forms of online learning exhibit the transmission, interaction, and transaction modes of communication in diverse ways. At its best, online learning can become *online augmentation*, in which the online tools amplify or extend other modes of learning in the classroom or beyond.

## SHUTTING DOWN OR OPENING UP?

Imagine a Grade 4 class in early spring, about to embark on a unit about the seasons. The teacher recognizes the auspicious emergence of cherry blossoms on a tree in the playground. She also checks the coat area and verifies that few of the students are still wearing jackets to school. This provides an opening to a discussion about the signs of spring and, from there, of the characteristics of the seasons in their geographic area.

The unit proceeds, with lists and diagrams on the board, individual drawings by students, identification of questions that can be answered through scientific inquiry, as well as those important questions about feelings and meanings that can be discussed, but not given simple answers. Perhaps the students create physical models, or they make measurements on the inner solar system replica painted on the playground asphalt.

There is a discussion about the local farms: What crops do they grow? What stage are they today? What produce do we see in the grocery store? Can you tell where it comes from? Is any of it local, or different at this time of year? If the school is in an urban area, the teacher might still lead an investigation into what plants are growing through the cracks in the sidewalk. Or, possibly, the class might consider the effects of local microclimate, such as that caused by the shade of a tall building.

The unit grows to consider the changing pattern of stars seen locally. They take a field trip to the local planetarium and learn more about how the local season compares to seasons in other states or countries, especially hemispheres. Students explore theories about the cause of the seasons, for example, is it the earth's position in its elliptical orbit or the tilt of the axis? They learn more about the solar system, the inner versus the outer planets. The unit grows without bounds.

## FILLING A VESSEL

Now, consider that this classroom adds online learning. There are two ways this could go. One is to conceptualize learning as filling a vessel. In this case, the district purchases a set of online lessons about the seasons. It probably comes as part of a complete Grade 4 package, or even an all elementary school bundle. Online lessons are necessitated by the pandemic, but in some cases districts expand the online use for budget reasons. Perhaps class size can be increased if some students learn at home, or lower-paid teaching paraprofessionals can be hired to manage the class if the software "manages the learning."

This is *online substitution learning*. In the best case, the online lessons transmit their information effectively. Of course, they cannot adjust for unexpected student questions, such as "Why are the planets shaped like balls?" or "When I went to North Carolina, it was really hot. Why?"

There could be a simulation in which the student enters a zip code, but otherwise the online lessons are insensitive to the cherry blossoms, the need for jackets, the produce from local farms, the urban canyons, or anything else tied to place. The lessons, dissociated from the local environment and the students' lives, become abstract and hollow. Students can be tested on their content acquisition. They may do even better than those in some fully in-person classes. But their learning is constricted. It is hard to relate to, hard to make sense of, and hard to remember.

Online substitution learning takes the already overly proscribed classroom learning environment, with its scope and sequence charts, curricular, district, and state goals, textbook mandates, and more, then restricts the learning possibilities even further, funneling the learning process into ever narrower channels. It is easy to understand why it appeals to administrators and to some novice teachers; the rules are clear and predictable. The point here is not to criticize educational practitioners but to critique the system we all operate in.

The outcomes of substitution learning are limited and known in advance. Bits of learning are isolated, purified, and deposited in the supposed empty brain of the student. The effects of this are not only limiting; they can shut down questioning and wonder. What is the alternative?

## ADDING KINDLING TO A FIRE

A second way is to adopt Plutarch's view of teaching as adding kindling to a fire, with each idea sparking another idea, and further questions. Our hypothetical classroom might employ online tools mostly in response to student inquiries. They offer "what if" simulations: What if we could alter the tilt of the earth's axis? What if we could change the nearly circular path of the earth's journey into an elongated ellipse?

In a web of online learning, students could investigate local plants using *iNaturalist*. They could set up experiments involving shadows and occlusions, then use online tools to analyze their data. They could search databases of seasonal data (rainfall, temperatures, extreme weather events, etc.).

Rather than narrowing the possibilities for learning, the online tools in this scenario expand those possibilities, building on the community of inquiry in the classroom and connecting to larger webs of inquiry. They do what experts recommend as the goals of scientific inquiry, to develop knowledge and skills that all students should acquire from their total school experience from kindergarten through high school. This includes attitudes of curiosity, wonder, experimentalism, and skepticism. These recommendations downplay traditional subject categories and instead highlight the connections between them.[4]

The diversity of online innovations presents problems for traditional models of teacher education in which teachers are "trained" in the use of specific methods, approaches, or innovations. The training model misses the most salient fact about implementation: that it is a creative process involving critical analysis of the innovation's potential in the light of institutional and sociocultural context, physical resources, student needs, and pedagogical goals. The innovation process doesn't end, but begins, with the teacher.

> When an innovation that calls for significant changes in teacher practices meets an established classroom system, "something has to give." Often, what gives is that the innovation is simply not used. Rarely is an innovation adopted in exactly the way the developers intended . . . the process of re-creation of the innovation is not only unavoidable, but a vital part of the process of educational change . . . a deeper understanding of this process will highlight the fact that teachers need more support in attempting these re-creations. Their role in the innovation process is as innovators, not as recipients of completed products.[5]

Although most teachers see their role as expanding the possibilities for learning and connecting to ever-expanding webs of meaning, most school districts will eventually choose buckets over fires. One issue is cost. A single comprehensive package is assumed to be cost-effective, even with little evidence to support that. As more students already have access to mobile devices and new software packages are generally free and open source, there is at least a good case to be made for web-like online tools actually saving money.

But a more compelling issue is that of control. Fires after all are dangerous and unpredictable. Districts worry that students with free inquiry might start to ask questions about human-caused climate disruption or that an investigation of local agriculture could lead to embarrassing questions about agricultural pollution or monoculture farming. They ask, what if the students learn about Saturn's rings but do not actually learn the reason for the seasons?

The latter can become a compelling worry despite the evidence that few fourth-grade students actually learn the reasons for the seasons in any pedagogical format. Few adults can give even a roughly accurate response to this question.

There are also few well-reasoned arguments that knowing the reasons for seasons is more important than knowing about planetary rings, life on Mars, radiation belts, or endless other possibilities. If students are engaged in genuine inquiry, they will explore and answer many questions that matter to them. They do not need to be funneled into what is likely to be a faulty answer to one question on a standardized test.

## UNTETHERED FROM TIME OR PLACE

Most of the free university education around the world is now offered online through Massive Open Online Courses (MOOCs).[6] The universities use platforms such as Coursera, Udacity, FutureLearn, edX, or Udemy to host the courses through campus websites. Universities offer free online college classes that include recordings of lectures as well as interactive courses with assignments and final projects.

These learning opportunities can be a great way for job seekers to boost their skill set, gain valuable knowledge, and enhance their likelihood of career progression. In return, the institutions are able to compile research that can be used to improve their courses and develop better technologies for online and classroom-based learning. The offerings are usually noncredit, but some provide a (digital) certificate of achievement or completion.

A platform such as the Khan Academy offers practice exercises, instructional videos, and a personalized learning dashboard that empower learners to study at their own pace in and outside of the classroom, for subjects such as math, science, computing, history, art history, economics, and more, including K-14 and test preparation (e.g., SAT, Praxis, LSAT) content. They focus on skill mastery to help learners establish strong foundations, with no preset limits on what to learn next. Millions of students from all over the world, each with their own unique story, learn at their own pace at Khan Academy every day. The resources are available in more than thirty-six languages.

Launched in January 2012, Coursera is now the largest MOOC provider in the world. It offers 5,500 online courses. The platform also hosts fully online master's degrees in fields such as computer science, data science, business, and public health. Over the last decade, more than 900 universities around the world have launched free online courses. In addition to the larger global platforms (Coursera, edX, and FutureLearn), many national governments around the world have launched their own country-specific platforms.[7]

The growth of MOOCs appears to fulfill the promise of the earlier free universities. Even the 8,500 annual registrations at the UKMC Communiversity pales in comparison with more than a million registrations in some individual online courses. These appear to offer a way to bring education to everyone, thus realizing the full potential of communiversity.[8]

But there is a key difference. Free university offerings reflect the interests of particular communities and help to strengthen them. In a region with a significant indigenous population, they might offer courses about, or even taught by, Native people. An area with a serious river pollution problem might offer target chemistry courses, or courses on water pollution. The UKMC Communiversity supported community radio and the local not-for-profit dance school, City in Motion. These activities are extremely important now to the local community but might have little relevance to those in, say, the Philippines, or even those in Kansas City a decade from now.

Free university courses thus typically reflect local history, industry, and culture. Over the years, the course offerings would be grounded in time and place, providing a map of life in the community. At best they could become a public forum for addressing issues of concern and help to build common ground.

In contrast, part of the appeal of MOOCs is that they are not tied to a time and place. A student in Indonesia can take a computer science course from Harvard, without needing to know the instructor or even how to find Cambridge, Massachusetts. MOOCs thus offer the democratizing potential of individual development, but they undermine the complementary democratic potential of dialogue and developing a common purpose.

One project with great promise is Wikiversity, a Wikimedia Foundation project devoted to learning resources, learning projects, and research for use in all levels, types, and styles of education from preschool to university, including professional training and informal learning. Teachers, students, and researchers are invited to join and create open educational resources and collaborative learning communities.

## TELEHEALTH

Discussions of online learning usually focus on online courses intended to supplement or replace courses already being taught in formal learning situations, such as calculus or history, or perhaps training for some new procedure or equipment. But in our increasingly complex world, people need to learn new things to manage their finances, do a better job gardening, repair a faucet, play a musical instrument, or find a mate. Online learning is becoming the norm in all of these areas. "Find a youtube on that," meaning to locate an online tutorial video, is almost as common as "google it" to locate some fact.

As an example, consider telemedicine. Data analytics using population-level data makes possible personalized care strategies for individual patients.

Health care becomes more personal by addressing social determinants of health. Machine learning and artificial intelligence are now used to identify and personally reach out to customers who may need greater assistance in accessing health care.[9]

In addition to population-level data, online telemedicine has meant better access to one's personal health data. Many people now regularly use patient gateways that maintain a record of visits and medications. Lab results are made available shortly after the blood draw or scan. There are tools to look at trends over time and anomalous findings.

Gateways are beginning to facilitate the access by health care providers in other networks, family members, or other relevant parties. They also offer messaging services and private communication channels for the patient and provider. Thus, the online service can actually enhance person-to-person communication.

Meanwhile, inexpensive electronics for temperature, blood pressure, O2 saturation, blood sugar, and EKG monitors built into smart watches have given another boost. Much of the routine monitoring done before only in a health clinic or hospital can now be done at home, with greater privacy, at much lower cost, and with equal accuracy.

Online tools in medicine now provide transmission-like communication through videos, websites, and fully online courses. They also provide more interaction-like communication through fully online means such as FAQs or search and browse features, but also by linking individuals together through phone or video connections. The latter can be especially useful for counseling for mental health, nutrition, or other lifestyle issues.

These online tools make it much more feasible for older adults to receive care in their homes.[10] Home health care is not just possible but increasingly normalized, often saving costly emergency room and hospital visits, and coordinating medications from the local pharmacy.

The coronavirus pandemic only added to the already growing patient demand for opportunities to connect with health care providers remotely. As a result, there has been a huge jump in the utilization of telehealth. This has in turn created new demands. One is to provide adequate broadband access at home. Another is to develop better procedures for ethical management of data.

## LEARNING IN THE WILD

Learning on and through social media is becoming essential for lifelong learning. This can be for transmission-like communication, such as accessing information, but also for interaction- or transaction-like communication through finding other self-motivated learners.

A good example is Reddit, the online news-sharing site that is also a forum for asking and answering questions. Caroline Haythornthwaite et al. studied these learning practices found in "Ask" subreddits, such as those devoted to science, politics, or history, and developed a coding schema for informal learning. They examined the discourse, exploratory talk, and conversational dialogue, as well as the norms and practices on Reddit and the support for communities of inquiry.

Their *learning in the wild* coding schema contributes to an understanding of how knowledge, ideas, and resources are shared in open, online learning forums. For example, "providing resources" includes "comments that include direct reference to a URL, book, article . . ."[11] This implies a transmission mode of communication.

But most of their categories fit more in the interaction mode. Various kinds of "explanation" (with or without agreement) explicitly entail the feedback loop of interaction, as do references to "Subreddit rules and norms." "Information seeking" initiates a loop of communication, leading to multiple back and forth exchanges. Some of these interchanges could be considered as transactional communication in which participants create meaning together. The "socializing interactions" (saying "thanks" or "you're an idiot") fit that mode quite well.

Haythornthwaite et al. describe the communication on these subreddits as *social learning*. This contrasts with the transmission mode that dominates formal learning situations:

> Social learning is demonstrated in a number of ways in these Ask communities. Explanations represent the practice of learning from and with others. Equally important are the opening forays into seeking information, where individuals begin the process of engaging with others in the service of learning.

Participants adopt and shift roles as the conversations proceed, with teachers responding to learners as well as the other way around: "Experts who respond, for example, through explanation, do so in a reciprocal social learning role, the teacher role in response to the learner."

In these conversations, there is also meta-talk, in which participants define and shape the very discourse they are constructing: "In keeping with ideas of apprenticeship, experts and moderators also model and instruct in proper answering, e.g., in providing resources to justify claims, and sanctioning off-topic or non-conforming answers."[12]

Reddit saw on average 52 million daily users in late 2020, marking a 44 percent jump from the same time the previous year. But there are problems as well. In fall of 2021, Reddit moderators of more than seventy subreddits with millions of collective subscribers went private in a coordinated effort to protest the coronavirus disinformation they say runs rampant on the platform, as well as Reddit's refusal to delete subreddits dedicated to undermining the severity of the pandemic.

## WRITING TO LEARN

Online learning plays an important role as a transmitter or deliverer of information. But the learning occurs through writing as well. One can see this by a quick look at Wikipedia, which might otherwise be deemed the greatest transmitter of information there has ever been.

Wikipedia began with its first edit on January 15, 2001. It now appears in 323 languages. There are nearly 300,000 active editors and almost 100,000,000 users. The size of Wikipedia can be measured in various ways. As of September 6, 2021, there are 6,371,102 articles in the English Wikipedia alone containing nearly 4 billion words on over 54 million pages. The current version of all the articles compressed is about 20 gigabytes. Wikipedia continues to grow, and the number of articles on Wikipedia is increasing by over 17,000 a month. The amount of text added to Wikipedia articles every year has been constant since 2006, at roughly 1 gigabyte of (compressed) text per year.

Users, anyone with internet access, can add new articles or contribute to the millions of existing articles. Students do this for course assignments; ordinary citizens do it through Wikipedia parties; hobbyists do it to further their passions; scholars do it as part of their public engagement. Although not every article is carefully researched by the individual, it is collectively, as other Wikipedia users edit and add to the entries of others. An enormous amount of learning occurs in this way.

An extreme example is Sverker Johansson, by one estimate, the world's most prolific author.[13] In parallel to his studies in the origins of language, he also maintains a web-crawling bot that scrapes geographical, meteorological, and other data and automatically creates short Wikipedia articles. He estimates that, to date, nearly 20 percent of the articles on Wikipedia, or more than 1.5 million, were first created by this bot. On the positive side, Johansson's bot helps to redress some inequities in Wikipedia coverage:

> "Wikipedia has excellent geographic coverage where young white males live," he explains drily. "North America, Europe, generally industrialized countries—but Africa was basically a blank spot. Suppose there is a disaster in some village somewhere. What do you do as a journalist? You look the village up on Wikipedia, and if you have a stub [a short article] there, you can at least see which province it is in, the rough location, the nearest city."[14]

These stubs provide a useful service, but they also reveal how Wikipedia works, what it does well, and where it falls short. So, creating this content is a way of learning for us all.

The discussion thus far barely touches on the possibilities for learning inherent in massive sets of data, freely accessible and searchable with new data analytic tools. For example, the emergence of large multi-institutional digital libraries has opened the door to aggregate-level examination of the published word.

Peter Organisciak, Benjamin Schmidt, and Stephen Downie describe such large-scale analysis as a way to pursue traditional problems in the humanities and social sciences. The basic idea is to use digital methods to ask questions of large corpora. They work with the HathiTrust Digital Library, a digital repository of over 17 million volumes of digitized materials contributed by dozens of university and public libraries. Their work examines the role that exploratory data analysis and visualization tools can play in understanding these datasets. Their tool, HathiTrust+Bookworm, "allows multi-faceted exploration of the HathiTrust Digital Library, and centers it in the broader space of scholarly tools for exploratory data analysis."[15] Similar projects are underway to analyze not only other text corpora but also corpora of images, music, maps, protein and genetic sequence databases, and other media.

Various display tools in HathiTrust+Bookworm allow the analyst to look at questions such as the use of the word "Beijing" in English-language countries over the last fifty years. This shows an upsurge in the mid-1990s, especially in Australia, and a few years later in the UK. Another example shows the use of "burned" versus "burnt" over the years since 1750. There is a peak for "burnt" around 1820, with a steady decline since, but still a significant use today. Another query shows the relative rise in the use of "coffee" over "tea."

The graphical displays are interesting per se, but the meaning of them still requires the analyst to apply historical, cultural, linguistic, and other contextual knowledge. For example, is the shift from "burnt" to "burned" part of an overall trend of regularization of English spelling and pronunciation or does it reflect some other cultural trend?

Large databases such as the HathiTrust Digital Library are now freely accessible anywhere in the world. They offer sophisticated tools for browsing and searching and use graphical displays that are more informative and user-friendly. Digital humanists can benefit from computational access to these massive, era-spanning digital libraries. The scale of such collections presents technical hurdles.[16] Nevertheless, they may transform education more than the simple movement of in-classroom lessons to an online format.

Transforming education in that way poses a challenge at least as designing new tools. The very power and appeal of the corpus are for open-ended or web-like learning. Students can venture anywhere in their explorations. But that grates against the education system's need for control: How do we specify learning outcomes in advance if no one, not even the designers of the corpus or the analysis tools, can tell us what students might learn?

Others may choose to explore the natural world through platforms such as *iNaturalist*.[17] It combines literal learning in the wild with a massive global database and a social network for collaborative learning. Imagine a field guide, a very large one, which can identify a bird by one feather, a shrub by its berries and a couple of leaves, a small mammal by its tracks, or any other living thing. Further imagine that if you are unsure what you have seen, it can look up your observation based on a photo from your phone in a database of over 90 million observations. You can receive suggestions for a generic classification and consider more specific options. Imagine further that if the automatic identification is insufficient, you can draw on the knowledge of over a million observers.[18]

*iNaturalist* began in 2008 as a graduate school project. It later became a joint initiative between the California Academy of Sciences and the National Geographic Society. Today, it hosts a social network of naturalists, citizen scientists, and biologists built on the concept of mapping and sharing observations of biodiversity across the globe. It combines multiple technologies: the camera on mobile devices, a large database of observations, and crowdsourcing.

Since 2012, the number of participants and observations has roughly doubled each year. In 2014, *iNaturalist* reached 1 million observations. As of February 2021, *iNaturalist* users had contributed approximately 66 million observations of plants, animals, fungi, and other organisms worldwide. They can use *iNaturalist* to find online nature groups or citizen science projects in their local area and contribute photos and data directly,

Although not a science project per se, *iNaturalist* is a platform for science and conservation efforts, providing valuable open data to research projects, land managers, other organizations, and the public. It is the primary application for crowd-sourced biodiversity data in places such as Mexico, southern Africa, and Australia, and the project has been called "a standard-bearer for natural history mobile applications."[19]

Users have created and contributed to tens of thousands of different projects. It is commonly used to record observations during bioblitzes—biological surveying events that attempt to record all the species that occur within a designated area. Other projects include collections of observations by location or taxon or documenting specific types of observations such as animal tracks and signs, the spread of invasive species, roadkill, fishing catches, or identification of new species.

## SUBSTITUTE OR REJUVENATE?

Unlike what we call here online substitution learning, *iNaturalist* invites the user to get outside, to explore nature, and become a problem solver. It promotes self-directed learning in which the user can investigate entirely on their own or connect with a large community of others interested in nature. *iNaturalist* is not part of most standard scope and sequence curriculum guides; it is too unpredictable. Yet, it is one of many examples showing the promise of online learning outside the physical walls of the classroom or the virtual walls of online substitution learning.

Learning in the wild comes with attendant risks. Unplanned and unwanted material can intrude, as in the Reddit example. There will be inaccuracies, incompleteness, disorder, even deliberate misinformation, hatred, and vile ideas. We expect our standard curriculum to protect us from these, although it does at best so imperfectly. Moreover, the very protection, to the extent that it is possible, means that students are not afforded opportunities to learn how to sort the wheat from the chaff, nor what to do with the chaff.

The best learning environments satisfy curiosity by presenting new things to be curious about. They engage learners in exploring, thinking, reading, writing, researching, inventing, problem-solving, and experiencing the world.[20] This echoes Ivan Illich's call for education webs, not funnels.[21] Education should expand the possibilities for experience, not funnel them into ever narrower boxes (or earthen vessels).

Online learning, in some circles, represents the future of education. It builds on the latest technologies to present new modes of learning, with advantages such as the possibility of distance learning, customization to specific learners and situations, interactive simulations, multimedia, and more.

At the same time, online learning takes us back to a mode of learning that places mind over body: Playstation replaces the playground. Learning from direct social interaction, through nature, through hands-on manipulation of water, clay, fabrics, electronics, plants and animals, or one's own body are all subordinated to interactions with a screen. When many learners suffer from decreased interaction with the physical and social worlds, they are offered at best simulations of those.

Online learning often means learning outside of the classroom walls. Indeed, it can make those walls irrelevant, even when the computer is physically in that classroom. But serious questions remain about how far that sort of beyond-the-walls learning can go to expand or enhance in-class learning. If online learning can provide us with new things to be curious about, it can be a vital part of rejuvenating public education. If on the other hand, it simply replicates or worse, funnels current modes of education into ever narrower spaces, it is something we must fight against.

## NOTES

1. *Cape Cod Times*, September 7, 2021.
2. Bertram C. Bruce and Andee Rubin, *Electronic Quills A Situated Evaluation of Using Computers for Writing in Classrooms* (Hillsdale, NJ: Lawrence Erlbaum, 1993).
3. Robert P. Taylor, II, ed., *The Computer in the School: Tutor, Tool, Tutee* (New York: Teachers College Press, 1980).
4. F. James Rutherford and Andrew Ahlgren, *Science for All Americans* (New York: Oxford University Press, 1990); Project 2061 (American Association for the Advancement of Science), ed. *Science for All Americans: A Project 2061 Report on Literacy Goals in Science, Mathematics, and Technology* (Washington, DC: American Association for the Advancement of Science, 1989).
5. Bruce and Rubin, *Electronic Quills A Situated Evaluation of Using Computers*, 218.
6. "MOOC (Massive Open Online Course): The Key Facts," *Edukatico* (blog), n.d., https://www.edukatico.org/en/report/mooc-massive-open-online-course-the-key-facts.
7. See also Barbara A. Oakley, *Mindshift: Break through Obstacles to Learning and Discover Your Hidden Potential* (New York: TarcherPerigee, 2017).
8. Dhawal Shah and Laurie Pickard, "Massive List of MOOC Providers Around The World," *The Report by Class Central* (blog), February 3, 2021.
9. Heather Cox, "The Future of Home Health Care Is Now," *Boston Globe*, September 6, 2021.
10. Joanne Binette and Kerri Vasold, "2018 Home and Community Preferences: A National Survey of Adults Age 18-Plus," AARP Research, 2018.
11. Caroline Haythornthwaite et al., "Learning in the Wild," 1. Original manuscript for paper published in *Learning, Media and Technology* 43(3).
12. Haythornthwaite et al.: 17.
13. Toby Skinner, "The Most Prolific Writer on Earth," *N by Norwegian Magazine*, September 2014.
14. Steven Poole, "Passing the 'Chimp Test': How Women Were Key to the Birth of Language," *The Guardian*, August 28, 2021.
15. Peter Organisciak, Benjamin M. Schmidt, and J. Stephen Downie, 2021. "Giving Shape to Large Digital Libraries through Exploratory Data Analysis," *Journal of the Association for Information Science and Technology*, July, asi.24547.
16. Ibid: 12.
17. Layal Liverpool, "Identify Local Wildlife and Aid Research with the INaturalist App," *New Scientist*, February 9, 2022.
18. Scott Loarie, "We've Reached 1,000,000 Observers!," i*Naturalist* (blog), May 15, 2020, https://www.inaturalist.org/blog/35758-we-ve-reached-1-000-000-observers#summary.
19. G. R. Goldsmith, "The Field Guide, Rebooted," *Science* 349, no. 6248 (2015): 594.

20. Peter Marin, *Freedom & Its Discontents: Reflections on Four Decades of American Moral Experience*, 1st ed. (South Royalton, VT: Steerforth Press, 1995).

21. Ivan Illich proposes an idea, funnels versus webs, which is similar in intent to buckets versus fires, in *Deschooling Society*. 1st ed. World Perspectives, v. 44 (New York: Harper & Row, 1971); later, *After Deschooling, What?* (London: Writers and Readers Publ. Cooperative, 1976).

# Profile
## *Ching-Chiu Lin*

A popular idea is to bring art to those perceived to be outside of participation in culturally sanctioned discourse. Often described as bringing the center to the margins, the idea presumes that lack of access to mainstream ideas, art, music, and general discourse limits opportunities for those on the margins of society.

The approach has led to opening up museums and concert halls, as well as to university-based arts outreach. The effects of these efforts have on the whole been positive. But despite the benefits, this can become little more than a transmissive solution to equity in art and culture. As Jane Addams warned, that one-way transmission of culture can be a disservice to both the people involved and the common good itself especially when it positions one aspect of culture as superior to all others:

> We have learned to say that the good must be extended to all of society before it can be held secure by any one person or any one class; but we have not yet learned to add to that statement, that unless all men and all classes contribute to a good, we cannot even be sure that it is worth having. In spite of many attempts we do not really act upon either statement.[1]

Ching-Chiu Lin has devoted her career to helping all people contribute to that common good.[2] Her teaching and research on connecting community life and the classroom enrich both. This effects the transformation that Maxine Greene calls for:

> It is not only a matter of admission and inclusion in predefined public spaces; it is . . . a matter of transformation of our institutions and public spaces. . . . We need to make audible and visible the diverse ways in which identity is

negotiated in our country and the manner in which it is affected by fairness, equity opportunities for free expression, and by the existence or the nonexistence of democracy.[3]

Ching-Chiu argues that "community arts education is not simply an end, but a means to develop social relationships and collective action in the community." This kind of communication is not simply transmissive, but transactive. Ching-Chiu elaborates,

> I was a public school teacher in Taiwan for seven years before pursuing my Ph.D. in the United States, so working within the school system is something I was familiar with. My dissertation was about three Illinois high school art teachers' uses of technologies in their classroom. I was exposed to teaching and learning outside the public school system as a Research Assistant in the Youth Community Inquiry project.[4] It gave me a taste of out-of-the-school educational programs.
> 
> That experience probably was the first time I got a sense of "the alternative space" of learning that is situated in between the public school structure, flexible curriculum and community focus. Meanwhile, I was traveling to three public schools in Illinois for my dissertation fieldwork, so I was able to compare the difference between two learning settings while reflecting upon my own positioning. It is interesting that because of this experience, I actually switched my research interest to more community focus than the school in terms of research settings when I moved to Canada. I felt that public schools have more bureaucracies that I have to go through if I want to conduct research in the school contexts.
> 
> Being new to Canada and having my previous experience in U.S. schools, I thought researching outside of the school context may be easier. With my postdoctoral fellowship in Canada, I tried to find a research site to study young people's digital engagement through arts. I didn't want to involve public school settings as I felt it was exhausting to navigate the layers of bureaucracy. However, later I realized that navigating community was even more intense because the structure and program were more spontaneous and organic. For the school system, I found there was an organizational commonality across school system that I could find my ways to navigate hierarchy.
> 
> I learned that for community, there were no roadmaps. Community is a relational practice in which the navigation is through the intersections of collegial interaction, shared commitment, and other factors. This was a space calling for transactional communication. Now working with community partners on community arts education projects for many years, conducting research in the community is like a self-therapy for me. Working with people on the margins in the society has given me a sense of fulfillment.

I often feel that have learned from the community more than I can offer. Recently I worked with a community of seniors, trying to understand their views on coping with COVID. By talking to the seniors, I thought of my own father and my childhood memory with him.

Meanwhile, working with diverse populations in the communities have opened my eyes to varied viewpoints. It's fascinating talking to people with rich experience, to learn from them, to see the resilience for dealing with their hardships. My encounter with community members has allowed me to recognize the dynamic relationship entangled with life itself. The performing of living is celebrated through stories, action, and relationships among community members. Artmaking becomes an active performative space of community living.

## NOTES

1. Jane Addams, *Democracy and Social Ethics* (Urbana, IL: University of Illinois Press, 2002), 97.

2. Ching-Chiu teaches in the Faculty of Education at Simon Fraser University, Canada. She has worked on community arts education, including digital media. Her work shows how learning occurs in community life and arises from lived experience. She focuses on the alternative space of learning situated between the public school structure and the community. See Ching-Chiu Lin and Anita Prest, "Frames Film Project" (Frog Hollow Neighbourhood House, May 26, 2015); Joanna Black, Juan Carlos Castro, and Ching-Chiu Lin, *Youth Practices in Digital Arts and New Media* (New York: Palgrave Macmillan US, 2015); Ching-Chiu Lin, "How Art Teacher Disengagement with Visual Literacy Discourse Reveals the Gap between Research and Practice in Art Education," November 20, 2009.

3. Maxine Greene, "Moral and Political Perspectives: The Tensions of Choice," *Educational Researcher* 27, no. 9 (1998): 19.

4. Bertram C. Bruce, Ann Peterson Bishop, and Nama Raj Budhathoki, eds., *Youth Community Inquiry: New Media for Community and Personal Growth* (New York: Peter Lang, 2014).

*Chapter 7*

# Community Engagement through Work

> The dichotomy of mental versus manual didn't arise spontaneously. Rather, the twentieth century saw concerted *efforts* to separate thinking from doing. Those efforts achieved a great deal of success in order in our economic life, and it is this success that perhaps explains the plausibility the distinction now enjoys. Yet to call this "success" is deeply perverse, for wherever the separation of thinking from doing has been achieved, it has been responsible for the degradation of work. If we can understand the process by which so many jobs get fragmented, we will be better able to recognize those areas of work that have resisted the process, and identify jobs in which the human capacities may be more fully engaged.
>
> —Michael Crawford, *Shop Class as Soulcraft*[1]

In *Shop Class as Soulcraft*, Michael Crawford seeks to redefine the nature of work and its value for self and community. He points out that his work on motorcycles situates him in a particular community:

> The narrow mechanical things that I concern myself with are inscribed within the larger circle of meaning; they are in the service of an activity that *we* recognize is part of a life well lived. This common recognition, which needn't to be spoken, is the basis for a friendship that orients by concrete images of excellence.[2]

He further points out that the degradation of work has come about from "concerted *efforts* to separate thinking from doing, mind from body" (emphasis in original). We must work to undo those efforts and to restore the dignity of work, both physical and intellectual.

## FRAMES FILM PROJECT

An example of work with dignity, combining both learning and doing, is the Frames Film Project, located in Vancouver, British Columbia, Canada. It provides opportunities for youth (ages sixteen to thirty) to learn the basics of filmmaking in a supportive, safe, and fun environment.

> Using film as an artistic medium, youth receive a wide range of skill building workshops on life and technical skills related to film making, leading to the creation of film pieces expressing their thoughts, experiences, and ideas for change. Frames' films [have] addressed youth issues of substance misuse, mental health, multi-culturalism, and crime prevention . . . this approach has been effective in assisting those youth with significant barriers to develop a wide range of skills and take the necessary steps towards employment and community attachment.[3]

Multi-barriered (i.e., mental health, homelessness, and unemployment) youth receive support from a full youth Case Management Team, a Frames' Social Worker, and a Film Instructor. Each cycle involves ten weeks of lessons plus two shooting and editing weekends. Participants gain life and employment skills, industry knowledge from guest speakers, and technical filmmaking skills. It is an excellent example of bringing together mind and body in action.

A toolkit for service providers opens with an argument for the value of film in this context:

> Film is current, inclusive and culturally relevant, and it provides youth with an effective medium for self-expression and social change. Through the lens of film, we endeavor to reduce the stigma and isolation experienced by people living with a mental health diagnosis and/or addiction.[4]

Youth collaboratively create short film projects expressing their thoughts and ideas for change. In some cases, they conceptualize and produce a film for a partnered non-profit organization to gain hands-on work experience and build community engagement. All projects are shared with the community via numerous events and media channels subsequent to each course. Several of the participants' short films have had great success on the film festival circuit. The approach has proven to help youth with significant barriers develop a wide range of skills and begin to take necessary steps toward employment and community attachment.

Storytelling is central to the Frames experience:

> Storytelling through film is a process that traverses between overcoming personal challenges and learning to be team players in order to meet production deadlines and ensure quality. Such a creative endeavor moves beyond the personal pleasure of digital-making. Instead, it creates and fosters a culture of professionalism in which youth are expected to act professionally like those working in the film industry or the arts community.[5]

Participants in Frames spoke of feeling more connected to their community: "Frames got us out in the community." For example, participants working on the documentary "Where we sleep" visited Single Room Occupancy facilities and got to know residents. One youth stated that "it was a chance to connect with people from the Downtown Eastside community. It felt like it was a huge bridge for them and me." Some referred to the Frames program itself as their community and said that they became very close while working together: "This program felt like a community."[6]

Frames is an alternative to transmission models for academy-community interaction. More interactive communication can lead to deeper community engagement. One feature is to assume feedback as a necessary component of communication. A full interaction model starts with the idea of a two-way conversation.

These interactions support learning in multiple dimensions:

> Through the lens of Frames as an informal site of learning, we may see the importance of fostering a relational understanding of youth creative practice that is unfolding, evolving and emerging. These stories illustrate that artistic practice, specifically film making, is a viable methodology in which youth can explore, express, and communicate their personal values and their collective commitment to the community in which they live.[7]

The Frames model emphasizes context, both physical and psychological. This means that programs are designed to accommodate the local conditions and to fit with local needs and backgrounds. Going outside can lead to multiple relationships with community organizations. The links become two-way communication is shown in figure 7.1.

With interaction can come the alignment of academic practices with life and work in the community. There are now a variety of practical guides for educators to help identify constituent groups and to devise strategies for working with them. Most of these are directed at educators to help them work with families and other groups in the local community.[8]

## INTERNSHIPS ADDRESSING COMMUNITY PROBLEMS

Most formal higher educational organizations in the United States offer some forms of practicums or internships. For example, West Valley College (1963), a public community college in Saratoga, California, has partnered with the World Innovations Network (WIN) to form the United Community Alliance. The Alliance involves West Valley students and faculty, local government officials, accomplished entrepreneurs, high-tech leaders, and the venture capital community.

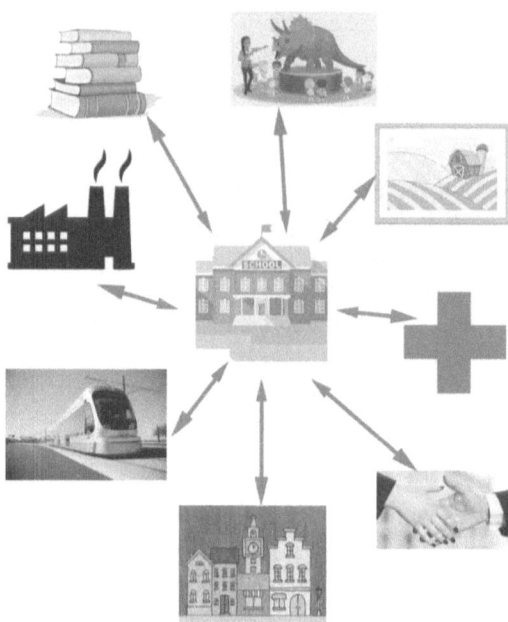

**Figure 7.1 Interactions between the Academy and Community Organizations.** *Source*: Author created. Note: A similar image appears in Dewey's *School and Society*, MW 1:45. It has explicit two-way links suggesting at least an interaction model.

It provides students a chance to help solve real-world problems through sponsored paid internship programs. Through these internships, students work on community issues. They become interns for local businesses with mentors from those businesses. They learn how to apply their skills to real problems in the community using problem-based learning (PBL), case approach, and inquiry-based learning. They also make connections that can help them obtain good jobs; the companies show how they are good citizens; the college offers more relevant learning.

In a recent semester, students identified three areas on which to focus their first efforts: Covid-19, student homelessness, and clean water. This could be viewed as a Silicon Valley version of a communiversity, one in which students learned by focusing on important problems in the community and employed local resources to address these.

## THE LAB STUDIO MODEL

King's College, Kathmandu, is one of many institutions experimenting with new curricula, instructional approaches, and modes of assessment. One such approach has included an emphasis on entrepreneurship. A good example is the LAB studio model as established at the Oulu University of Applied Sciences in Finland.[9] It is grounded in a constructivist view of learning with problem-based education at its core and draws from traditional studio models for training.[10] The model merges work life experience with studio training in a multidisciplinary and multi-professional environment.

Compared with other studio models, the LAB studio model is more closely aligned with industry needs and workplace reality, "because it focuses on instruction in a competitive structure; integrates experienced professionals and coaches from the industry; includes problems or ideas from industry; and builds multidisciplinary project teams."[11]

A version of the LAB studio model, called DoLAB, has been implemented at King's College. The program brings experiences of working with the industry into the classroom and innovation and design practices from the classroom to industry. Activities are based on principles of human-centered design, merging education, design, and entrepreneurship.

The projects are diverse since DoLAB collaborates with schools, businesses, non-profits, and a wide variety of other organizations, essentially anyone with a problem. For example, one project worked with the FabLab, a digital fabrication laboratory located in Kathmandu.[12] In the FabLab, students and entrepreneurs use new technologies to make prototypes for their business ideas.

One student group came up with an idea to produce and sell organic lip balms. Theirs would be eco-friendly and use innovative packaging—aluminum containers, keyrings, and pop sockets to make it more convenient for users. The keyring and pop socket lip balms are new concepts in the Nepalese market, so they had to work to explain the idea to potential customers.

In their first visit to the FabLab, they learned about different work areas, such as 3D printing, molding, textile, and laser. Using 3D printing they made one prototype for each type of packaging. The aim was to make them less bulky and easily portable. They learned much during the iteration process, including collaboration, the design process, and multiple technologies.

## CREDIT FOR WORK AND LIFE EXPERIENCE?

Former Illinois Governor Jim Edgar was a graduate of Eastern Illinois University, an institution that he continued to support in many ways through the years. It was at Eastern that he met fellow student Brenda Smith of Anna, Illinois. The two married while still students at the university, and Ms. Edgar put her own education on hold while supporting her husband's political career and raising the couple's two children.

Over the years, Brenda worked with Jim on many initiatives including one seeking to partially equalize funding for education in the state. The initiative would place a very modest floor on the funding for schools, mostly those in downstate Illinois. At the time, there was a tenfold disparity in funding between rural public schools and schools in wealthy Chicago districts.

This was a brilliant initiative. However, it was opposed by politicians from Chicago, who fought for every advantage for their region, by the Democrats who rebelled against anything Edgar would propose, and by his own Republicans who saw it as a giveaway to go to the poor and could not countenance a progressive income tax.

In the 1990s, while serving as Illinois' First Lady, Brenda Edgar contacted Eastern to see what would be needed to complete her degree. Working with the School of Continuing Education, she finished her coursework and received what is now known as the bachelor of arts degree in general studies during commencement ceremonies in May 1998. Within months, Mrs. Edgar, in conjunction with Ronald McDonald Charities, had established the Brenda Edgar Scholarship for Women, to be awarded to returning adult female parents over the age of twenty-five.

Although she actually completed all the coursework required, many people thought that she should have been awarded the degree outright based on her lifetime of service at her husband's side. Surely, she had learned more than any ordinary graduate of the school based on endless studies of the state's economy, education, and health care systems, not to mention its bizarre politics. She undoubtedly helped with speeches that went beyond the usual undergraduate essay. As a woman, she had set aside her own career advancement goals in favor of service to the governor and the state.

There are many negatives to digital credentialing and its impact on ordinary life. But one positive is that one can envision ways to credit someone like Brenda Edgar for the wide variety of work she did that fell outside of the regular education credentialing system. Could we move toward credentialing of work and community service in a way that recognizes how important learning through doing can be?

Whether in rural Mississippi, Appalachia, coastal Alaska, or Silicon Valley, programs integrating classroom and work life show how learning, democratic community, and work can be integrated for the full development of the individual and the development of the community.

## NOTES

1. Matthew B. Crawford, *Shop Class as Soulcraft: An Inquiry Into the Value of Work* (New York: Penguin, 2009), 37.

2. Ibid: 197.

3. Ching-Chiu Lin and Anita Prest, "Frames Film Project" (Frog Hollow Neighbourhood House, May 26, 2015): 10.

4. Frog Hollow Neighborhood House, "Frames Film Project: Engaging and Empowering Youth through Film: A Toolkit for Service Providers," n.d.: 2.

5. Lin and Prest, "Frames Film Project," 24.

6. McCreary Centre Society, "Final Evaluation Report—January, 2014: Frog Hollow's Frames Film Project," January 2014: 21.

7. Lin and Prest, "Frames Film Project," 28.

8. Kathy Gardner Chadwick, *Improving Schools through Community Engagement: A Practical Guide for Educators* (Thousand Oaks, CA: Corwin Press, 2004); Joyce Levy Epstein, ed., *School, Family, and Community Partnerships: Your Handbook for Action*, 2nd ed. (Thousand Oaks, CA: Corwin Press, 2002); Donald R. Gallagher, Don Bagin, and Leslie W. Kindred, *The School and Community Relations*, 6th ed. (Boston: Allyn and Bacon, 1997); Carol Gestwicki, *Home, School & Community Relations*, Ninth Edition (Boston, MA: Cengage Learning, 2016).

9. Kari Pekka Heikkinen and Blair Stevenson, "The LAB Studio Model: Enhancing Entrepreneurship Skills in Higher Education," *International Journal of Innovation and Learning* 20, no. 2 (2016): 154.

10. Donald Schön, *Educating the Reflective Practitioner* (San Francisco, CA: Jossey-Bass, 1987); *The Design Studio: An Exploration of Its Traditions and Potentials* (International Specialized Book Service, 1985); *The Reflective Practitioner. How Professionals Think In Action* (New York, NY: Basic Books, 1983).

11. Heikkinen and Stevenson, "The LAB Studio Model," 154.

12. The fabrication laboratory is at Nepal Communitere in Kathmandu. This is a not-for-profit organization devoted to helping community members address practical problems and learn new skills. The space is made from sixteen donated shipping containers. It values "growth, learning and safe failure." https://nepal.communitere.org/.

*Part IV*

# THE THIRD MISSION

The university has traditionally been considered as an institution devoted to preserving cultural heritage and generating new knowledge. Equally important is its role in transmitting that knowledge to the next generation. Primary and secondary schools have similar roles in preserving heritage and teaching, though perhaps less so for generating new knowledge. But ordinary community life can be an equal partner or even lead the way in defining the new academy, pointing to radical changes in education for the future.

Following the land-grant vision as it developed within the United States and subsequent developments in the later nineteenth and twentieth centuries, a *third mission* has emerged for education at all levels. It means extending the academy's mission to include community or public engagement:

> Even though teaching and research are still considered as the pivotal functions of universities, other activities such as technology transfer, lifelong learning or social engagement have broadened the scope of their actions. These activities, labelled as third mission, are supposed to strengthen the impact of science in society and epitomize the changing role of universities.[1]

At the pre-college levels, this third mission is most often realized through the concept of community schools, or various forms of school-community engagement. But the concept is similar: The academy should not stand isolated from the life around it.

## NOTE

1. This is an international phenomenon, for example, Hendrik Berghaeuser and Michael Hoelscher, "Reinventing the Third Mission of Higher Education in Germany: Political Frameworks and Universities' Reactions," *Tertiary Education and Management* 26, no. 1 (March 2020): 57.

# Profile
## *Ebru Aktan*

Believing early childhood education to be the earliest opportunity to address social injustice, Ebru Aktan Acar founded a multifaceted program to provide early childhood education services to Turkish children and their families, especially those stressed by economics, racism, or immigrant status. These services create opportunities for student teachers to bring together theory and practice, to create an ecosystem where the individual empowers the society and vice versa.[1]

The work is ground-breaking: It engages future teachers in working with children from diverse backgrounds; it offers support to refugees and others who are too often left out of supportive social services; it helps all involved to develop a better understanding of ethnic, linguistic, and social class differences; and it provides a research base for improving early childhood education anywhere.

Her program, Çaba-Çam, becomes a prototype of a communiversity, bringing together academicians and community members in equal partnership to address problems in the community. It represents a commitment to cross-cultural understanding to supporting people without power, building on transactive communication.

Çaba-Çam not only transfers knowledge from the college to the community but also highlights community knowledge to help build more robust understanding and teaching practices. Changes in living and learning emerge from creating with people, by people, and for people.[2] Ebru says,

> My mother is a very kind person and my father also. They want to help people all the time. So, they were my role models. And maybe this is the reason [I developed a commitment to extending teacher education into the community]. Secondly, I went to Germany in 2002 to work with Turkish people in Germany.

I stayed three months in Berlin, where I met with the persona dolls approach. I received a grant and worked with Turkish German bilingual kids.

When I was at the university in 1990, I went to England to work in a coffee shop for two summer holidays. And then, there were various conferences in New Zealand, Canada, and Mexico. I met with many people from all over the world. I was the representative of a community, the world for early care and education. There were people from Nepal, Philippines, and Congo. I heard their stories. Later, I went to the eastern part of Turkey and visited all the villages.

I noticed that most of the children could not speak Turkish, but rather Arabic or Kurdish. These experiences influenced my teaching in Turkey, a huge, multicultural country. I was also working in teacher training. I realized that it wasn't until the fourth year that a teacher candidate could have hands-on experiences with diverse students.

I saw that teacher candidates needed more practice and we needed parental education. Around the same time, I visited a teacher training college at the University of Helsinki. It was a wonderful experience for me. All of the teacher candidates worked with children all week. And they become very successful preschool teachers. Why didn't we have a place to educate children from low-income families along with their families, using teacher candidates?

Everyone wins in this situation. Soon we started to get some children from refugee families, from China, Congo, Iraq, and Syria. Now we have, more than 500 Çaba-Çam teachers all over Turkey, but they affect many more families, some children and many lives.

## NOTES

1. Ebru Aktan Acar graduated from the Boğaziçi University, Turkey, in 1993. She completed her master's and doctorate degrees on preschool education at the same university and then joined the faculty of Çanakkale Onsekiz Mart University. Following an initial focus on literacy skills, she has worked on varied early childhood education models and approaches throughout the world, emphasizing peace education and respect for diversity. Her work shows how one can enhance education through the alternative or third space between formal education and the community.

2. As Elsie Clapp showed in the 1930s.

*Chapter 8*

# Community Schools

A community school forgoes its separateness. It is influential because it belongs to its people. They share its ideals and its work. It takes from them and gives to them. There are no bounds as far as I can see to what it could accomplish in social reconstruction if it had enough wisdom and insight and devotion and energy. It demands all these for changes in living and learning of people are not produced by imparting information about different conditions or by gathering statistical data about what exists, but by creating with people, by people, for people.
—Elsie Ripley Clapp, "A Rural School in Kentucky"[1]

The Homestead Act of 1862 gave 160 acres to anyone over 18 who stayed on the land for 4 years. At least 1.5 million homesteaders were granted a total of 420,000 square miles, equal to almost 10 percent of the land in the current United States.[2] The act brought many settlers and soon the need to educate children. The first schools were typically one-room schools, located in dugouts, sod houses, abandoned houses, and people's homes. A one-room school with the teacher living in parents' homes was a kind of community school.

## ONE-ROOM SCHOOLS

Mostly serving isolated communities, the schools required one teacher to educate children of varying ages at the same time in a single classroom.[3] There were typically few students, resulting in an enviable student-teacher ratio. The older students often helped the younger ones. It was not unusual for students to have the same teacher for many years in a row.[4]

One-room schools were unique centers of learning. They were often important centers of community activity. Many schools served as the local chapel on Sunday, and during the evening or on Saturday as meeting places for local activities. Town meetings and picnics were often held there. Community involvement of the kind that Elsie Clapp advocated was a given.

In the early days of the county schools, teachers were sometimes as young as sixteen-years-old with no formal training. Often they were girls with an eighth-grade diploma who could teach reading, writing, and arithmetic. More than two-thirds were young, unmarried women, expected to serve their community as the personification of "Wisdom and Virtue." A rule that prevented married women from teaching was a factor in female teacher turnover. This rule was maintained into the 1950s.

Some teacher accounts from Morgan County, Colorado, provide a sense of life in the schools:[5]

- Sylva (Kula) Biddle taught around 10 miles north of Weldona in "a God-forsaken place" and lived with an "an old maid in a claim shanty." The fifteen students in Grades 1–8 were a challenge. When she first saw her school, the classroom was covered with paper wads, and the students had "run the previous teacher back to Denver." It was a lonesome, hard job. She had to sweep, pump water, pick up and plan activities, as well as teach every subject.
- Margaret Dewey was a teacher from Brush.

    > I taught at Golden School 1932–34 about 5 or 6 miles south of the Woodrow store in Washington County. . . . The teacher was not only a teacher—she was a playground supervisor at recess and noon, a nurse, a janitor and a disciplinarian.

- Helen Underwood taught in 1914, 9 miles north of Snyder, Colorado.

    > I began to teach in January. The school was held in a one-room homestead house. It was heated mostly with corn cobs and some coal. I tacked sheets of wrapping paper on the walls for blackboards and wrote with Crayons. No books were available, so I borrowed some from the Brush school. I stayed with a family of five, and three of them were my pupils. The house had one room, and a corner was curtained off for me. Coyotes howled most of the time.

Dorothy Wickenden gives us a detailed look into the life of two teachers who came to Colorado to teach in a one-room school in the mountains. Her book is based on letters written in 1916–1917 by one of the teachers, her grandmother Dorothy Woodruff.[6] The two teachers lived with the Harrisons (homesteaders) on their ranch with two of their eight children. The ranch cabin was a large room with two bedrooms with blankets covering the doors, and a loft.

The teachers' room was in a small loft, and if they fell out of bed they would tumble down the stairs. There was no indoor water and only an outhouse.

Elkhead School was 2 miles from the homestead, accessible only by horseback. It was actually a two-room school, or three-, counting the barn. The main room had a folding door to separate the classrooms and could later be used for community events. Woodruff had ten students, Grades 1–5, and the other teacher, Underwood, had Grades 6–8. The teachers never missed a day of school because they knew their students would be waiting for them in the cold with little warm clothing. They bought books, clothes, shoes, and food and opened the door to education for many students in the remote mountains of Colorado.

In Clinton County, Kentucky, a former student relates his experience as a pupil in Kentucky:

> The experience . . . is something that I will remember and cherish forever. . . . At that time one teacher taught nine grades—primer through 8th. . . . The teachers . . . would get to the school early to get a fire started in the potbelly stove. . . . On many occasions they would prepare a hot, noon meal on top of the stove. . . . I like to consider that they taught the five "R's" instead of the traditional three—the last two being *respect and responsibility.*
>
> Drinking water was obtained from a well on the school ground or carried from a farmhouse close by. . . . The older students were given the responsibility of bringing in water, carrying in coal or wood for the stove. The younger students would be given responsibilities according to their size and gender such as cleaning the black board (chalkboard), taking the erasers outside for dusting plus other duties that they were capable of doing. (Emphasis in original)[7]

The one-room schools lacked in terms of facilities and materials. Teachers were poorly prepared by modern US standards. Most importantly, they failed at exposing children to the diversity of American life. Nevertheless, they made it possible for children in rural areas to learn from the classroom as well as life on the farm.

These schools still exist in the United States, a legacy of a less mobile, more rural time. In 1919 there were 190,000; there are fewer than 400 left. De-population has forced the closure of many. Others have been lost as districts seek economies of scale through consolidation.

## HULL-HOUSE

Jane Addams and Ellen Gates Starr founded Hull-House in Chicago in 1889 to offer social services to the community, which comprised mostly recent immigrants. The services included legal aid and an employment bureau, plus action for women's rights, child labor laws, and provision of city services.

Although Hull-House is not usually classified as a community school, it performed many similar functions. It was certainly an educational institution. In addition to the art gallery and libraries, it offered training in crafting and domestic skills; kindergarten and day care facilities for the children of working mothers; English and citizenship classes; theater, music, and art classes.

Writing about Hull-House, the pioneering social settlement in Chicago, Jane Addams writes that "educational matters are more democratic in their political than in their social aspect."[8] She had learned that the social world in which one lives determines the real meaning of educational activities. As one example, she relates:

> A typical street boy who was utterly absorbed in a wood-carving class, abruptly left never to return when he was told to use some simple calculations in the laying out of the points. He evidently scented the approach of his old enemy, arithmetic, and fled the field.

Addams learned that teaching in a settlement required distinct methods, especially for those who had been denied educational opportunity, those who "cannot take their learning heavily." She writes,

> [Education] has to be diffused in a social atmosphere, information must be held in solution, in a medium of fellowship and good will. Intellectual life requires for its expansion and manifestation the influences and assimilation of the interests and affections of others.

The social atmosphere of education becomes a site to bring together mind and body in action.

Hull-House developed many ways to enact "socialized education," in which learning activities enlarged, rather than constricted the social worlds of participants. For example, a Hull-House summer school was instituted at Rockford College. For ten years, one hundred women, and some men, gathered there for six weeks.

> The outdoor classes in bird study and botany, the serious reading of literary masterpieces, the boat excursions on the Rock River, the coöperative spirit of doing the housework together, the satirical commencements in parti-colored caps and gowns, lent themselves toward a reproduction of the comradeship which college life fosters.[9]

Hull-House is not usually considered to be a community school, but it embodied the principles that have guided the community school movement throughout its history: the belief that education should be diffused in a social atmosphere, that community members set the terms for learning, and that intellectual life starts with the community.

Addams wrote about this.

> It is because of a lack of democracy that we do not really incorporate him in the hopes and advantages of society, and give him the place which is his by simple right. We have learned to say that the good must be extended to all of society before it can be held secure by any one person or any one class; but we have not yet learned to add to that statement, that unless all men and all classes contribute to a good, we cannot even be sure that it is worth having. In spite of many attempts we do not really act upon either statement.[10]

Community schools seek to ensure that all members of a community have a say in its future, to contribute to its good, and, by implication, to create and maintain its schools.

## THE ARTHURDALE SCHOOL

Through her work at the Rosemary Junior School in Connecticut, Ballard Memorial School in Kentucky, and the Arthurdale School in West Virginia, Elsie Ripley Clapp developed and articulated the ideas that John Dewey had proposed about building on the child's natural capacity for activity and learning.[11]

Charlene Siegfried describes her as one of the lost women pragmatists "who exposed the deleterious effects of the artificial boundaries that isolated the school from its environing community." She sees Clapp as going

> one step further [than Dewey] by adopting the radical position that scholars ought to be or become members of communities played by the problems their theories are supposed to solve. . . . Their experiments were experiments in community living as well as in community problem-solving.[12]

An important relation for Clapp was the pragmatic challenge to the dualism of the empirical, or a posteriori, and the rational, or a priori. This epistemology was deeply lodged in the approach of American schools to knowledge or subject matter. Like Dewey, Clapp and her colleagues saw thought as only a tentative hypothesis, itself being formed through experience. It was subjective, not absolute or objective outside of experience. Accordingly, they sought to relate the subject matter to the real-life experiences of children.[13]

> For Elsie, the key to reform—be at social, economic, or political—was education. For her it would always be the key. Elsie approached progressive reform by nurturing children and meeting their needs. For Elsie, education was the key to social

betterment. . . . She had learned through experience about racism, class conflict, and the plight of the working class, political corruption, and sexism. . . . Soon she had the opportunity to shape her own version of community within a school. . . . She described these difficult years in her memoirs as "learning by living."[14]

Dewey wrote to Clapp in 1911:

> I do not think it is possible to overstate the degree to which in which traditional education is dead; the trouble is that we educators having been ourselves educated in it are too dead to bury it and start afresh. Student activities indicate the necessity that mind can be employed only upon the activities of life.[15]

In the 1930s, Clapp set out to bury traditional education and to turn vision into reality in the Ballard School near Louisville, Kentucky. She emphasized the transformative potential of the school.

The plan for these schools was emergent, a working hypothesis that changed based on experiences. Working in the schools led to Clapp's understanding of what a "functioning school" ought to be. A crucial feature was to have teachers dedicated and experienced in applying progressive methods. Teachers should make full use of the local environment, including paying attention to the traditions and customs of the community. The school should address health concerns, especially malnutrition and the lack of professional care. It would serve as a medium for sharing experiences.[16]

It must be noted that at Ballard, there were separate (and unequal) schools for African American children. There was no attempt made by Clapp or the other Ballard teachers to bridge between these two communities, a necessary step in building true democratic education.

Clapp's most notable work occurred at Scott's Run, a 5-mile-long hollow near Morgantown, West Virginia. It was once a thriving place, laid over some of the richest coalfields in the world. Its rapid growth during the 1920s meant that it was an anomaly in Jim Crow America, a diverse mix of racial and national groups living together in relative peace. A survey by missionaries in the 1930s put the population at 60 percent foreign-born, 20 percent Native-born whites, and 20 percent blacks.[17]

This idyllic scene dissolved along with the collapse of the great bubble following World War I and the easy money policy of the Federal Reserve. That collapse led to the Coal Wars, a period of labor violence unmatched anywhere else in the United States. Because the coal mines were located in remote areas, the companies had to provide housing, stores, and even a church in order to attract workers. When the mines failed, these resources disappeared. The Joads from Steinbeck's *The Grapes of Wrath* had US dollars to seek opportunity elsewhere, but many families in Scott's Run and other such towns were "stranded" with only worthless company scrip.

In the community, it was typical for girls to marry at fifteen and to have eight children by age twenty-seven. They could not read. There was endemic domestic violence. Water supplies were contaminated. Children experienced malnutrition. Many could not get to feeding programs because they lacked clothing and shoes. There was widespread preventable disease, leading to a childhood mortality rate more than three times that of the nation.

> The crushing debt burdens, isolation, endemic property, and suffering of the coal camps created frequent strikes and long periods of labor violence between the miners in the coal operators. . . . The famous massacre at Matewan was born of the labor strife, and while colorful characters such as Old Mother Jones and Sheriff Sid Hatfield fought for union names, equally colorful (and violent) men such as "Boss" Don Chafin and the Felts Brothers stood opposite them.[18]

This all occurred as the nation entered the Great Depression. One response to Scott's Run was the federal homestead assistance project of the New Deal. This back-to-the-land movement carried a democratic concept of community, fraternity, equality, and solidarity. In 1933, Eleanor Roosevelt had become aware of the plight of people in Scott's Run. She saw both opportunity and need there. The homestead assistance project would also keep demographic and economic pressure off of urban areas. It reached its apotheosis in the small town of Scott's Run.

Eleanor Roosevelt referred to Scott's Run as a "human experiment station." The Arthurdale project would not only help local people directly; it would serve as a model for progressive change elsewhere. She spoke with Elsie Clapp who recommended a community school based on her experience in Kentucky. One miner said to her, "You ain't never goin' to make notin of us. We're like them old apple trees out there, all gnarled and twisted."[19]

Clapp began her work in Arthurdale with the children.

> An integral part of the community school was the nursery school, which opened in the fall of 1934 with thirty-two children, two teachers, and a dietitian. Elsie believed that the nursery school was one of the most significant contributions of the homestead. It helped create a sense of pride, joy, and hope for the community.[20]

The school came to be the center for health care and recreation in the community. It offered warm clothes, food, and social events.

> The second graders decided that they wanted to build the village of Arthurdale. They decided their village needed a store, bank, barn, and post office. In constructing the village with scrap lumber collected throughout the project, the children learned to measure and use a square and level. In the process they enhanced

their understanding of fractions, addition, and subtraction. They also learned to work together for a common end, and this meant cooperation of communication to solve problems as they literally build a village. They constructed maps of their village, price charts for their store, and eventually made deposits tat the bank. They learned cents and decimals in the process. They elected a mayor, assistant mayor, and town council. . . . By the end of the first year the children increased their confidence and self reliance, so much that they took control over their own learning consulting [the teacher] only when necessary.[21]

The older children conducted even more elaborate projects, all exemplifying learning by doing problems and activities relevant to their own lives. Clapp claimed that scholars in the community ranged from ages two to seventy-two. Adults learned how to manage and farm their home states including animal husbandry and budgeting for the purchase of food, cows, pigs, and chickens. There were singing groups and square dancing.

Teachers were to be an active part of the community. They assisted on the fire committee, the well-baby clinic, and other activities. The school design was simple, homelike in character, and the school buildings were similar to the local houses. They were detached to prevent the spread of disease and to leave room for future expansion. The plans included playgrounds, gardens, and proximity to woods.

Based upon the freedom to explore, to ask questions, to reflect, and to initiate, with teachers serving as guides seeking to capture the interest of the students and integrate traditional subject matter as part of the process, the ideal community school was a living, vital component of the community and met the educational, health, and recreational needs of the people it served. Elsie saw no dualism between learning and living, and the school was to service as an agency of sharing, mutual effort, and transformation. The community school was a society in itself.[22]

John Dewey believed that the Arthurdale school program was one of the best public schools in the nation. Although short in duration (two years) the school stands today as a model for what a community school could be as well as a reminder of the challenges facing community schools.

A harsh critic of the program, C. J. Maloney, nevertheless writes that

It is time that Americans grant Arthurdale the respect it deserves. Our world is the one created by Franklin Delano Roosevelt's new deal, and the dramatic rise of federal power in everyday life was given its purest expression in the resettlement colonies of the subsistence homestead program. Arthurdale was that program's crown jewel; it is the cradle of modern America.[23]

## HIGHLANDER SCHOOL

Academic-initiated communiversity models often assume that there are meaningful work opportunities everywhere outside of the academy. While it may be true that one can learn from any kind of work, the possibilities are enhanced when the work itself holds significant meaning, especially when that stretches the assumptions of the academy. The site for an internship can shape its value.

A good example of this is the Highlander Folk School founded in 1932 in Monteagle, Tennessee, by Myles Horton.[24] Horton's early experiences showed him that when community people discussed their problems, he was unable to answer their questions. However, when he induced them to share their experiences, they discovered that they already had many of the answers. They understood at a visceral level how the economy worked to disadvantage them and how they were denied voting and other civil rights.

At the University of Chicago, Horton studied with sociologist Robert Park. He was impressed by Park's view that conflict can be used to encourage people to work for a better society and by Lester Ward's view that education requires action. He also met Jane Addams and visited Hull-House.

Later, he encountered the model of the Danish folk schools, admiring their informality, their close student-teacher interaction, and their use of culture as a tool for learning. These played a vital role in revitalizing Danish culture and addressing the country's social and economic problems in the late nineteenth century. Horton wanted to create a similar school in the south where teachers would work with both black and white students to address community problems, thus reifying the action-based view of learning promoted in Chicago. Like Hull-House, Highlander would not ordinarily be listed as a community school, but it has in fact been a major force for learning in the community.

Highlander focused first on organizing unemployed and working people, and by the late 1930s it served as the de facto Congress of Industrial Organizations education center for the region, training union organizers and leaders across the southern states.[25] During this period, Highlander also fought segregation in the labor movement, holding its first integrated workshop in 1944.

It then became an important incubator of the civil rights movement. Workshops and training sessions at Highlander helped lay the groundwork for many of the movement's most important initiatives, including the Montgomery bus boycott, the Citizenship Schools, and the founding of the Student Nonviolent Coordinating Committee. After struggles with the State of Tennessee, Highlander eventually became the Highlander Research and Education Center and moved to its current location near New Market, Tennessee.

In the late 1960s and 1970s, Highlander played a vital role in support of anti-strip mining and worker health and safety struggles. In the 1980s and 1990s, it expanded its work to support grassroots groups fighting pollution and toxic dumping, and later sponsored workshops on human rights in the context of trade and globalization issues.

Today, Highlander continues to fight for justice and equality, supporting organizing and leadership development among Latinx immigrants. It builds on indigenous culture as a resource to enhance social justice efforts and helps other organizations develop new strategies and alliances.[26] Interns learn how to advance multiracial, intergenerational movements for social and economic justice.

In addition to internships, Highlander offers structured learning opportunities. For example, Mapping Our Futures: Economics and Governance is a curriculum that "explores economic and governance systems through a participatory community-based process to create knowledge and share solutions that foster healthy communities." It is designed to be used by organizers and community members to examine how these systems are designed, how they work, how they impact communities, and to imagine and practice solutions based on a solidarity economy. "Through political education, community mapping, and shared knowledge building, participants learn about how economy and governance impact their lives and work, and importantly, how to develop strategies to change the economies in their communities."[27]

There are many other examples of community-based education, showing how academic learning can pair with action in the community to enhance both individual and community development. Earlier models such as Hull-House, Arthurdale, New Market, and the Nordic folk schools have been extended and revised for contemporary situations.

Community schools have a long history, but assume increasing importance in our pluralistic society.[28] The Coalition for Community Schools defines community school as

> a place and a set of partnerships, connecting a school, the families of students, and the surrounding community. A community school is distinguished by an integrated focus on academics, youth development, family support, health and social services, and community development.[29]

There is potential for an intrinsic emphasis on equity:

> Equitable collaborations ask us—both formal leaders and families and communities—to lead change and realize more just schools in ways that fundamentally depart from the ways we are accustomed to interacting. We can no longer easily check off the tidy box marked "family engagement" or compartmentalize it as someone else's responsibility.[30]

On the other hand, community schools can invoke the worst of modern society. They invite pernicious parental (or even nonparent activist) involvement in determining curriculum, setting health policies, and choosing books for the school library. Some community involvement has led to bans on teaching about slavery and reinforced anti-black discrimination. It has promoted prejudice against immigrants and non-Christians, essentially stigmatizing anyone who does not appear to fit the currently dominant culture. In other cases, it has endangered LGBTQ youth and prevented them and their teachers from reading about or discussing their life issues. These sorts of involvement can reify and institutionalize beliefs and practices that oppress already marginalized people.

## LISTENING TO STUDENTS

A model for community involvement is the system of "small schools" started by Deborah Meier at Central Park East school in New York. It demonstrated how community involvement could create environments in which all kids could learn. She found that doing so meant unsettling our notions of what schools are and how they should be organized:

> The task of creating environments where all kids can experience the power of their ideas requires unsettling not only our accepted organization of schooling and our unspoken and unacknowledged agreement about the purposes of schools. Taking this task seriously also means calling into question our definitions of intelligence and the ways in which we judge each other. And taking it seriously means accepting public responsibility for the shared future of the next generation.[31]

Schools that work to improve learning for all students inevitably find that they must consider the students' parents and families, soon their neighborhoods, and the socioeconomic conditions under which they live. Whether one starts with the community and moves to the school, as Elsie Clapp did, or starts with the school per se, one is led to a community school's perspective.

Community schools have expanded considerably since the days of Hull-House or Arthurdale.[32] In a small, but increasingly important minority of these schools, youth have come to play a role as planners, advocates, evaluators, and decision-makers.[33] Community-based research has emerged as both a means of improving community life and as an important pedagogical strategy.[34] Youth have also employed art to tell the story of their own lives and their communities.[35] Their participation can be a powerful force for transforming the institutional norms and power relations that cause youth disengagement and alienation.[36]

Fehrer and Lopez describe the transformation of the Oakland school district into a full-service community school district and the part that youth have played. Their story tells of an awakening of a sociopolitical consciousness, positive racial identities, and the power of collective action. It also describes a rich civic fabric of youth organizations that enabled both the infrastructure and the political will for constructing a meaningful role for youth. Finally, it describes an unrelenting focus on equity and how community schools emerged as a strategy to disrupt persistent inequalities for Oakland youth.

The model followed at Oakland shifts authority away from the school per se. As Ishimaru states,

> Rather than operating from the premise that schools are the central actors with the agency to involve or engage families, a journey of *equitable collaboration* asks that we recognize schools as *part* of broader community within which we foster new kinds of relationships between families and schools, premised on a different paradigm. (Emphasis in original)[37]

In a campaign in 2007–2008, youth in Oakland found that the district's high school graduation requirements were not aligned with the California state standards. As a result, many low-income students of color were graduating from high school ill-prepared and ineligible for admittance to the state's public university system. They called for a complete overhaul of the graduation requirements. They also saw the need for tutoring, health care, transportation, and especially improvements to create a safe positive school culture and climate.

Community schools reimagined youth government as a training ground for youth researchers, organizers, and advocates. As one teacher put it, it means acknowledging that "our students aren't disrespectful because they advocate for what they need. If they disagree with you appropriately, what is the problem? You have to hear what they say. You need to have a conversation."[38]

The Oakland experience shows how participation in democracy, experiencing democratic schooling, and having more integrated, caring schools can be one and the same. It also shows how community schools are not simply add-ons to formal education, nor yet another way to structure schooling, but a rethinking of the education process, a burying of the traditional schooling as Dewey would say.

## ÇABA-ÇAM EARLY CHILDHOOD EDUCATION CENTER

The Çaba-Çam center in Çanakkale, Turkey, shows a way to get beyond the walls while staying within them. It addresses several problems simultaneously. One is an overly theoretical teacher preparation program, which provided scarce opportunities to learn by doing. A second is the refugee crisis and the unequal education opportunities for refugees, especially at the early childhood level. A third is the need for parental education.

The schooling rate for children between the ages of three and five in Turkey is approximately 33 percent. The participation rate for early childhood is even lower for Syrian refugee children. On the other hand, early childhood education is known to be important for the completion of children's mental and physical development. The founder Ebru Aktan says that her dream was to reach socioeconomically disadvantaged families and children. She envisioned the project which brings together families, children, and prospective teachers.

In 2008, Çaba-Çam launched its first class. It can be considered not only as a child and family-centered project but also as an early intervention program. A total of 250 students from the department of early childhood education teach disadvantaged children. At the same time, they find the opportunity to put theory into practice. One university student said,

> Most of our courses are theoretical. Until our implementation course in the last year of the university, there was no practice part of the curriculum directly with children. That's why we cannot be aware of what and how children can learn. So we're astonished. Now, we start to work earlier and we specialize in how children learn through experience.

The center provides education for more than 130 children at the age of early education. It includes their parents through seminars. A parent said,

> Our children like this place so much, their self-confidence increased here. They can speak more. They can draw. Their sources of communication became more effective. Their self-confidence increased. They were like a baby before now, but now they are like an adult. Their behaviors changed and they want something. They put themselves forward.

Volunteers implemented a questionnaire at the local level in order to identify disadvantaged families with the support of the campus municipality. Another parent says,

> This is a very good place. I'm very pleased, Sound and learn many things here. And it helped him to be, be more disciplined. Before he was naughty and he was not listening to me. But after coming here, his behaviors were positively affected. He learned to draw, to use scissors and to become familiar with different hand works.

The center is affiliated with Çanakkale Onsekiz Mart University. Preschool teacher candidates conducted neighborhood-based surveys and codesigned a model to expand early childhood education while transforming their own training into practice. The program especially addresses the needs of low-income families, including refugees from Syria, Iraq, Afghanistan, and, more recently, Congo and China. Students in the university education program volunteer to work with the children, many of whom have suffered greatly from poverty and war and would otherwise have little access to early education.

The program now offers a model that anyone could use and values that ought to remind all of us of how we could better interact with one another. It makes a difference in the lives of young children, their parents, and future teachers. Its impact will continue for generations, both in the lives of prospective teachers and children.[39]

We now have ample models, some historically based such as Hull-House and the depression era community schools, many in diverse neighborhoods throughout the United States, and large numbers in other countries, such as Spain (*Misiones Pedagogicas*)[40] and Turkey (*Köy Enstitüleri*, or Village Institutes).[41] Each of these shows the value of connecting school and community and, conversely, how much we lose when we maintain a wall between them. Collectively, they pose the question: Could community schools be not just the odd alliance, but the future of all education?

## NOTES

1. Elsie Ripley Clapp, "A Rural School in Kentucky," *Progressive Education* 10 (March 1933): 128.

2. The Homestead Act of 1862 granted land claims in thirty states. The land was taken from the traditional or treaty lands of many Native American tribes. At least 93 million living white Americans continue to benefit from the Homestead Act land patents. Following the 1866 Civil Rights Act and the Fourteenth Amendment, African Americans were eligible as well, although their numbers were few in comparison with the millions of white settlers. There were many barriers, including that the act specifically excluded agricultural workers and domestic servants, who were predominately African American, Mexican, and Asian. See National Park Service, "FREE LAND Was the Cry!" August 21, 2021, https://www.nps.gov/home/; Natasha Hicks et al., "Still Running Up the Down Escalators: How Narratives Shape Our Understanding of Racial Wealth Inequality" (Insight Center for Community economic development, Samuel DuBois Cook Center on Social Equity, 2021).

3. Neenah Ellis, "One-Room Schools Holding on in Rural America" (National Public Radio, December 22, 2005); "One-Room Schoolhouse Center," 2022, 1998, http://oneroomschoolhousecenter.weebly.com/.

4. This plan is known as looping in larger schools.

5. Community History Writers, "Portraits of the Past: Revisiting the Days of One-Room School Houses," *The Fort Morgan Times*, September 5, 2019.

6. Dorothy Wickenden, *Nothing Daunted: The Unexpected Education of Two Society Girls in the West* (New York, NY: Scribner, 2011).

7. Harold L. Stearns, "One Room School," 2000, https://web.archive.org/web/20111003174603/http://www.snowkentucky.com/one_room_school.htm.

8. Jane Addams, *Twenty Years at Hull-House with Autobiographical Notes* (New York: Macmillan, 1912).

9. Jane Addams, "Socialized Education," in *Twenty Years at Hull-House with Autobiographical Notes* (New York: Macmillan, 1912), 427.

10. Jane Addams, *Democracy and Social Ethics*, edited by Anne Firor Scott (Cambridge, MA: Harvard University Press, 1964), 219–20.

11. Mustafa Yunus Eryaman and Bertram C. Bruce, *International Handbook of Progressive Education* (New York: Peter Lang, 2015).

12. Charlene Haddock Seigfried, *Pragmatism and Feminism: Reweaving the Social Fabric* (Chicago: University of Chicago Press, 1996), 58 (cited in Stack).

13. Sam F. Stack, *Elsie Ripley Clapp (1879–1965): Her Life and the Community School*, History of Schools & Schooling, v. 42 (New York: P. Lang, 2004), 83.

14. Ibid: 109.

15. Ibid: 78.

16. Ibid: 186.

17. C. J. Maloney, *Back to the Land: Arthurdale, FDR's New Deal, and the Costs of Economic Planning* (Hoboken, NJ: Wiley, 2011), 11.

18. Ibid: 16.

19. Elsie Ripley Clapp, *Community Schools in Action* (New York: Viking, 1939), 116.

20. Stack, *Elsie Ripley Clapp*, 191.

21. Stack, *Elsie Ripley Clapp*, 193.

22. Stack, *Elsie Ripley Clapp*, 204.

23. Maloney, *Back to the Land*, 10.

24. Myles Horton, *The Long Haul: An Autobiography* (New York: Teachers College Press, 1997).

25. The CIO was a federation of unions that organized workers in industrial unions in the United States and Canada from 1935 to 1955.

26. This summary draws from and builds upon the Highlander Research and Education Center website, https://highlandercenter.org/our-history-timeline.

27. https://highlandercenter.org/our-impact/economics-governance/.

28. JoAnne Ferrara and Reuben Jacobson, eds., *Community Schools: People and Places Transforming Education and Communities* (Lanham: Rowman & Littlefield, 2019), 17.

29. Martin J. Blank, Reuben Jacobson, and Atelia Melaville, "Achieving Results Through Community School Partnerships," Center for American Progress, January 2012: 1.

30. Ann M. Ishimaru, *Just Schools: Building Equitable Collaborations with Families and Communities*, Multicultural Education Series (New York, NY: Teachers College Press, 2020), 140.

31. Deborah Meier, *The Power of Their Ideas: Lessons for America from a Small School in Harlem*, 2nd ed. (Boston: Beacon Press, 2003), 4.

32. Atelia Melaville, Amy C. Berg, and Martin J. Blank, *Community-Based Learning: Engaging Students for Success and Citizenship* (Washington, DC: Coalition for Community Schools. Institute for Educational Leadership, 2006); Martin J. Blank, Reuben Jacobson, and Atelia Melaville, "Achieving Results Through Community School Partnerships" (Center for American Progress, January 2012).

33. Kendra Fehrer and Aurora Lopez, "Voices for Equity: Youth Leadership in Oakland Community Schools," in *Community Schools: People and Places Transforming Education and Communities*, edited by JoAnne Ferrara and Reuben Jacobson (Lanham, MD: Rowman & Littlefield, 2019), 111–40.

34. K. J. Strand, "Community-Based Research as Pedagogy," *Michigan Journal of Community Service Learning* 7, no. 1 (2000).

35. Ching-Chiu Lin and Bertram C. Bruce, "Engaging Youth in Underserved Communities Through Digital-Mediated Arts Learning Experiences for Community Inquiry," *Studies in Art Education: A Journal of Issues and Research* 54, no. 4 (July 27, 2013): 335–48.

36. Fehrer and Lopez, "Voices for Equity," 112.

37. Ishimaru, *Just Schools*, 33.

38. Fehrer and Lopez, "Voices for Equity," 127.

39. *Fark Yaratanlar (Difference Makers): ÇABA-ÇAM*, 2017. https://youtu.be/OdpBfLKhPco.

40. Francisco Canes Garrido, "Las Misiones Pedagógicas: Educación y Tiempo Libre En La Segunda República," *Revista Complutense de Educación* 4, no. 1 (1993): 147–68.

41. Selcuk Uygun, "John Dewey and Village Institute Model in Teacher Training System in Turkey," in *International Handbook of Progressive Education*, ed. Mustafa Yunus Eryaman and Bertram C. Bruce (New York: Peter Lang, 2015), 75–90.

# Profile
## *Dave Leake*

Community colleges go far beyond offering listed course options. One can see this by examining the career of one faculty member, Dave Leake. His career path shows how one can start with community-based work and then connect it with the academy.[1] His diverse projects show how education can thrive in the third space between the formal classroom and daily life, especially when the communication is transactive, respecting and valuing the contribution of all the parties. He says,

> I actually did things in reverse order of what other people might do. Some might start out in the classroom and then expand to do some extra-curricular or co-curricular. I started out doing the opposite. I owe a lot of my success, believe it or not, to Halley's Comet. Halley's Comet last visited our part of the solar system in 1985 and 1986 and I was working in industry at the time. I was employed after graduation from the university at Anderson Physics Laboratories in Urbana.
>
> When I was a senior, a gentleman approached me about a local job and I thought he was joking as all of my physics friends were either attending graduate school or pursuing employment on either coast. Since it was a local job with no travel, I figured I would be remiss for not looking into it and I ended up taking the job.
>
> When comets approach the Sun they typically brighten, but, due to the position of the Earth, when Halley's was at its brightest it was going to be on the other side of the Sun. So the astronomical "powers that be" wanted to get the word to the public that there would only be a few good opportunities to see the comet. The general public needed to know what was happening and why. Astronomy had been a hobby of mine since the fifth grade. A colleague of mine from the physics lab suggested I should teach some sort of class. There weren't a

lot of community education classes at the time, so I approached the Champaign Park District and offered to teach a six-weeks class in basic astronomy.

I soon came to realize that I was pretty good at teaching. I enjoyed it and had a passion for it. Now if you had told me, when I was a senior in high school, that I was going to teach in any sort of classroom for thirty years, I would have told you you're nuts! I repeated the class several times and even taught a sequel with many repeat students. And the students were adults and kids—a very mixed group.

From this group of "lifelong learners," we founded the Champaign-Urbana Astronomical Society in 1986. I did not get the job at Parkland College until the fall of 1989. The Society was very good at engaging kids at events like the farmer's market and displays in the parks, plus offering views of the Moon and planets through club telescopes. So, I did public education before I went into the formal classroom.

I was born with a defect, that being the inability to say "no." If a project comes along, instead of saying that I don't really have time for it, I usually explore it further. When I was approached to participate in a grant project, I rarely said no. When I got to the planetarium, I wanted to continue where I left off educating the public about the sky, no matter their age. That led to the work with teachers.

In some planetariums, they produce a show about a topic and then say "here it is, take it or leave it." My personal feeling is that we, as a planetarium, should be supporting classroom instruction as best we can. When a school district adopted a new unit that included astronomy, I wanted to meet with the teachers and find out where they were having problems.

With this kind of collaboration, the visiting teachers then know what they are going to see and can prepare their students and the planetarium show operator can ask where the class is at in the unit. If they are just starting it, then we can do an introduction. If they have finished the unit, we can emphasize reflection or assessment. The dialogue with the teachers is key. The teachers essentially co-write the program and then I would create a workshop to help with content and classroom activities.

I loved being involved in the process and I think the teachers appreciated it, too. I learned to be open minded to listen to any and all ideas. We even did thirteen weddings in the dome during my watch!

## NOTE

1. Dave was the director of the Staerkel Planetarium at Parkland Community College from 2000 to 2019. In addition to teaching Astronomy and Physics for the college, he presented public programs, outreach programs, handled field trips for

K-12 students, worked with scout groups, and worked with local schools on curriculum development.

He has been a guest on many radio shows, cohosted a radio show called "Sky Guys" on the local public radio station, and has hosted his own television program on Parkland College television. Dave taught all ages. He might teach two or three community college classes but then perform a program teaching kindergarteners. Then he would give talks to civic groups and do workshops for the public and teachers. He has also taught eight-week virtual workshops for The Osher Lifelong Learning Institute meeting the learning needs of seniors. And he worked to establish the first and only dark sky preserve in Illinois in 2018.

See David C. Leake, "The Planetarium versus the Traditional Classroom: A Study of Language in Diverse Learning Environments" (Champaign, Illinois: University of Illinois, Curriculum & Instruction 490 DWS, Spring 1994).

*Chapter 9*

# Precursors of the Communiversity

> There are a set of societal groups for whom engagement with the university is problematic, despite its apparent potential value to benefit both these communities and the university in terms of creating context-specific knowledges of societal challenges, issues and problems. . . . All too often universities default to engaging with easy-to-reach communities with which it is intrinsically attractive to engage.
> 
> —Benneworth et al.[1]

Benneworth et al. note that "the definition of community engagement is notoriously difficult to pin down."[2] There are many communities to consider as well as diverse relationships between those communities and the academy. One might focus on immediate physical neighbors around campuses, on those with a philosophical overlap, such as for denominational universities, or on practical overlaps, such as medical schools with hospitals.[3] Some community engagement is with major industry partners, who offer employment for graduates and potential donors. Different academies, including K-12 schools, community colleges, research universities, professional training institutes, and so on, would each have their own definitions of community engagement.

The definitional problem is compounded by one of ambiguous purpose: Is the aim of community engagement to be charitable? Is it an extension of the academy's teaching mission? Is it an obligatory service to the public? Is it a means, as Benneworth et al. say, to obtain "context-specific knowledges of societal challenges, issues and problems"? Or, is it one of a large number of other purposes?

There are major efforts underway to develop more inclusive definitions of community engagement and classification systems for the different types.[4] These generally seek to highlight the hard-to-reach communities that support formal education but often derive minimal benefits. This chapter does not attempt to compete with those institutional efforts but instead to highlight some key examples and issues regarding what might be regarded as precursors to a communiversity.

## DEWEY'S DREAM

At the University of Pennsylvania and the local community of West Philadelphia, there has been a long tradition of emphasizing problem-solving as the foundation of education, awakening university students to their social responsibilities. Benson, Harkavy, and Puckett see the deeper engagement of that kind as essential for a thriving civil society and the development of democratic citizenship. They argue for the continued relevance of Dewey's philosophy, especially for a society made stronger by education at its center.[5]

Their analysis emphasizes community schools, and especially community tertiary institutions, as the best places to grow a democratic society based on racial, social, and economic justice. They assert that American colleges and universities bear a responsibility for, and would benefit substantially from, working with schools to develop democratic schools and communities.

Jean Bethke Elshtain takes up similar issues in her discussion of civil society. She argues that it does not solve problems, but "creates citizens." She sees this as essential "in an era [a generation ago] . . . when there is widespread agreement that American democracy is in some trouble, when a the mountain of data has been offered out displaying our civic depletion and cynicism."[6]

Her perspective emphasizes the formative role of institutions, especially schools, when they are connected to civic life:

> Government can help or hinder. But it is finally a test for the overlapping, plural associations of civic life in which citizens build and pass on those formative institutions—families, schools, churches, unions, and all the rest, including state and local governments—without which there is no democratic culture, and, indeed, nothing for the federal government to either correct or curb or serve.[7]

Figure 9.1 shows schematically the transition from the ivory tower style of connection between academy and community, first to the third mission type of engagement and then to a full transactional relationship as with a communiversity. In the first case, the academy focuses on its two primary functions of preserving and creating knowledge and then transmitting that to students.

In the second, the third mission adds technology transfer, lifelong learning, and social engagement. In the third, the communiversity incorporates

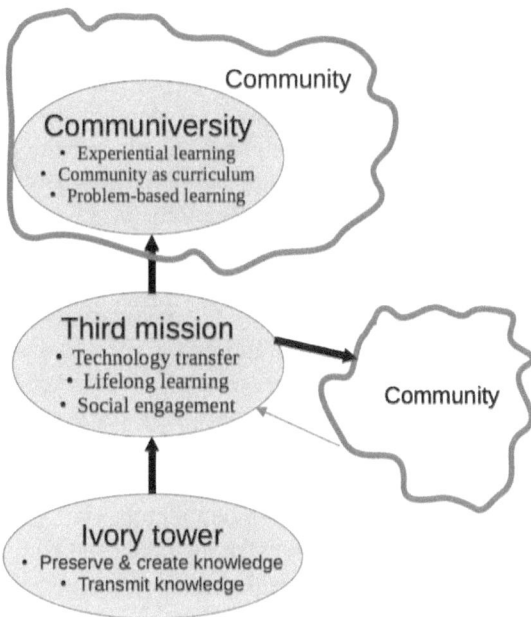

Figure 9.1  From Ivory Tower to Communiversity. *Source*: Author created.

experiential learning, community as curriculum, and problem-based learning through a full partnership.

## LINKING UNIVERSITIES WITH THE COMMUNITY

Gerhard Fischer et al. argue that community-based learning is a core competency for residential, research-based universities.[8] An example of their idea is the Physics Department at the University of Illinois. It could be described at first as a transmission model, one designed to share physics knowledge with a larger public. But it has incorporated interaction aspects as well. For example, "Saturday Physics for Everyone" is a series of free lectures on modern aspects of the physical sciences held Saturday mornings each fall. The program began in 1993. It offers high school students and the general public the opportunity to hear presentations from world-class scientists and researchers.

Attendees learn about recent advances in the physical sciences, gain an understanding of how physics affects development in modern technology, and how it influences daily life. A question and answer session is held at the end of each program. Participants may also communicate via email and obtain slides from the talks.

A related outreach activity is the Illinois Physics Van, a traveling science show for kids. By demonstrating and explaining fascinating physics principles, students and faculty from the Physics Department show audiences that science is fun and worthwhile for people who wonder about why the world acts the way it does. They challenge students' mental picture of what kind of people scientists are. They show them that as long as you want to learn and have fun, there is a world of physics waiting to be discovered.

The van travels to local elementary schools presenting to children and teachers. A middle school English teacher in one evaluation study of Physics Van saw connections between the inquiry process in physics and the writing process she teaches to her students. But, more importantly, she said that the experience was important to her professionally, because it validated her sense of herself as one who can learn new things. It reinforced her reasons for entering the profession in the first place, and the daily practice provided too little of that.[9]

Field stations are another way to extend the academy. This is a site (near a coast, along a river, in a forest, on a mountaintop, etc.) where researchers can study place-based phenomena with the materials and equipment they are likely to need for their studies. In recent years, field stations have been conceived as sites for learning as well, with internships, practicum experiences, on-site teaching of classes, and outreach programs.[10]

The field station at the University of Kentucky is located on a 60-acre, old-field tract in Lexington and surrounded by residential neighborhoods, agricultural land, and horse farms.[11] Biology faculty uses the facility for a broad range of ecological environmental and genomic research. The site also hosts classes and research experiences for undergraduates. There are multi-, inter-, and trans-disciplinary projects, involving art, literature, history, education, chemistry, astronomy, business, sociology, and other fields, as well as life sciences.

Other station facilities include trail networks or state-of-the-art laboratories. In addition to supporting research, teaching, and public engagement, a field station can address real problems in the community, such as pollution or biodiversity loss. They capitalize on rural settings, seeing them as a resource for learning, not just as a deficit for being far removed from an urban center or the main campus of a university.

Field stations can play a critical role in ensuring that environmental considerations are factored into local and regional planning and development decisions.[12] They can extend the curriculum beyond the rote material that makes up many standardized exams toward a deeper understanding of science as a process. That can mean an important role in promoting general science literacy.[13]

But many field stations offer only transmission-like communications, a one-way transfer of knowledge from the station to the public. Goals such as build community or make field station resources available to the public suggest more of an interactive model. One could easily imagine approaches in which the field station is driven by community needs and collaborates fully with community members to identify projects of local environmental concern. Doing so would make the field station operate more as a transaction model.

## COMMUNITY COLLEGES

Community colleges are an approximation of the communiversity. Their open-door admission policies "encourage students to enroll regardless of income level, sex, skin color, religion, or previous academic background. Half of all college students in the US attend these colleges."[14]

They offer adult education for job certification; they serve as junior colleges preparing students for four-year colleges and universities; and they offer a wide variety of courses for continuing education. Most of them offer a variety of other services for infants through the aged. Their offerings meet community needs in a way that large universities often do only indirectly. In this sense community colleges are automatically at least somewhat in the community school model, responding to community interests and needs.

Community colleges succeed when they value the individual student. Community building in which they bond with each other, faculty, and staff is also important. But this can be difficult. Most students spend very little time on campus, especially in Covid-19 times. They are likely to be part time, as are the instructors. For evening students, the administration and staff are practically nonexistent.[15]

William Rainey Harper was the major force behind the creation of the junior college and, later, community college system.[16] In the late nineteenth century, community boosterism arose along with the rise of the research university. Both of these fueled the community college movement. During the Progressive Era, additional sources were the advent of universal secondary education, professionalization of teacher education, and the vocational education movement. Following World War II, there was more open access to higher education[17] and the rise of adult and continuing education and community services. All of these contributed to a diverse movement.[18]

An examination of these trends reveals why community colleges have been primarily a US innovation. Community boosterism and the Progressive Era had parallels in other countries but did not develop as fully as they did in the United States. The same could be said for the early development of professional teacher education.

## PROGRESSIVE COLLEGES

Progressive colleges appear in many guises from junior and community colleges, to liberal arts colleges, to state-funded public colleges and universities, and many others. They include historically black colleges and universities (HBCUs) at least to the extent that they democratize learning opportunities.[19]

The HBCUs are concentrated in the Southern United States. Prior to 1964, higher education in the United States completely disqualified or limited African American enrollment. Even today, the overwhelming majority of higher education institutions are predominantly white and maintain de facto barriers to African Americans.

There are many definitions of progressive, but two common themes stand out: democratic education *within* and democratic education *beyond* the walls. For example, Green Mountain College (recently closed) had nearly two centuries of commitment to these goals. The college had a caring relationship with a diverse student body. It also had a close town-gown relationship. The capstone course, A Delicate Balance, culminated in a project that combined a student's academic area of focus with civic engagement. The Progressive Program let students develop their own program of study.

Progressive colleges have sought to achieve community engagement in a variety of ways. For example, Evergreen State College emphasizes local and global commitment to social justice, diversity, environmental stewardship, and service in the public interest. At Black Mountain College, students connected with the local community by participating in farm work, construction projects, and kitchen duty.[20] City University of New York was founded to "educate the whole people." It has maintained open access to all and is still tuition-free for nearly half of the students. It was the first to offer free education to women and has been welcoming to immigrants. Earlham College views education as a process of awakening the "teacher within," so that students become lifelong learners. At Warren Wilson College, students grow their our own food, till and harvest the farm, gardens, and forests using sustainable agricultural practices. Northeastern University's co-op program began over 100 years ago; students alternate classroom studies with full-time work in career-related jobs for six months.

A famous example is Berea College. Founded in 1855 by ardent abolitionists and radical reformers, Berea continues today firmly rooted in its historic religious mission. However, it can be a model well beyond that. It was the first interracial and coeducational college in the South. Its environment frees persons to be active learners, workers, and servers both as members of the academic community and as world citizens.

A primary goal is to provide an educational opportunity for students of all races, primarily those from Appalachia, who have great promise and limited economic resources. It seeks to create a democratic community dedicated to education and gender equality. This implies asserting the kinship of all people. The college emphasizes on understanding and equality among blacks and whites as a foundation for building community among all people.

Work is framed as being of practical benefit and as a way to promote learning and serving in community. The student Labor Program honors the dignity and utility of all work, mental and manual, emphasizing pride in work well done. Students graduate with little or no student loan debt. That work further engages Appalachian communities, families, and students in partnership for mutual learning, growth, and service.

bell hooks, a distinguished professor in Residence at Berea College, expresses the vision well in her book *Teaching Community*:

> Teachers who have a vision of democratic education assume that learning is never confined solely to an institutionalized classroom . . . the democratic educator . . . seeks to re-envision schooling as always a part of our real world experience, and our real life. Embracing the concept of a democratic education we see teaching and learning as taking place constantly. We share the knowledge gleaned in classrooms beyond those settings thereby working to challenge the construction of certain forms of knowledge is always and only available to the elite.[21]

Democratic education is essential to the survival of viable education at all levels. The New American Baccalaureate Project sees the character formation of individuals who can serve their communities as necessary for liberal arts colleges. It also emphasizes

> shifting curriculum away from mere breadth and depth in disciplinary knowledge and to breadth and depth of character development, supporting teacher tracks in higher education to foster this kind of student-centered learning, exploring the possibilities for liberal holistic learning in other contexts and at distance.[22]

Life on the community side provides the intellectual space, including both resources and challenges. The community provides the foundation of the curriculum and questions for inquiry-based learning. The academy side brings historically grounded disciplinary knowledge and tools for connecting to other communities, times, and places.

## CHARITY, CARING, EXTENSION, SERVICE, OUTREACH, OR PUBLIC ENGAGEMENT?

Terms such as charity, caring, extension, service, outreach, public engagement, and action-oriented learning reflect different stances toward connecting between the academy and the surrounding community. These terms have attained different levels of popularity and different meanings over the years. For some, the goal is the selfless mission to help others. Others critique any such concepts as elitist, one-way, or limited in scope.

Jane Addams saw the problem clearly:

> Probably there is no relation in life which our democracy is changing more rapidly than the charitable relation, that relation which obtains between benefactor and beneficiary; at the same time, there is no point of contact in our modern experience which reveals more clearly the lack of that equality which democracy implies. We have reached the moment when democracy has made such inroads upon this relationship that the complacency of the old-fashioned charitable man is gone forever; while the very need and existence of charity deny us the consolation and freedom which democracy will at last give.[23]

An examination of the use of these terms in a corpus of English-language text is revealing. "Service" is by far the most popular of these terms, peaking, as one might expect, during the two World Wars, then declining in use up to the present.[24] "Extension" is the next most popular, eclipsing "charity" around the time of the Morrill Land-Grant Acts, which mandated extension as a part of the university mission. Since then, its use has declined as "outreach" and "public engagement" have grown in use. "Charity" has seen a steady decline ever since around 1817, until only recently. "Caring" shows a strong rise starting around 1965. "Outreach" far surpasses "public engagement," but the gap began to narrow around the year 2000.

These trends reflect external events, such as wars or the Land-Grant Acts. They also suggest pendulum swings, as the use of a term reveals both its strengths and weaknesses. Outreach, for example, came to be seen in some circles as too much of a one-way relation, with some organizations transmitting its wisdom to the less informed. Public engagement was meant to imply a deeper connection to the beneficiary, more of an interactive or even transactive relationship.

Again, Jane Addams perceived the larger issue clearly. It is not to settle on one term or one way of viewing engagement with a community but to find the appropriate balance in real, living situations:

> The Hebrew prophet made three requirements from those who would join the great forward-moving procession led by Jehovah.[25] To love mercy, and at the same time to do justly, is the difficult task. To fulfill the first requirement alone is to fall into the error of indiscriminate giving, with all its disastrous results; to fulfill the second exclusively is to obtain the stern policy of withholding, and it

results in such a dreary lack of sympathy and understanding that the establishment of justice is impossible.[26]

Addams understood, and saw in practice, that there are problems with mercy or caring per se. Although it seems like something to strive for, it can lead to "disastrous results." Torrents of blame, judgment, dependency, superiority, inferiority, and obligation overcome what might have been natural, human relations of care. There are equal challenges to the otherwise obvious call to do justly. Adherence to rules and fundamental principles of justice can get in the way of natural human relations. And these two requirements can work against each other.

Addams warns that we can never resolve the conflicting requirements of mercy or caring against the tough love mandate of acting justly within the frame of just these two mandates. Instead we need to follow the third requirement, which moves us from essentially transmissive to fully transactive relationships:

> It may be that the combination of the two can never be attained save as we fulfill still the third requirement, to walk humbly with God, which may mean to walk for many dreary miles beside the lowliest of his creatures, not even in peace of mind, that the companionship of the humble is popularly supposed to give, but rather with the pangs and misgivings to which the poor human understanding is subjected whenever it attempts to comprehend the meaning of life.[27]

## NOTES

1. Paul Stephen Benneworth et al., *Mapping and Critical Synthesis of Current State-of-the-Art on Community Engagement in Higher Education* (Institute for the Development of Education, 2018), 18.

2. Ibid: 10.

3. Ibid: 27.

4. "National Inventory for Institutional Infrastructure on Community Engagement (NIIICE)," *Commission on Public Purpose in Higher Education* (blog), 2022, https://public-purpose.org/initiatives/national-institutional-inventory-of-infrastructure-for-community-engagement/.

5. Lee Benson, John Puckett, and Ira Harkavy, *Dewey's Dream: Universities and Democracies in an Age of Education Reform* (Philadelphia: Temple University Press, 2007).

6. Jean Bethke Elshtain, "Not a Cure-All," in *Community Works: The Revival of Civil Society in America*, edited by E. J. Dionne, Jr. (Washington, DC: Brookings Institution Press, 2000), 28.

7. Ibid: 29.

8. Gerhard Fischer, Markus Rohde, and Volker Wulf, "Community-Based Learning: The Core Competency of Residential, Research-Based Universities," *International Journal of Computer-Supported Collaborative Learning* 2, no. 1 (October 16, 2006): 9.

9. Bertram C. Bruce, Michael Weissman, and Michael Novak, "Science Education Outreach: Physics Demonstrations, Lectures, and Workshops," *Spectrum: The Journal of the Illinois Science Teachers Association* 23, no. 2 (1997): 8–12; Michael Novak, n.d. "Evaluating the Impact of the Physics Van on Its Target Audience."

10. https://www.obfs.org/.

11. https://bio.as.uky.edu/erf.

12. https://obfst.memberclicks.net/.

13. Rhonda Struminger, Jill Zarestky, Rachel A. Short, and A. Michelle Lawing, "A Framework for Informal STEM Education Outreach at Field Stations," *BioScience* 68, no. 12 (December 1, 2018): 977. The paragraph to follow summarizes their study.

14. S. deBoef, *It's Time to Complete Community College: Student Outcome Studies Show What It Takes to Succeed* (Lanham: Rowman & Littlefield, 2018).

15. Vanessa Smith Morest, *Community College Student Success: From Boardrooms to Classrooms*, American Council on Education Series on Community Colleges (Lanham: Rowman & Littlefield, Publishers, Inc, 2013): 106.

16. Richard L. Drury, "Community Colleges in America: A Historical Perspective," *Inquiry* 8, no. 1 (Spring 2003): 6. Drury cites Steven Brint and Jerome Karabel, *The Diverted Dream: Community Colleges and the Promise of Educational Opportunity* (New York, NY: Oxford University Press, 1989).

17. There are world-class tuition-free universities, including for international students, in many European countries.

18. James L. Ratcliff, "Community Colleges: The History of Community Colleges, The Junior College and the Research University, The Community College Mission," in *Education Encyclopedia-StateUniversity.Com*, 2021, https://education.stateuniversity.com/pages/1873/Community-Colleges.html.

19. HBCUs are institutions of higher education in the United States established after the Civil War and before the Civil Rights Act of 1964.

20. The college closed in 1957. See Katherine Chaddock Reynolds, *Visions and Vanities: John Andrew Rice of Black Mountain College* (Baton Rouge, Louisiana: Louisiana State University Press, 1998); Martin Duberman, *Black Mountain: An Exploration in Community* (Evanston, IL: Northwestern UP, 2009).

21. bell hooks, *Teaching Community: A Pedagogy of Hope* (New York: Routledge, 2003), 41.

22. Robert L. Fried and Eli O. Kramer, "The Meaning of a Liberal Arts and Sciences Education in the United States: Anachronistic Lessons from a Parochial Past," *The New American Baccalaureate Project* 3, no. 1 (April 2021).

23. Jane Addams, *Democracy and Social Ethics*, ed. Anne Firor Scott (Cambridge, MA: Harvard University Press, 1964), 13–14.

24. According to the Google Books Ngram Viewer <https://books.google.com/ngrams>.

25. Micah 6:8: "He has shown you, O man, what is good; and what does the Lord require of you but to do justly, love mercy, and to walk humbly with your God?"
26. Addams, *Democracy and Social Ethics*, 69–70.
27. Addams, *Democracy and Social Ethics*, 70.

*Part V*

# COMMUNIVERSITY

The use of the term *communiversity* reflects a belief about education more than a particular grade level, organization, or program. It integrates classroom learning with learning beyond the walls. It applies from early childhood learning as with Çaba-Çam discussed earlier, through K-12, to higher education, and lifelong learning.

The existing literature on *communiversity* exhibits multiple meanings, inspiring and aspirational in some cases, but merely descriptive of programs in others. Some communiversities emphasize noncredit classes. The one at the University of Cincinnati invites students to "enjoy non-credit classes for personal enrichment! . . . Classes are held in the evening, on weekends, online, and tailored with the adult learner in mind. . . . It is a great place to meet people who share your interests in class."[1] That is essentially an extracurricular program, like the University of Mississippi's Communiversity, where "community and university come together to share, learn, and experience new things—with no tests, papers, or grades."[2]

Others emphasize creating a bridge to higher education. For example, the communiversity of South Africa is a college-prep and training program that "bridges the gap between high school and college and/or a good career."[3] At Maynooth University,

> The Communiversity is a gateway for people to enter higher education . . . it can be the first point of contact for people who would not normally think of university as a place for them. . . . [They can] find out for themselves whether they would like to go further without having to commit to years of study or fees . . . to explore just who they are and where they fit in.[4]

These programs speak to the combination of classroom and daily life, without entailing major changes to the learning organization.

The programs discussed in Part V go beyond that and do imply major changes. The first profile included here (Udgum Khadka) is set in contemporary Nepal, where a radical transformation of higher education is underway. It foreshadows a chapter on Nepal that reminds us of a host of challenges to any education model. That case study brings together abstract theory with on-the-ground realities, including the effects of the Covid-19 pandemic. The result is not a how-to guide for connecting the academy and the community, or for integrating formal learning and experience. Instead, it is an effort to reveal the complexities and the possibilities of reimagining the future of education.

A second profile (Ann Peterson-Kemp) looks at an array of projects involving schools, universities, libraries, and community organizations. It introduces a contrasting model set in the community of Paseo Boricua, Chicago, which has been developing and experimenting with various modes of interaction between school, community, and college-level learning for over half a century.

## NOTES

1. https://www.uc.edu/about/continuing-ed/communiversity.html.
2. https://www.outreach.olemiss.edu/communiversity/.
3. https://communiversitysa.org/.
4. https://www.maynoothuniversity.ie/research/spotlight-research/how-communiversity-introduces-people-higher-education.

# Profile
## Udgum Khadka

Udgum Khadka is passionate about education at large, specifically in the areas of learning science and teacher development. His story shows how a young person with a variety of experiences integrating the classroom and daily life became committed to the community as a curriculum idea.[1] Udgum says,

> After I completed my undergrad, I started questioning where have I been applying the education, the knowledge, the information that I have gathered for almost 20 to 25 years. Where have I applied that knowledge and do I even remember some of the aspects that I was "taught" or that I learned. The answer I repeatedly got was probably I haven't used them that much.
>
> Some of the subjects that I was interested in, probably I was trying to see the relevance of it at my workplace, at my home, but the majority of them, the majority of the courses, subjects that I learned were limited to writing it on the paper for the sake of getting good grades, and after I get good grades, I'm done. I don't want to recall accounting anymore. I don't want to recall statistics anymore. I submitted the paper. Now I'm done! That's how I was spending my academic and formal educational life.
>
> Fortunately, after I went to Finland and got a taste of Finnish education, I started questioning, and saw how education can be more meaningful. There were companies who were working with researchers to find some aspects of 6G networks. The industry was working in 5G. Nokia networks were working with researcher at the university to understand how 6G networks work. They were even ahead of industry and practice.
>
> And the knowledge they were getting from the University, Nokia, the company, which was working with the researchers getting some insights was taking it back to their company and trying to explore what could be done beyond 5G.

So that was just one example, but I could start seeing how education can be made more relevant; education can be made more practical; education can be made more meaningful.

That's when I also started thinking of how can education go beyond four walls. How can we work in a more meaningful way so that we're not studying for the sake of getting good grades, but we're studying so that we could do something about it?

## NOTE

1. Udgum Khadka was born in 1990 in Kathmandu, Nepal. He studied business, focusing on Marketing and Entrepreneurship, and later worked at the University of Oulu, Finland. He is currently a Faculty and Educational Designer at King's College, Nepal. One of his significant life experiences was three months spent in Brazil in Teresina and Fortaleza.

*Chapter 10*

# Ruptures of Community Engagement

> I am 40 years old, married, and have two sons, 20 and 14 years old. As a married working mom (home caregiver) who finished matric in 1998, I never thought I would ever reach my goals of becoming a teacher....
> I was very skeptical to go in. I always just walked past the building, wondering what was really happening in there. My first time walking into the Communiversity was a real loving and warm experience.
> —Qwendie Soloman, student at the Communiversity of South Africa[1]

The integration of experience with formal education is a long-sought, but difficult to achieve, goal. Formal education tends to approach learning of various disciplines in silos, separate from one another and from ordinary experience.[2] This means that the experience from our everyday lives is rarely linked to the learning we do at schools. Furthermore, many students feel little connection between what they learn in class and the realities of the world.

## EDUCATION IN NEPAL

Nepal has many of the same challenges that other developing countries face, along with its own historical conditions. Education was for a long time based on homeschooling and gurukulas, a type of residential schooling system from ancient India with shishya (students) living near or with the guru (teacher).[3] The first formal school, established in 1853, was intended for the elite. From its inception, formal education was modeled on the Indian system, itself a legacy of the British Raj.

Chandra Shamsher established the first institute of higher learning in 1918, naming it after himself.[4] During the inauguration, he lamented that opening up education in even a modest way foretold the end of Rana rule. Later he felt personally responsible for the downfall of the Rana dynasty.

The modern education system in Nepal started in 1951 after the fall of the Ranas. At that time the adult literacy rate was 5 percent, most of those being male. Although education has expanded rapidly since then, there is still limited education in the villages. Even in Kathmandu, schools are under-resourced by Western standards and operate through a confusing array of public and private organizations. Recent decades have seen major changes and improvement in literacy, but there are many remaining challenges in areas such as teacher preparation and resources for learning.[5]

Endemic poverty has consequences for health, education, and general welfare. In recent years the country has changed governments on a more than yearly basis, making it difficult to sustain any campaigns for human rights or accountability. Disasters such as the May 2015 earthquake, which would be devastating anywhere, act with renewed vengeance on a nation ill-equipped to repair roads or rebuild.

There is also discrimination based on gender, caste, religion, or language. This oppression is often seen as unavoidable, part of the fatalism often attributed to Nepal.[6] It stands in contrast to the aspiration of unity through diversity alluded to in the national anthem: "Diverse races, languages, religions, and cultures of incredible sprawl / This progressive nation of ours, all hail Nepal!"[7]

For some students, the issue is whether they have a school at all, or a teacher. Books, computers, and electricity are often lacking. Even private schools are under-resourced by US standards. A series of studies led by Narendra Prasad Phuyal et al. has documented many of these problems in areas such as difficult geography, inadequate facilities, outdated curriculum, language diversity, restrictive pedagogy, lack of informal learning opportunities, demands of agricultural work, attitudes, and social relations.[8]

Despite these problems, Nepal has an amazing array of innovative projects promoting learning across all ages. These occur in schools, colleges, informal learning centers, civic groups, and other organizations. Although each project has its own story to tell, there is a common thread: They conceive that the individual can develop only in a supportive community and conversely that the community requires the full participation of critical, socially engaged citizens. There are many examples that embody a progressive vision and resist the factory model, even in the face of limited material resources.[9]

## THE INTEGRATED COURSE

To make things worse, it is not easy to build programs that connect within-the-walls and beyond-the-walls learning. An example of both the challenges and the benefits of this linking is the four-month-long *Integrated Course* at King's College, Nepal.[10] This is an experimental project-based learning program, which aims to integrate learning and action in the community with classroom-based education. Although the case discussed below is just one iteration of one course, it represents a crucial first step toward creating a *communiversity* in Nepal. As such it helps us to understand both the promise and the perils of community-based learning.

In the course, action in the community is brought to the center. It is not a practice to employ subsequent to academic learning. Instead, action in the community is both where learning begins and where it is applied. The community is the intellectual space for student engagement and growth as an understanding of problems and solutions to them comes from involvement in the real problems in the community. The course developers write, "Connecting classroom learning with the world beyond academia can increase motivation for students, provide familiar examples for study, open the classroom to a trove of resources, promote integration across subject areas, and facilitate transfer of learning."[11] The course thus integrates mind and body in action. Life in the community is conceived as an intellectual source, but it incorporates aspects of body, whether through agricultural work, interacting with community members, or visiting sites in the community.

The first iteration of the course was offered as part of an undergraduate program in the business. It is integrated between college and community, between research and practice, and across the disciplines of Entrepreneurship, Ethics, and Communication. This entailed a completely different system of assessment, in which learning was more self-directed. In addition to students and community members, there were *course facilitators* responsible for overall coordination, *teachers* who conducted classes for the three disciplines—Entrepreneurship, Communication, and Ethics—and *mentors* responsible for checking in on a team's progress, ensuring smooth teamwork, and facilitating team discussions outside the classroom environment.

The course promoted five kinds of integration:

1. Community life was the curriculum; the learning process and outcomes were derived from knowledge and practices in the community.[12] Four themes—Education, Livelihood, Local Business, and Agriculture—were chosen in collaboration with community members.
2. Student learning was integrated with that of their peers. Sixteen undergraduate business students were divided into four teams, one for each theme.

3. Students integrated their classroom and experiential learning under guidance from mentors.
4. There was integration across the disciplines of Entrepreneurship, Ethics, and Communication, each of which was already interdisciplinary.
5. Finally, there was a goal of integrating this new approach to learning and community engagement with the traditional university-established procedures for assessment and accreditation.

The plan was that the students would visit the community for at least a week and then periodically after that.[13] Projects were the common ground on which students could bring their learning experiences from all three disciplines together. Various small projects would add up to the final project, namely the creation of a prototype solution for a problem identified under the theme. Learning occurred through collaborative problem-solving—among the community, students, and teachers.[14] For example, under the theme "Education," students found that the issues were closely tied with the earning capacity of children's guardians as well as community social norms.

## INQUIRY AND DISCOVERY

Some students enrolled in the course were literally lost while riding their motorbikes to the community where the course was based. They were trying to find Shikharpa, a small village in mountainous terrain. There are very few good maps of that region and none of the signposts that one might expect in the United States or Europe. The usual resort to online maps was not much help. With spotty cell service that map might not be available, and even if it were, it could easily be incomplete or inaccurate.

The students were also lost in their journey through a completely new way of teaching and learning. The course was designed to begin with the knowledge and needs of the community, one quite different from the bustling, urban environment of Kathmandu, the home of most of the students. But as one said, "being lost was fun."[15]

In both the literal and the metaphorical senses, the students experienced venturing into an unknown terrain. They had to invent their own ways to navigate that unfamiliar terrain and to make sense of strange phenomena. In the end, they eventually found their way out and reported benefiting from the initial disorientation. One said that he had for the first time felt truly responsible for his own learning. This experience recalls the Grand Inquisitor tale: The students might have preferred the "bread" of simple directions to the site, but relying on their own resources led to a deeper learning.

In line with the idea that the community is the heart of the curriculum, the initial month of the course was dedicated to inquiry and discovery with the students immersing themselves in community life. That immersion enabled them to identify and test real-world problems, reflect on these problems, validate existing theories, and create solutions for the community. For example, it was difficult to find data, such as on demographics or types of work, but could be done through home visits.

The choice of community was based on various practical considerations such as meeting accessibility, potential learning opportunities, safety, and security. Shikharpa, with several hundred inhabitants, met most of these requirements. Visitors would find small shops, agricultural land, and walking trails amid its natural beauty.

The ten miles from Kathmandu to Shikharpa might seem trivial to most readers. But in Nepal, due to road conditions and traffic, that distance can entail a journey of an hour or more by bus or motorbike. The cultural and socioeconomic distances are even greater—students, for example, often referred to how many people from the community sought to leave for employment and education in Kathmandu.

Students visited the community during the second week of the course. It was important to do so despite the difficulties. Initially, their time there was more akin to a group of young people enjoying an outing. However, once the workshops began, they took group discussions and community visits more seriously. They met people, asked questions, observed, and experienced community life.

One student said that "the first few weeks of the course stayed in my memory the most because what we learned on paper, we got to see for ourselves" and that "we used to study about [other's experiences] but this course felt like studying things we saw right in front of us." Students' attitudes toward the course were likely influenced by the novelty.[16] However, the students also felt strongly that in-person and real-world experiences helped them make sense of their learning throughout the course.

The Covid-19 pandemic threw a major wrench into a course intended to integrate college and community. All of the workshops, sessions, and classes suddenly needed to be delivered online. More importantly, for the students, the change came at a crucial point in their course. Students could not maintain in-person visits. Teachers were preoccupied with the new demands to deliver lessons online. Integrating the content with student projects and across disciplines suffered.

## RUPTURES AS SOURCES OF INSIGHTS

The problems for the course reveal more than a completely smooth implementation would have done. Heidegger famously makes this point regarding tools: While engaged in trouble-free hammering, the skilled carpenter has no conscious recognition of the hammer, or that matter, the lumber, nails, or workbench, or even herself. A tool-in-use thus becomes phenomenologically transparent.[17] Bruce and Hogan write about a simple example of this process in our use of telephones. Initially a novelty, the tool soon becomes a habit:

> Soon it is treated as part of daily activity. We might say, "I talked to my friend today," without feeling any need to mention that the telephone was a necessary tool for that conversation to occur. Through this process, we move from looking at the technology as an addition to life to looking at life through that technology. The embedding of the technology in the matrix of our lives makes it invisible. In fact, the greater its integration into daily practices, the less it is seen as a technology at all.[18]

In this case, the Integrated Course functions as a tool, or a technology, one that is transparent when it works flawlessly. Disturbances to its ideal mode of action help us to see it directly, rather than through it, and to understand better how and why it works as it does. Specifically, five "ruptures" in the course became apparent, each being relevant to the overall course goal of integration: (1) between students and community, (2) among students, (3) between mentors and teachers, (4) between students and the intended curriculum, and (5) between educational philosophies.

A densely connected network of participants assumed communication among all, with some connection between any two nodes (figure 10.1). But there were crucial breakdowns in some key areas as it was implemented. These breakdowns were exacerbated by the pandemic in which a collaborative, high-touch approach was more challenging to accomplish.

First, the Covid-19 lockdown came at a critical point in the course. The students were not able to access the richness of knowledge in the community as intended. Despite their attempts to keep in touch with the community through the internet and telephone, it was evident that hearing alone (rather than experiencing and seeing) was insufficient for students to appreciate the wealth of knowledge in the community. For instance, students working in the agriculture theme would not understand the rationale for each step of the agricultural process.

This rupture made more evident the idea that the community is in fact a valuable source of knowledge for students. Classroom discussions emphasized theoretical perspectives on how entrepreneurs may source funding for their businesses in the initial stages. However, when students interacted with the community, they gained a better understanding of what it took for entrepreneurs to convince financial institutions, their friends and family to lend them money for their businesses and the legal liabilities they would incur. Students developed a self-directed and accountable mindset through

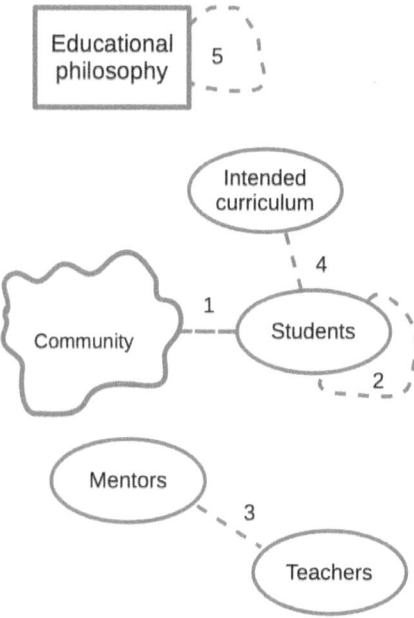

Figure 10.1 Five Ruptures That Stood Out in a Densely Integrated Course. *Source*: Author created.

their projects. They were not simply accountable for their own learning and growth, but also to real people outside the curriculum.

Second, the course revealed different degrees of collaboration among the student teams. One student team met only when they needed to work on the project. In contrast, another team would have non-course-related discussions during mentor check-ins where, for instance, they once talked about multi-player games they could play together online. The second team built better social relationships over the four months. It was noticeably more open to feedback, discussed more creative ideas, and had more productive conversations within the team. It did far better in areas of collaborative teamwork, community engagements, and stepping outside the comfort zone.

Third, there was also a rupture between mentors and teachers. Mentors felt that in most cases, their discussions with students were anchored on teamwork and the students' projects. This opened up possibilities for guided knowledge seeking outside the formal course content, thus further enhancing the students' opportunities to connect the curriculum with the community-based project. But whereas mentors focused on the "doing" side of things, teachers felt compelled to focus on the "content."

Fourth, transitioning to online learning due to the lockdown required the teachers to shift their focus from integrated learning to remote instruction.

This meant that efforts to link concepts across disciplines as well as to link concepts with community-based projects suffered. The effort to link learning to the real world brought the chaos, complexity, and unpredictability of the real world to the curriculum as well.

A final rupture was between educational philosophies. King's College offers its degrees through a university in the United States. Questions about the "equivalence" of credits between universities, including those in Nepal, can become contentious. With universities operating in different settings, differences in priorities, fundamental beliefs, and processes become apparent. While the course sought real-world experiences, community centricity, student independence, and student growth, the existing system focused on content delivery and quantitative measures of performance. Interdisciplinary approaches led to learning outcomes that differed from, and often exceeded, predefined learning outcomes.[19]

## INTEGRATED LEARNING

The Integrated Course had high aspirations related to a vision of the communiversity: It sought to link school and community, urban and rural life, academic study with concrete work on real community problems, research and practice, students with their peers and community members, and subject areas as diverse as communications, ethics, and entrepreneurship.

There were inherent challenges deriving from the course complexity, its elision of boundaries, difficulties of timing and distance, and, perhaps most of all, the knowledge that this was not the way it had always been done. The Covid-19 pandemic, which disrupted education everywhere, was particularly damaging to a project premised on close, in-person collaboration and learning through life in the field. Nevertheless, the goals were at least partially achieved.

Teachers found that their pedagogy evolved as a result of the course. They shifted from one-way knowledge transmission to a more transactional mode of teaching. This meant aiding the students' discovery of knowledge and valuing the understanding of diverse perspectives. Students found the assignments in the course to be relevant and connected to their learning. They drew from community experiences, projects, and ideas well beyond the course itself. This more open framing meant that the questions they asked were in context of the projects rather than on a particular week's topic from a syllabus.

None of the students had prior first-hand experience of life in a community so different from that of Kathmandu. As one said, the multiple community visits enabled them to experience a different environment. This "changed our mindset to take more seriousness in our work than we were learning in the classroom." Through meeting different people they came to understand that their own experience provided just one perspective: "It made us realize that the situation might be different from what we think of. . . . It has made us think critically and not from one side."

One student wrote, "Since I spent 12 years studying conventionally where I had to do assignments and [take] exams, this course was a new way of learning which I really wished I got to experience more." In a discussion he went on to add that nowhere in his prior formal learning did he see that what he was learning made any difference for others.[20]

Despite curtailing village visits because of the lockdown, students found innovative ways to use tools to work on their projects online. One stated that she felt "more responsible" in the course. Multiple teachers, mentors, and teammates presented a variety of perspectives. The unintended messiness of the design was exacerbated by its being a first-time implementation, by the complexities of working across different organizational realities, and, of course, by the pandemic. One student noted that this put her in a position where she had to make extra effort to link the course content to her experiences in the community for the sake of the project.

When asked about their thoughts on self-directed learning and the concepts discussed in class, students said that they felt lost initially during the course because there were too many possible ideas to explore. But they discovered that needing to find the relevant knowledge made them feel more involved in the learning process and resulted in better understanding.

In such self-directed learning, motivation plays a significant role.[21] One important source of motivation was the realization that their work had an impact on others. If the students did not go beyond the classroom and make an effort to actively seek out relevant knowledge, their projects would ultimately suffer. They needed to bring their knowledge alive, to take charge of their own learning.

> A good example of this process can be seen in the work of the agriculture team. They figured out that farmers devoted much of their time and energy to transporting goods to market. They devised a new system in which the farmers could bring their produce to a central location in the village, then have one person take that produce to Kathmandu. This was a classic business school problem related to allocation of resources. When they presented their "solution" to the farmers, they learned to their dismay that the farmers had tried that approach before. It had failed because of a lack of trust in the driver who delivered the produce.
> 
> The students learned about the real world complexity that is often omitted in textbook examples. They also saw the importance of communication. If the farmers had been directing the problem solving throughout, that particular

solution path might have been avoided. . . . This apparent failure of their specific solution was actually a powerful means for student learning, one that was not possible in a conventional course.[22]

The students learned things they would have never seen in ordinary classes. They learned to collaborate, to understand the perspectives of others, to be more socially responsible, to carry through on projects, and to take charge of their own learning. Many teachers and parents would say that the educational process succeeded, regardless of whether they acquired the specific knowledge and skills covered in traditional courses.

The Integrated Course sought to connect curriculum and college learning with the real world outside the classroom. It is noteworthy that validation for the approach occurred not so much when things went well, but when they did not. Only then was the function and value of the components revealed. Developers saw that the role of a mentor was pivotal in helping students make sense of classroom knowledge in the context of their projects. Similarly, the community's sharing of their realities was crucial. Robust relationships among various participants were crucial.

The Integrated Course was an awkward hybrid. It needed to accord with strict institutional rules. In doing so, it was successful in a conventional sense: Students learned the prescribed content. At the same time, the course invited open interaction with the world, thereby stepping beyond the banking model of education and instead promoting Freire's call for the practice of freedom.[23]

## DECOLONIZING EDUCATION

Much of the work on communiversities has been done in developing nations, such as Nepal, and especially in nations that have suffered directly under colonization, as in Africa. In these countries, education was first denied, then the lack of education has been used to rationalize injustice. When local people sought formal education, they found a neocolonial model that perpetuated their subaltern status.

> The tragedy of education in Africa is that the university system, which was inherited from the colonial rulers, has become an effective tool of re-colonization. The African university system is so deeply entrenched in the western world view that it is unable to critique its relevance within the local, political, economic and cultural settings.[24]

Compounding the colonial framing of Western education, individual students discover that their success requires cultural transformation.

Students who come to the university are made to feel that they are being introduced to a different world from their native world and the path to progress lies in how quickly they can imbibe this new world. They are expected to adopt the dress codes and research methodology of their academic disciplines, as a mark of induction into the new academic community.[25]

A communiversity is a deliberate hybrid, one that incorporates traditional university coursework with attention to local situations, cultural heritage, and problems. The example of King's College Nepal shows us both the possibility of communiversities for decolonizing education and the challenges that await.

# NOTES

1. https://communiversitysa.org/student/qwendie-soloman/. The communiversity's twelve-course college-prep and pre-professional program supports stress management, emotional intelligence, and experiential learning along with academics. Qualified high school leavers and matriculants are introduced to relevant career fields and further English, Maths, and Computer skills.

2. Lee Benson, John Puckett, and Ira Harkavy, *Dewey's Dream: Universities and Democracies in an Age of Education Reform* (Philadelphia: Temple University Press, 2007).

3. One could consider the gurukula as a kind of community school.

4. Tri-Chandra College.

5. E. Garner, "Education in Nepal: Meeting or Missing the Millennium Development Goals?" *Contributions to Nepalese Studies* 33, no. 2 (2006); Panth, Brajesh, and Hinchliffe, Keith, "Nepal: Priorities and Strategies for Education Reform," Human Development Unit, South Asia Region (Washington, DC: World Bank, July 18, 2001).

6. Dor Bahudur Bista, *Fatalism and Development: Nepal's Struggle for Modernization* (New York: Orient Blackswan, 1991).

7. Byakul Maila, Nepali national anthem, 2006.

8. Narendra Prasad Phuyal et al., "Access of Disadvantaged Children to Education" (Balkhu, Kathmandu, Nepal: Tribhuvan University Research Centre for Educational Innovation and Development, 2005).

9. Bertram C. Bruce, *Progressive Education In Nepal: The Community Is the Curriculum* (Wellfleet, MA: Chequessett Neck Books, 2018).

10. Raunak Chaudhari, Smriti Karanjit Manandhar, and Bertram C Bruce, "Realities of Implementing Community- Based Learning during Lockdown," *Schools: Studies in Education* 19, no. 1 (Spring 2022): 109–36.

11. Ibid.

12. Bertram C. Bruce, "Community as Curriculum: Nurturing the Ecosystem of Education," *Schools Studies in Education* 15, no. 1 (April 2018): 122–39.

13. Most chose the option to remain in the community. However, due to Covid-19, they could not return to consolidate or extend their initial impressions. In some cases, they were able to communicate with villagers through cell phones.

14. Gitta Domik and Gerhard Fischer, "Coping with Complex Real-World Problems: Strategies for Developing the Competency of Transdisciplinary Collaboration," in *Key Competencies in the Knowledge Society*, edited by Nicholas Reynolds and Márta Turcsányi-Szabó, 324:90–101, IFIP Advances in Information and Communication Technology (Berlin, Heidelberg: Springer Berlin Heidelberg, 2010).

15. Chaudhari et al., "Realities of Implementing Community Based Learning during Lockdown," 130.

16. Sulaiman M. Al-Balushi and Shamsa S. Al-Aamri, "The Effect of Environmental Science Projects on Students Environmental Knowledge and Science Attitudes," *Journal of International Research in Geographical and Environmental Education* 23, no. 3 (2014).

17. Martin Michael Wheeler, "Martin Heidegger," in *Stanford Encyclopedia of Philosophy (Fall 2020 Edition)*, ed. Edward N. Zalta, https://plato.stanford.edu/archives/fall2020/entries/heidegger/.

18. Bertram C. Bruce and Maureen P. Hogan, "The Disappearance of Technology: Toward an Ecological Model of Literacy," in *Handbook of Literacy and Technology: Transformations in a Post-Typographic World*, ed. David Reinking et al. (Florence, KY: Routledge, 1998), 269–81.

19. Susan M. Drake and Joanne L. Reid, "Integrated Curriculum for the Twenty-First Century," in *International Handbook of Holistic Education*, edited by John P. Miller et al. (New York, NY: Routledge, 2018).

20. Student quotes here are from a video interview on January 8, 2022.

21. D. R. Garrison, "Self-Directed Learning: Toward a Comprehensive Model," *Adult Education Quarterly* 48, no. 1 (November 1997): 18–33.

22. Chaudhari et al., "Realities of Implementing Community Based Learning during Lockdown," 130.

23. Paulo Freire, *Pedagogy of the Oppressed* (New York: Continuum, 1970).

24. Samanyanga Ronnie Lessem, Anselm Adodo, and Tony Bradley, *The Idea of the Communiversity: Releasing the Natural, Cultural, Technological and Economic GENE-Ius of Societies* (Manchester, United Kingdom: Beacon Books and Media, 2019), 330.

25. Ibid.

# Profile
## *Ann Peterson-Kemp*

One leader in community partnerships for learning is Ann Peterson-Kemp, cofounder of the Community Informatics Initiative at the University of Illinois.[1] She received a university career award that, as she says,

> speaks to the university's civic commitment, the importance we place on meaningful research and learning partnerships with communities such as north Champaign, East St. Louis, and Paseo Boricua in Chicago . . . it also acknowledges the important contributions of our community partners to generating new knowledge crucial to the life of the academy and to society at large.

She also cofounded Prairienet,[2] one of the earliest freenets.[3] Ann says,

> It's really like a whole life story, or at least a whole professional life story. It wasn't one thing, but a path strewn. An underlying essence is that it's just very self-serving. You want to do something that's interesting, engaging, fun, and meaningful.
>
> My academic background was in Russian literature, I got into library and information science with a blank slate in terms of research approaches and theories to guide professional practice. I didn't know anything about social science. I didn't know anything about methodology. I didn't have any relevant theories about how people learn or how people communicate or anything like that. So I was coming to it without a background in any particular area that might have channeled me to a certain way of thinking about fundamental phenomena in the field.
>
> I remember in my masters and PhD programs, I had some very good methods courses, but they were very traditional, positivistic, and quantitatively oriented . . . like statistics and survey methods. That, along with the lack of personal

experience in deep community or social action, puts you in a pretty small box. And for the most part, anything community-based or action-oriented was kind of suspect and viewed as not very rigorous. So when I started as a professor, that's all I had. But the great mentors I had showed me how research could have a major impact on everyday life.

I had just moved to Illinois and didn't know anyone. I thought that working with Prairienet would be a good way for me to get to know Champaign-Urbana. The first thing that shook my brain up was related to a Prairienet project to bring the Internet to low-income communities in our area. One of the students working on the project mentioned Paulo Freire and said "Hey, maybe we should look at this approach. This might be relevant here." And I had never even heard of him. So I read *Pedagogy of the Oppressed* and it just clicked.

Another life story intersection was when my daughter was born. I remember realizing that community-based work with Sisternet women, families at Shadowwood (a residential neighborhood where many recent Spanish-speaking immigrants live), and community activists in Paseo Boricua was great because it was the kind of work that they could be included in. So it's a kind of work that doesn't further separate me from my child. I was finding a space to work that recognized the importance of motherhood and family, that cherished children and was devoted to their welfare.

Beginning an after-school homework help program at an under-resourced public school brought me to another important influence . . . a little girl brought me home one day to meet her mother and we ended up forming a life-long family friendship. When we met that first day, I think I was doing an evaluation of our program or something so I wanted her to answer some questions, complete a form. She didn't trust me much, and had little reason to, but she was generous enough to give me a chance. It didn't take me long to realize that I was learning much more through our friendship than from any questionnaire. Sharon's mom is a natural coach, teacher, and mentor and I've learned a lot from her about how good and supportive learning happens in homes and communities.

And then being drawn to *community inquiry* was a major factor in my development as a scholar.[4] Again, I had this really immediate and strong feeling that this really fits what I'm seeing, what I'm experiencing, and how I'd like the world to be. Jane Addams presented a powerful and rigorous praxis that was grounded in everyday life, explained complex information science phenomena, and illuminated how positive social change happens in individuals, communities, and society as a whole.

Involvement with various community-based education and learning projects fueled my dissatisfaction with deficit-based framings of reality. I didn't feel they were advancing my understanding or contributing much to social justice. I was lucky to have really brilliant and mentors and colleagues in both the university and in the community. The community inquiry group at the university created the right kind of space to nurture knowledge that I was gaining from relationships with successful community-based institutions for learning, such as Sisternet, TAP-In Academy, and the Puerto Rican Cultural Center.

You'd be out in the community and there would be specific instances, just little things that would hit you hard and make a huge impact on your understanding. We were teaching the kids how to use computers and to make *Inquiry Units* and the first two sentences one of the boys (who was always getting in trouble) typed were "My name is Steven. I'm a good person." Something like that causes you to really reflect, and you just keep turning that little marble over in your brain and thinking of all that it signifies.

I went to the local premiere of a documentary about a music program in Champaign-Urbana, Illinois.[5] That was a decades-long program where adult and teen volunteers from the neighborhood taught the children how to play drums, just outside in the park, apart from any formal educational institution. They went on to win a national championship. Seeing the documentary and talking with those involved in the music and the film-making highlighted for me the power of local communities.

Steven was one of the kids handing out programs for the movie. I said "Oh, hi, Steven! I didn't know that you were in the Drum Corps." And it turned out that he knew dozens of music pieces that he could play from memory. And it's like, okay, this is the kid who supposedly has zero attention span and doesn't learn well. So things like that, you're never going to forget. And it allows you to learn more and develop a better understanding of community action, youth development and education, everything.

A more recent example is the study of immigrant youth information behavior that I was lucky enough to be a part of at the University of Washington. Instead of doing a traditional survey or focus group, one of the grad students suggested we try a "design thinking" methodology in which teens design information technology tools—just using arts and crafts supplies—to help with problematic situations in their daily lives.

The teens were totally engaged in the process and really had fun. And we learned so much more from their creative expressions. One young man designed an "empathy helmet" that would help bullies understand the pain they inflicted on other kids. Another teen designed an app to track public busses—he felt that drivers sometimes passed him by because he looked "scary."

I mostly learned from scholar-activists in the community. If the outcome you're looking for is improving education and well-being for youth who are furthest from educational and economic justice, and you're trying to capitalize on the greatness in these children that is too often wasted and squashed, these community-based approaches work. I'm a prime example of someone who was educated in and by the community. Thank goodness people were tolerant and helped me grow from my mistakes.

## NOTES

1. Ann Peterson Bishop, Bertram C. Bruce, and Sunny Jeong, "Beyond Service Learning: Toward Community Schools and Reflective Community Learners," in *Service Learning: Linking Library Education and Practice*, edited by Loriene Roy, Kelly Jensen, and Alex Hershey Meyers (Chicago: American Library Association, 2009), 16–31.

2. Sally van der Graaf, "From Prairienet to the CDI: Writing the History" (Charleston, IL: Eastern Illinois University, 2015).

3. Also known as a "free-net," a freenet was a text-based community computer network which offered internet services, at little or no cost, providing access to low-income communities.

4. Bertram C. Bruce, Ann Peterson Bishop, and Nama Raj Budhathoki, eds., *Youth Community Inquiry: New Media for Community and Personal Growth* (New York: Peter Lang, 2014).

5. The documentary focuses on the award-winning Douglass Center Drum Corps and Drill Team from the late 1960s. "The Beat Goes On," *Illinois Youth Media* (blog), n.d., https://will.illinois.edu/illinoisyouthmedia/beatgoeson.

## Chapter 11
# Community as Curriculum

> Our students don't come here because they are consciously seeking a liberating education or because they support Puerto Rican independence. They come here because they know that this school will work hard not to neglect them and because they'll find out who they are.
> —René Antrop-González,
> quoting a PACHS teacher[1]

Community-initiated engagement between the academy and the community often employs the idea of *the community as the curriculum*.[2] These build upon the idea of *funds of knowledge*, that most important knowledge derives from our lived experience in communities. The community is not simply a recipient of vetted knowledge from the academy, nor of problems to overcome, but is the primary source of ideas.[3]

These approaches are built upon a set of perspectives on how learning occurs and how it can be best facilitated. Learning has begun to be seen as *rhizomatic*, constructed by the learners involved in a nonlinear process.[4] Their most meaningful experiences come through active engagement in problem-solving on challenging projects. This posits learning as a lifelong process and part of everyday affairs in life.[5]

When the community becomes the curriculum, not simply a backdrop to it, issues from the community are brought to the curriculum and academic work returns to the community. Among other things, this can mean attempting to bridge the gap between the classroom and the outside world by introducing course projects and investing in innovative learning programs aimed at fostering creative and critical thinking and innovative teacher education programs. Most fundamentally, it means seeing the community as the intellectual center for learning, and a full partner in the educational process.

Both the academy and the community are essential; how they connect is the key. Oversimplifying a bit, one can say that the academy offers a space for reflection on community life and work, connection to work of others, including those in faraway places and times, and learning codified knowledge and skills. Similarly, the community not only offers funds of local knowledge, an intellectual space for learning and problem-solving, and problems or issues that need immediate attention but also provides a foundation for problem-based learning. In this model, both the academy (including pre-K to lifelong learning) and the community have something to offer; neither can be fully successful without the other. They come together through focused action in the world.

## PUERTO RICAN CULTURAL CENTER, CHICAGO

A contemporary version of this approach, one that has gone far in connecting community and curriculum surrounds the Puerto Rican Cultural Center (PRCC), a coordinating institution in the Paseo Boricua community in Chicago. The center draws from the ideas of innovators such as Eugenio María de Hostos, known as "El Gran Ciudadano de las Américas." He was a Puerto Rican educator, philosopher, intellectual, lawyer, sociologist, and independence advocate. In the Dominican Republic, he founded the first teachers' college and introduced advanced teaching methods. He opposed religious instruction in the educational process and promoted women's rights.[6]

Building on the ideas of Paulo Freire, the PRCC represents well the idea of *Popular Education* (*La educación popular*). Learning is based on everyday practices, experiences, and social context. The individual learns from the surrounding environment, not necessarily in formal settings. Popular education asserts that in the context of social injustice, education can never be politically neutral. If it does not side with the oppressed in an attempt to transform society, then it effectively sides with the oppressors, maintaining the existing structures of oppression. The approach is widely used in social justice efforts, including, for example, in immigrant rights groups.[7]

There is both informal learning through lived experiences and more formal elements, such as a daycare center, a family learning center, a library, and a community museum. A centerpiece is the Pedro Albizu Campos High School (PACHS).[8] The diversity of learning is amplified by the interactions among the activities in the learning spaces. There is a network of connections across formal schooling, after-school and community-based activities, political work, social development, and lived experience.

Many communities struggle with problems that the PRCC has faced—gangs, drug and alcohol abuse, violence, racism, gentrification, homelessness, alienation, poor job prospects, pollution, isolation, and other problems—but with far less success. And most communities are in the big middle ground, with small victories laid against those problems. The lack of communication and shared effort toward a common good makes many of these problems intractable.

## SOCIAL JUSTICE YOUTH DEVELOPMENT

In her ethnographic account of youth attending a comprehensive, virtually all-Mexican, inner-city high school in Houston, Angela Valenzuela found that schools actually *subtract* resources from youth by dismissing their definition of education and minimizing their culture and language. Students understand this well:

> They oppose a schooling process that disrespects them; they oppose not education, but *schooling*. [Many schools] are organized formally and informally in ways that fracture students' cultural and ethnic identities, creating social, linguistic, and cultural divisions among the students in between the students and the staff. (Emphasis in original)[9]

Leaders in Paseo Boricua found similar conditions; only one in four of their young people completed high school.

In response to these dysfunctions for students in marginalized communities, Shawn Ginwright and Julio Cammarota propose a *social justice youth development* model. A defining aspect of this model is to help youth develop awareness of their own circumstances as a prerequisite for addressing them. They argue that to promote this praxis of critical consciousness and social action, youth need to progress through three stages of awareness.

The first stage, self-awareness, focuses on helping youth achieve a positive sense of self, in terms of social and cultural identity. It encourages them to explore identity issues related to race, class, gender, and sexuality. For the PACHS curriculum, this means learning about the world in a connected way. Literacy follows Paulo Freire's idea of learning to read the word in order to read the world.[10] This means actively participating in that world as both a critic and creator. Each student is viewed as a whole, living being; one rarely hears talk of deficits, but rather of caring, strengths, and potentials for growth.[11]

The second stage is social awareness, which fosters an understanding of how their immediate social world functions. It encourages the capacity to think critically about issues in their own communities. The curriculum emphasizes learning how to act responsibly in the world, building on understanding themselves and their Latinx heritage.

As the school became known for its open and supportive community, it began to attract students from more diverse backgrounds, including African American and LGBTQ students. This led over time to conflicts and a reevaluation of the school's priorities. The effort to affirm specific cultural identities while becoming more inclusive is an ongoing one. This ensures that the continuity of lived experiences is a present reality for students and that their daily challenges can be conceived in relation to the larger world and the experiences of others.

The third stage is global awareness, which encourages youth to practice critical reflection in order to empathize with the struggles of oppressed people throughout the world.[12] The curriculum leads to learning how to transform the world, to give back to the community. Classes include video, *bomba y plena*,[13] dance, guitar, and journalism, as well as analysis of community resources and challenges. For example, students make podcasts about the history of their school and community. Across disciplines of history, biology, English, mathematics, and others, they learn about themselves as active and responsible participants in civic life.

The PACHS curriculum can be seen as a realization of the social justice youth development model in which self-awareness, social awareness, and global awareness guide growth.[14] Students write and share reflections about work in the community as a way of learning the language. They are encouraged to think critically about their learning experiences and to participate actively in their community.

An example of the three levels in practice and in interaction arises in history class. When students are taught about Spanish imperialism in the sixteenth century, the ideas may seem very abstract. But if those same students are engaged in a community project to resist gentrification, itself a modern form of colonialism, they understand their self, their social identity, and global dynamics in a more connected way. Applying that awareness in community action furthers their understanding and embodies it.

## CONNECT LEARNING AND COMMUNITY LIFE

Paseo Boricua community leaders advocate for Puerto Rican independence, community resistance against violence, and solidarity with Puerto Ricans and other oppressed people. However, they recognize that young people, first of all, need a nurturing environment for learning.[15] Most of the students there now complete high school and many have gone on to college.

PACHS and the family learning center for young mothers and their children build instruction around students' lives. There are many factors in their success, including dedicated teachers and a curriculum relevant to students' lives. Most of all is the sense of a school community connected to a neighborhood community, with an opportunity to grow in socially meaningful ways.

Dr. Melissa Lewis, the school principal, says the school "was really founded from the needs of students. I think that's probably the strongest legacy that we have. You always center the needs of students." She adds that the school "is focused on flexibility, a healing-centered approach and meeting students where they're at."

PACHS has about 200 students, all of them learning remotely for now. They are often dealing with food and housing insecurity. Some are parents, many are working and under stress worsened by the pandemic.

Aalyah Parks, a nineteen-year-old junior, describes her situation:

> I got kicked out [of the previous school] due to my lack of interest. I was fighting a lot. I was skipping school. I wasn't really motivated. When I automatically heard Campos I was thinking bad. I thought alternative no I don't want to go to an alternative school. But it was the only option I had.

Parks said she was struggling with life at home. At school, she found guidance and support. Lewis responds: "I see you, I hear you and I'm going to do whatever I can to make this work for you because you need a high school diploma. You need to start thinking far beyond that to be successful."[16]

The success of the program has also attracted non–Puerto Rican students. One might predict this would pose a problem in Paseo Boricua, given the emphasis on strengthening Puerto Rican identity and community. But PACHS thrives on diverse interests. It now provides a successful alternative to dominant deficit models employed elsewhere and meets "the affective and cultural needs of the Puerto Rican, Mexican, and African-American students that call it their academic home."[17]

## FIND INQUIRY PROBLEMS IN DAILY LIFE

Rather than using hypothetical problems constructed from remote situations, students at PACHS find real, contemporary problems in the community to initiate learning. Examples might include water pollution, racism, economic difficulties, substance abuse, or disputes about building a rail trail. Participation in community life then becomes the hidden resource of the curriculum.

Schooling becomes more productive by shifting to a transaction mode of communication. In that case, the communication is not for the purpose of the school informing the community but for true collaboration in making new meaning. Transaction implies that the school and community do not simply send messages to one another, but collaborate to construct the message. This can lead to a mutually transforming relationship.

These activities are most effective when learning organizations work together. Community centers, clubs, museums, libraries, zoos, hospitals, workplaces, online spaces, religious organizations, and other settings, as well as schools and universities, can all be opportunities for learning. When they are connected, their impact amplifies.

In this way, community problems are not an impediment to education but a resource that leads to knowledge growth. At PACHS, community members enact this through a variety of organizations, such as the PRCC and the community newspaper, *La Voz*, which plays a central role in a participatory democracy project. Community action is supported through a healthy lifestyles program, a health center, and Batey Urbano, a club/study center for young people and a venue for social action, where they present poetry with a purpose, hip-hop, videos they have produced, and other cultural expressions.[18]

There is also collaborative work to foster the development of economic and commercial projects including a Puerto Rican–focused restaurant district. Many of these activities are designed and run by young people in the community. All of them are conceived as sites for learning for community members of all ages and for visitors as well.

## URBAN AGRICULTURE

A large, ongoing project at PACHS is an excellent example of the outside community becoming the curriculum. PACHS embodies the community school idea, as well as ideas of transformation and collaborative inquiry, to address community needs. In this case, the "seedbed" that Harry Boyte writes about has a literal meaning as well. Education becomes about transforming both ourselves and our institutions.

The project, Urban Agriculture in the Context of Social Ecology,[19] began as a way for students to address community problems, such as the high rate of diabetes (see figure 11.1). In an *Inquiry Cycle*, their initial *Ask* might be to see whether they could do something to improve the local environment. Through *Investigations* in history class, they learned why the neighborhood had become a food desert. They also learned the history of the neighborhood and why there was so little safe, outdoor space for exercise and play.

This led to a *Create* phase in which they explored various solutions. In science class, they did hands-on investigations of hydroponics and soil-based gardening. *Discussion* led to specific projects such as growing produce on a vacant lot and setting up a farmer's market. *Reflection* soon expanded to

Community as Curriculum

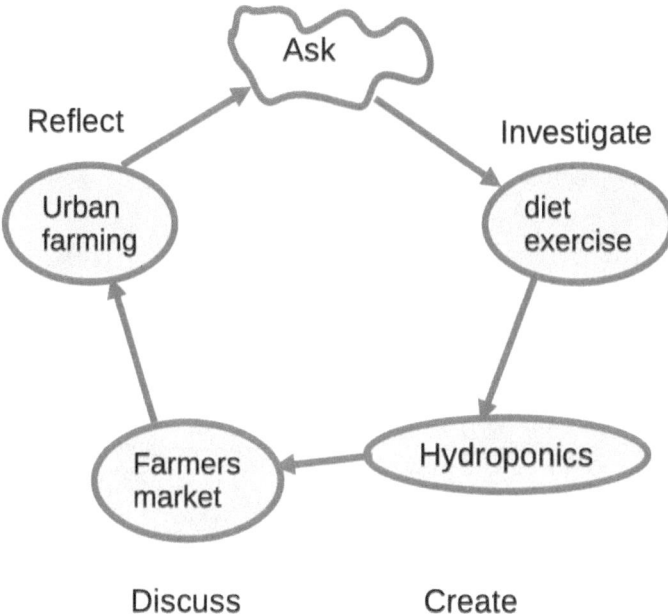

**Figure 11.1 The Inquiry Cycle for the Urban Agriculture Project.** *Source*: Author created.

include the study of urban agriculture worldwide, community wellness, and economic development, and then to more *Asks*.

As one example, students learned that there was an issue with getting fresh produce to consumers, especially to the bodegas and to invalids. Not everyone could make it to the local farmers' market. For the bodegas, they learned that they needed a packaging scheme that fit the bodegas' business model. A standard box with a mix of produce could be sold for $8 and met that need.

For invalids and those far away, they needed a delivery scheme. They saw bicycles as an environmentally friendly means for this, but to carry large loads they would need trailers. So, they learned how to build trailers out of pipes and tires. This led to a class on welding, which recalls the local history. Many Puerto Ricans came to Chicago during and after World War II to work in the pipe-fitting industry. Thus the practical effort led back to history and English classes. See figure 11.2.

As another example, students used the urban agriculture plot and hydroponics to grow the ingredients needed for *sofrito*, a sauce used as a base in cooking. These include tomatoes, onions, garlic, green bell peppers, ajíes dulces, oregano, cilantro, and other spices. Growing these and making the sauce contribute to understanding their cultural heritage. Bottling and selling the sauce furthers community economic development, as well as affords

**Figure 11.2 Students Working on the Bicycle and Trailers Program.** *Source*: Public domain.

an understanding of economics and food processing. But the project is not merely about student learning, as important as that is. It is also a central activity of the community, which is seen as a way to address issues of economic development, cultural awareness, and environmental responsibility.[20]

## LIFELONG LEARNING

Although most of the prior examples centered on the high school, the community as curriculum approach touches all ages and people both in and out of formal learning. Even preschoolers are involved in community projects and are taught that it is important to learn about their community. College students bring special experience and expertise. Retired people, including the aforementioned invalids, also have a role to play.

This is a good example of how the ideas of community schools, community college, and communiversity share a fundamental spirit, despite institutional differences. A community motto is "Live and Help Others to Live." This shows up on banners and coffee cups. It contrasts with the more common and pithier "Live and Let Live." The latter suggests that everyone is out for themselves; the former emphasizes the community as both worthy of care and as a source of strength for individuals.

## COMMUNITY AS INTELLECTUAL SPACE

Through these projects, the community is seen as a source of knowledge, not simply a place to apply what has been learned. Because it is the arena in which we make sense of the world and ourselves, community becomes the starting point for understanding the sociocultural and natural processes we experience. Thus, community becomes the entrée into the whole curriculum—the map that guides our knowledge and how we obtain it. It also reminds us how education can draw from the problems and the resources of daily life as well as give back to life.

The Paseo Boricua community in Chicago hosted an annual Community as Intellectual Space Symposium for several years.[21] One year, the theme was Critical Pedagogy: Community Building as Curriculum. The conference examined how community building and critical pedagogy can offer effective and sustainable change, locally and among collaborators as well.

There were presentations and workshops on topics such as community-based research, urban agriculture, community informatics, service learning, social-emotional learning, critical pedagogy, community health, and community archiving. There were also Batey Urbano's production of *Crime against Humanity*, screenings of original documentaries filmed on Paseo Boricua, community tours, and art exhibits.

The concept for the conference has emerged from discussions among progressive scholars and community leaders. The discussions are meant to cut across disciplines and explore cultural, social, educational, or economic intersections among various issues. An underlying aim is to bring people from a variety of occupations and perspectives to apply critical inquiry to community-wide issues.

## LEARNING SPACES AND COMMUNITIES

Students at PACHS meet together, typically on a Monday morning, to discuss their school and out-of-school experiences. Typical questions include "Are you learning?" and "If not, why not?" The answer might be that the textbook is boring or seems irrelevant. Students then take on the responsibility of finding a better text, since the goal of learning remains, even if the approach to it is mutable.

One year students complained about the history text. They were then assigned the task of finding a better one. It could be more lively or culturally relevant but needed to support learning to meet state or college requirements. By taking on a major curricular assignment, the students learned more than they would if they had been assigned any text. After reviewing several books, they chose Howard Zinn's *A People's History of the United States: 1492 to Present*.[22] Through projects such as this, the classroom becomes an incubator to engage students and teachers as active participants in democratic living, advancing critical dialogue and promoting diversity, equity, and justice.

PACHS is a member of the Alternative Schools Network (ASN) in Chicago, comprising forty-three not-for-profit, independent, and self-governing alternative schools, as well as youth and adult education organizations. It serves more than 3,500 Chicago students between the ages of sixteen and twenty-one, primarily African American and Latinx. The ASN serves students who are at risk of dropping out, have been previously incarcerated, experienced violence that interrupted their learning, or have disabilities. The ASN programs typically involve students in decision-making, as PACHS does.

PRCC also initiated Humboldt Park's Community as a Campus.[23] This cross-institutional organization seeks to transform all the schools in the area into "safe and inviting places to explore the world." In terms of structure, it connects the Roberto Clemente Community Academy and multiple elementary schools and preschools. It provides support for K-16 education in the neighborhood, framed within the International Baccalaureate model. It emphasizes family involvement and whole family learning. Housing for teachers enables them to be more a part of the community.

## NOTES

1. René Antrop-González, "'This School Is My Sanctuary': The Dr. Pedro Albizu Campos Alternative High School," Julian Samora Research Institute working paper no. 57, June 2003, University of Wisconsin–Milwaukee: 1.

2. Bertram C. Bruce, "Community as Curriculum: Nurturing the Ecosystem of Education," *Schools Studies in Education* 15, no. 1 (April 2018): 122–39; Bertram C. Bruce, *Education's Ecosystems: Learning through Life* (Lanham, MD: Rowman & Littlefield, 2020); Bertram C. Bruce, Ann Peterson Bishop, and Nama Raj Budhathoki, eds., *Youth Community Inquiry: New Media for Community and Personal Growth* (New York: Peter Lang, 2014).

3. Luis C. Moll et al., "Funds of Knowledge for Teaching: Using a Qualitative Approach to Connect Homes and Classrooms," *Theory into Practice* 31, no. 2 (October 1, 1992): 132–41; Norma Gonzalez, Luis C. Moll, and Cathy Amanti, eds., *Funds of Knowledge: Theorizing Practices in Households, Communities, and Classrooms* (New York: Routledge, 2005).

4. Dave Cormier, "Rhizomatic Education: Community as Curriculum," *Innovate: Journal of Online Education* 4, no. 5 (July 2008), http://nsuworks.nova.edu/innovate/vol4/iss5/2.

5. Bertram C. Bruce, "Community as Curriculum: Nurturing the Ecosystem of Education," *Schools Studies in Education* 15, no. 1 (April 2018): 122–39.

6. See, for example, Paulo Freire, *Pedagogy of the Oppressed* (New York: Continuum, 1970); Paulo Freire and Donald Macedo, *Literacy: Reading the Word and the World* (South Hadley, MA: Bergin & Garvey, 1987); and Liam Kane, *Popular Education and Social Change in Latin America*, 1. publ (London: LAB, Latin America Bureau, 2001).

7. Angel Villarini Jusino and Carlos Antonio Torre, "Eugenio María de Hostos, 1839–1903," in *Fifty Major Thinkers on Education: From Confucius to Dewey*, edited by Joy A. Palmer (London; New York: Routledge, 2001), 161–69.

8. This section draws on material first presented in Bertram C. Bruce, *Education's Ecosystems: Learning through Life* (Lanham, MD: Rowman & Littlefield, 2020), 87–92.

9. Angela Valenzuela, *Subtractive Schooling: U.S.-Mexican Youth and the Politics of Caring* (Albany, NY: State University of New York Press, 1999), 5.

10. Freire, *Pedagogy of the Oppressed*.

11. Laura Ruth Johnson, "Challenging 'Best Practices' in Family Literacy and Parent Education Programs: The Development and Enactment of Mothering Knowledge among Puerto Rican and Latina Mothers in Chicago," *Anthropology & Education Quarterly* 40, no. 3 (2009): 257–76.

12. Shawn Ginwright and Julio Cammarota, "New Terrain in Youth Development: The Promise of a Social Justice Approach," *Social Justice* 29, no. 4 (2002): 82–95.

13. Two percussion-driven musical traditions.

14. Jeannie Oakes and John Rogers develop similar ideas, showing that engaging K-12 students in community-based research in collaboration with universities can be a powerful mechanism for both education and social change. *Learning Power: Organizing for Education and Justice* (New York: Teachers College Press, 2006).

15. This is a good example of Nel Noddings' care theory, as in *Caring: A Feminine Approach to Ethics and Moral Education* (Berkeley, CA: University of California Press, 1984); Mark K. Smith, "Nel Noddings: The Ethics of Care and Education," *The Encyclopedia of Informal Education*, January 1, 2004.

16. Gaynor Hall, "Humboldt Park School Helping Students Who Are on Verge of Dropping Out," *WGN9 News*, March 26, 2021.

17. René Antrop-González, *Schools as Radical Sanctuaries: Decolonizing Urban Education through the Eyes of Youth of Color* (Charlotte, NC: Information Age Publishing, 2011), 106.

18. Nilda Flores-Gonzalez, Matthew Rodriguez, and Michael Rodriguez-Muniz, "From Hip-Hop to Humanization: Batey Urbana as a Space for Latino Youth Culture and Community Action," in *Beyond Resistance! Youth Activism and Community Change*, edited by Shawn Ginwright, Pedro Noguera, and Julio Cammarota (New York: Routledge, 2006), 175–96.

19. Michelle L. Torrise, "Role of the Library Media Specialist in Greening the Curriculum: A Community-Based Approach to Teaching 21st Century Skills Outside of the School Library through the Practice of Urban Agriculture," *Library Media Connection* 28, no. 4 (February 2010): 18–20.

20. Bertram C. Bruce and Naomi Bloch, "Pragmatism and Community Inquiry: A Case Study of Community-Based Learning," *Education and Culture: The Journal of the John Dewey Society* 29, no. 1 (2013): 27–45; Mihye Won and Bertram C. Bruce, "Community as Curriculum: Dewey's Theory of Inquiry in the Context of an Urban Agriculture Project," in *Teaching and Learning in Urban Agricultural Community Contexts*, edited by Isha DeCoito et al. (Amsterdam: Springer, 2021).

21. Alejandro Luis Molina and Ann Peterson Bishop, "Community as Intellectual Space: Preliminary Program," June 14, 2005. A fiftieth anniversary event is now being planned.

22. Howard Zinn, *A People's History of the United States: 1492 to Present* (New York: Harper Collins, 2010).

23. Community Action Council of Humboldt Park Chicago, "Greater Humboldt Park 'Community as a Campus' Executive Summary," August 8, 2014, https://prcc-chgo.org/blog/2014/10/29/community-as-campus/.

# Conclusion
## "Walk Beside" versus "Talk To"

> Universal education through schooling is not feasible. It would be no more feasible if it were attempted by means of alternative institutions built on the style of present schools. . . . The current search for new educational *funnels* must be reversed into the search for their institutional inverse: educational *webs* which heighten the opportunity for each one to transform each moment of his living into one of learning, sharing, and caring.
>
> —Ivan Illich, *Deschooling Society*[1]

Learning beyond the walls, exemplifying Illich's webs, includes not only the workplace learning lauded by James Gannon in *Teacher's Pet* but also learning in many other real and virtual spaces, from early childhood to senior learning, individual and collective endeavors, free form or connected to schools, universities, libraries, and other organizations. Can beyond-the-walls learning be connected to formal education, especially that of the sort represented by Erica Stone, Gannon's counterpart? That would aid her efforts to make classroom learning engaged, relevant, and connected to real-world experience. Moreover, classroom learning can help to make sense of daily life experiences.

But individual teachers can only do so much. To bring together the classroom and daily life, we need an educational system that does that as well. That requires a kind of communication between the academy and the community that is flexible, equitable, and open to the co-construction of new ideas. It needs to be built upon Jane Addams's idea of walking beside, not simply that of talking to.

## STULTIFIED PEDAGOGY

Our schooling system has stultified. Observers from diverse corners report that it does not meet their expectations. Employers see the need for "twenty-first-century skills," not just coding and fluency with information technology. Learning defined by well-structured syllabi and well-ordered problem sets may be useful up to a point, but ultimately it is poor preparation for a world in which disruptive technologies change the rules of the game on a regular basis, and where everyday problem-solving depends on knowledge created after the textbooks were written.

The so-called twenty-first-century skills include the ability to communicate across cultural and national boundaries, the experience of following through on complex, challenging projects, and the ability to find problems within a messy space of possibilities, not just to solve well-defined problems with answers known in advance. We should call these skills multi-century, since they have been relevant ever since *Homo sapiens* could think.

Educators are frustrated as well. Outcomes-based evaluation, accreditation programs, and departmental reviews all push toward replicating a system that is obviously out-of-date and disconnected from the outside world. But it violates departmental norms to step outside the familiar patterns of teaching. Field trips, practica, and other beyond-the-walls experiences have become almost impossible to manage.

Policy makers wrongly expect education to solve all of society's problems; politicians use it as a convenient scapegoat. But formal education alone does little to address human-caused climate disruption, environmental destruction, endemic racism, economic inequality, global violence, misinformation, or other general concerns. Whatever education is doing, it seems not to be working on the things that matter to the larger public.

Above all, students are frustrated. Children in elementary school turn off of schooling when it should be the most fun. They learn all too soon the falsehood that they are not good at math, or English, or science. Secondary students drop out or sit in the classroom without any meaningful engagement with a curriculum that does not speak to their world.

At upper education levels, students long ago abandoned any hopes of general education, but they do not see the immediate job benefits either. They accumulate ever-greater debt only to find that their career preparation was off-kilter, out-of-date, or not what the job market needs today. There are dropouts, alienation, and general inability to see the meaning or relevance of what they are expected to study.

The general problem is that education is a self-perpetuating system, preparing early childhood students for elementary school, elementary students for secondary school, and so on. The students who succeed are happy or, at least, compliant with being integrated into that logic. They are taught not to think about what is missing outside the present system.

This is not just a problem for job preparation. It is also a challenge for democratic education. Where and how can students learn to become critical, socially engaged citizens? In the foreword to Paulo Freire's *Pedagogy of the Oppressed*, Richard Shaull observes that education is never neutral. It

> either functions as an instrument that is used to facilitate the integration of the younger generation into the logic of the present system and bring about conformity to it, or it becomes 'the practice of freedom,' the means by which men and women deal critically and creatively with reality and discover how to participate in the transformation of their world.[2]

Shaull and Freire seek an education in which people are able to confront the realities of their lives in order to bring about an intelligent transformation of those realities. Learning through texts is crucially linked to making sense of the world and acting within it.

## WHY WE NEED LEARNING BEYOND THE WALLS

We need learning beyond the walls because, as Illich says, "Universal education through schooling is not feasible." The system is designed to communicate and reinforce its logic, not to undermine that. It is transmission pedagogy. Connecting with the community, with the world of work, and with people in diverse settings does not guarantee that students can resist conforming to "the logic of the present system," nor does it mean that they automatically "deal critically and creatively with reality," much less transform their world, but it at least opens the door to a more engaged sense of community and self.

The good news is that learning beyond the walls works. As discussed earlier, when asked about their most meaningful learning experiences, few people cite some classroom lessons or even extended school-based units, even though some of these are very good. Even when they cite that formal activity, they point to the culminating activity—the trip to the planetarium or zoo, the community project, the building of a pioneer cabin, the mythology newspaper—as a memorable, life-changing experience.

For many of us, it is these experiences that we recall, orient our lives around, and upon which we build our foundation for further learning. They are different for each of us: one of these experiences might have been being advised by a caring supervisor at work, another planting a large tree at summer camp, meeting a researcher at the zoo and getting to interact with an exotic animal close up, working as an aide in a mental institution, going on a rare field trip to the beach, learning about an event of local lore that had been covered up or distorted in the official reports, and being introduced to a book excluded from the school curriculum. An experience such as one of these can hold a value unmatched by hours of classroom lessons.

People often refer to social interaction with a friend or relative, to a summer experience, to a hobby or club, to a valued mentor. The personal, emotional, and social bonds are what matters. Learning beyond the walls, amplified or extended through formal learning, is the key. Research-based evidence corroborates these individual experiences, especially in terms of promoting equitable education.[3]

## INTEGRATING CLASSROOM AND DAILY LIFE

Traditional skills and bits of knowledge are acquired equally well in an integrated learning approach, one which expands beyond the classroom. This can be seen in one of the best program evaluation studies ever conducted, the Eight-Year Study, based on research conducted between 1932 and 1940 by the Progressive Education Association.[4] Thirty high schools participated. Rather than focus on narrowly defined subjects, the most progressive schools emphasized broad themes of significance. "The starting point of the curriculum would be life as the student saw it." Moreover, the schools were community-based. "The schools believed they belonged to the citizens of the community."[5]

The students from the experimental schools performed slightly better on standardized test scores, but they showed major improvement in other areas, including intellectual competence, cultural development, practical competence, philosophy of life, character traits, emotional balance, social fitness, sensitivity to social problems, and physical fitness. Students from the most progressive schools showed the most improvement, more than those in the somewhat-progressive schools, and much more than those in traditional schools.

Outcomes of the study included better forms of student assessment, innovative research techniques, new ideas for curriculum, instruction, and teacher education. But above all, it provided an answer to a basic question: Is it possible to help the whole child develop, without losing basic skills? The answer is clearly yes.

The Eight-Year Study provides a blueprint for *eudaimonia* (or human flourishing), in which the individual student grows along every dimension.[6] In fact, education can be conceived in such a way that teachers and community members flourish as well.[7] Focusing on growth rather than on perceived deficits helps to develop the things almost every parent, teacher, student, or citizen truly values. Eudaimonia can also apply to the academy itself, or to the community. When they are in a transactive relationship, both become healthier and more productive.

## WALKING BESIDE

Classroom learning is always connected with daily life; there is no way to isolate one set of those experiences in school or college as standing in the way of their joy in life. Educators worry that daily life intrudes on "real learning." But when that connection is enriched, both classroom learning and daily life benefit.

There are many perspectives on extending education beyond the walls: community governance, extension, service, charity, outreach, and public engagement. Regardless of the terminology, the process should be treated as seriously as the research and teaching missions of the academy. This means providing adequate funding and seeking ways to certify outreach and community-based experiences so that they acquire the same validity as classroom or online learning. More importantly, it means working in a fully transactive manner that supports mutually transformative relationships, shifting from a "talking to" approach to one of "walking beside."

Culturally responsive teaching is one such effort to walk beside, to recognize that life outside the school is primary.[8] Place-based education is another such recognition.[9] Unfortunately, there is often great resistance to these approaches. For example, many states have introduced or enacted policies to ban educators from critically examining race and racism in the classroom.

Field trips can be another walking beside approach, especially when they support deep learning through experience.[10] But the frequency and length of field trips have declined, even more so with the pandemic. The difficulties of planning, liability issues, and the press of high-stakes testing have stood in the way.

We should recognize that online education in various forms is a vital, if not dominant, force within education today. However, we must reject the notion of online learning as limited to *online substitution*. It can be so much more. In Illich's terms, we should seek ways to expand the webs of education and not force everything into an ever-narrowing funnel.

Similarly, learning through work must be seen as a central part of the education process. We need better ways to certify field trips, museums, libraries, community centers, practica, internships, work experiences, clinical training, and other non-classroom forms of learning. This implies that the school is more than one among many activities in our society; it is, or can become, the social center of the community.[11] Community schools today fulfill many aspects of that function, but they are underfunded, and the work they do for the community is often seen as ancillary to the primary education function. We need to support and expand community schools. But most public schools are already underfunded. Support for engaging with the community rarely exists.

A large percentage of the students in postsecondary education in the United States attend community colleges. These colleges align their teaching with the needs of the community, and they also carry out significant outreach or public engagement roles. Community college education should be fully funded and free for all students, just as high school is today.

Comprehensive approaches to building a communiversity, such as we see in the work at King's College, Nepal, or Paseo Boricua, Chicago, ought to be supported, diversified, and expanded to meet a wide variety of needs. We need to nurture ongoing efforts and develop better models for others to follow.

Finally, making a commitment to expanding our capacity for democratic education is long overdue. We need first to work toward understanding the system we have created and then to understand how to make it work better, not simply point out its flaws. Spinoza reminds us to focus on understanding: "I have labored carefully, not to mock, lament, or execrate human actions, but to understand them." That understanding must involve not only abstract facts and logic but also concrete realities of daily life and "passions, such as love, hatred, anger, envy, ambition, pity, and the other perturbations of the mind."[12]

The understanding that Spinoza seeks cannot grow by simply talking to the other; nor can it be achieved by talking with. Instead, it requires *walking beside*. This applies to ordinary communication, to pedagogy, and to the relationship between the academy and community life. Walking beside enables understanding what the classroom is and how it fits into our historically constituted social, political, and economic systems, as well as into the vital life of the community.

Education calls on all the passions: "love, hatred, anger, envy, ambition, pity, and the other perturbations." But these are constrained by enormous societal and economic pressures, even buried by them. Perhaps this book can enhance understanding of what the classroom and daily life mean. Building on that understanding, we need action-based work deriving from daily life experience to develop the courage to make difficult changes, changes that can shape a better life for all.

## WHAT DO WE NEED TO DO?

A form of learning beyond the walls may be forced upon us. The decline in support for public education, the rise of digital credentialing, and an overly ample supply of racism and classism in the society may conspire to end public, place-based education as we know it. The communal function of education will then be lost. At that point, both the physical and the virtual walls will be gone, so all learning will be beyond the walls, whether we like it or not.

Can we generate a renewed commitment to democratic education? Although far from perfect in execution, the public education vision in the United States, and in many other countries around the world, has always at least claimed to promote values including, but going beyond, learning specific skills for further education and ultimately a paying job.

There has been an underlying principle of universal, democratic education throughout US history. Although far from fully realized, the principle has persisted, leading to models adopted around the world. During the days of Horace Mann, education came to be seen as an almost universal right. The Civil War led to initial education rights for blacks. The land-grant colleges opened higher education up to working classes. Community colleges offered multiple educational paths, conveniently located for affordable study. The GI Bill further expanded college education. The Brown decision said that "separate but equal" was not enough. Each of these changes had its limitations, but together they have opened up the possibilities for universal, democratic education.

There are various formulations of what that means, but it usually includes that students should have the opportunity to:

1 Learn through real-life problems, projects, and questions
2 Nourish awe of nature and life
3 Develop respect for diversity in all its forms
4 Learn how to communicate and collaborate across differences
5 Develop a critical, socially engaged intelligence
6 Grow an interest in lifelong learning, reading, thinking, and questioning
7 Understand the perspectives of others
8 Become not only good learners but also good people
9 Learn with and from one another in a caring community
10 Learn that interdependence is as valuable as independence
11 Locate oneself in widening circles of care, expanding from self, friends, and family, neighborhood, and country, to global awareness and care.[13]

These things cannot be taught in an abstract way through an online app; they need to be experienced in concert with others. Specifically, students need the opportunity to learn democratic education by participating in it directly. They need the right to participate in choices regarding everyday life and to share in the decision-making of their schools.[14] That is why democratic schools and teaching democracy are one and the same.

# NOTES

1. Ivan Illich, *Deschooling Society* (New York: Harper & Row, 1971), iv–v.
2. Richard Shaull, "Foreword," in *Paulo Freire, Pedagogy of the Oppressed* (New York: Continuum, 1970), 29–34: 34.
3. Anna Maier and Julia Daniel, "Community Schools: An Evidence-Based Strategy for Equitable School Improvement. Learning Policy Institute National Education Policy Center" (Boulder, CO: National Education Policy Center, 2017), nter. Retrieved [date] from http://nepc.colorado.edu/publication/equitable-community-schools.
4. Wilford M. Aikin, *The Story of the Eight-Year Study* (New York: Harper, 1942); Charles C. Ritchie, "The Eight-Year Study: Can We Afford to Ignore It?" *Educational Leadership*, February 1, 1971, 1–4.
5. Agnes E. Benedict, *Dare Our Secondary Schools Face the Atomic Age?* (New York: Hinds, Hayden and Eldredge, 1947), 17.
6. Veronika Huta, "Eudaimonia," in *Oxford Handbook of Happiness*, edited by S. David, I. Boniwell, and A. C. Ayers (Oxford, UK: Oxford University Press, 2013), 201–13.
7. In *The Good Life of Teaching: An Ethics of Professional Practice* (John Wiley & Sons, 2011), Chris Higgins talks of the importance of supporting eudaimonia for teachers if we want them to help students flourish.
8. Geneva Gay, *Culturally Responsive Teaching: Theory, Research, and Practice*, electronic resource, third edition, Multicultural Education Series (New York, NY: Teachers College Press, 2018).
9. David Sobel, *Place-Based Education: Connecting Classrooms and Communities*, 2nd ed., Nature Literacy Series (Great Barrington, MA: Orion Society, 2013); Sonya N. Martin, "Critical Pedagogy of Place: A Framework for Understanding Relationships Between People in (Contested) Shared Places," in *Cultural Studies and Environmentalism: The Confluence of EcoJustice, Place-Based (Science) Education, and Indigenous Knowledge Systems*, edited by Deborah J. Tippins et al., Cultural Studies of Science Education (Dordrecht: Springer Netherlands, 2010), 257–68.
10. Heidi H. Erickson, Angela R. Watson, and Jay P. Greene, "An Experimental Evaluation of Culturally Enriching Field Trips," *Journal of Human Resources*, February 4, 2022; Salvatore Vascellaro, *Out of the Classroom and into the World: Learning from Field Trips, Educating from Experience, and Unlocking the Potential of Our Students and Teachers* (New York: Bank Street College of Education, 2011).
11. John Dewey, "The School as Social Centre," MW 2: 80–93.
12. Benedict de Spinoza, 1677, *Tractatus Politicus*, translated by A. H. Gosset (1883), https://www.files.ethz.ch/isn/125506/5038_Spinoza_A_Political _Treatise.pdf.
13. Alfie Kohn, "Progressive Education: Why It's Hard to Beat, but Also Hard to Find," *Independent School*, April 1–9, 2008.
14. "What Is Democratic Education? – EUDEC," n.d., *European Democratic Education Community* (blog), https://eudec.org/democratic-education/what-is-democratic-education/ (accessed September 5, 2021).

# Glossary

*academy*: an organization incorporating usually accredited, formal learning. Examples include schools, colleges, universities, training institutes, and corporate training. The narrow meaning of *academy* is often restricted to a private high school or to a college in which special subjects or skills are taught. The use here is much broader, designed to apply to all organizations devoted to formal instruction, including pre- and elementary schools, college, universities, and corporate training. Much of the discussion in the book applies to both K-12 and college education.

*classroom learning*: formal instruction in co-located sessions, for example, lectures, discussions, seminars, tutorials, and hands-on activities.

*clinical training*: hands-on experience that replicates or simulates actual on-the-job work, for example, an elementary school field trip, CPR using a volunteer person or a dummy, supervised practice teaching, engineering teamwork on a project.

*community*: acknowledging the diverse meanings of "community," the examples here tend to imply place-based communities, with associated industry and agriculture, leisure activities, and more, essentially the life outside the academy. In most cases, these are also what Anthony Cohen calls communities of meaning, essentially what participants deem them to be.[1]

*community as curriculum*: posits learning as a lifelong process and part of everyday affairs in life. The community is seen not as surrounding context or a place to apply ideas but as the intellectual space from which knowledge and problems emerge and which is the ultimate recipient of new knowledge.

*community school*: a place and a set of partnerships connecting a school, families, and the surrounding community; an integrated focus on academics, youth development, family support, health and social services, and community development.[2]

*communiversity*: a venue for learning across and through the disciplines, building on local funds of knowledge, such as arts and culture of the community, local industry, and experiences of participants, as well as more formal expertise. It combines the best of community with the best of the academy. Its use in this book extends beyond offering noncredit courses to community members or college-prep experiences.

*credential (digital)*: a formal, widely accepted indicator of accomplishment or skill that can be displayed, accessed, and verified (online). Examples include driver's license, passport, credit card, training course completion certificate, certificate of proficiency with a computer language or a foreign language, and music performance exam certificate.

*credential process*: the process whereby credentials are authorized. For example, a high school certifying that a student has graduated based on courses taken on campus, or the GED Testing Service doing the same for study online or in a GED course and tests passed at the testing center.

*doxa*: the domain of opinion, belief, or probable knowledge represented in conventional practices; contrasts with episteme, the domain of true knowledge; in education it refers to self-evident assumptions such as that schools should certify learning (regardless of the validity of that assumption).

*eudaimonia*: literally "good spirit"; commonly translated as happiness, welfare, or flourishing; implies a growth model of pedagogy.

*experiential learning*: emphasizes learning from primary experience, especially sense experiences.

*guild*: organizations of workers in various occupations; controls entry to the field, ranks, promotion, and licensure. For example, a medical society that specifies who can work as a doctor and which subfields that person can operate in; a carpenters' union that specifies who can work as a union carpenter based on apprenticeship program. The term is used here in a broader than standard way. It usually means an association of persons of the same trade or pursuits, formed to protect mutual interests and maintain standards. Here, that definition is broadened to any society or organization that controls entry and advancement through some credentialing system.

*inquiry cycle*: a systemization of the process of inquiry, including elements of question asking, investigation, creation, discussion, and reflection.

*inquiry unit*: a web-based data structure in which users can represent elements of the Inquiry Cycle.

*interaction mode of communication*: a model of communication that emphasizes the context and feedback around the communication of a message.

*interaction pedagogy*: teaching and learning conceived in terms of the teacher sending knowledge into the student's mind, with possibilities for feedback.
*online augmentation*: use of new information and communication technologies to amplify or extend other modes of learning in the classroom or beyond.
*online learning*: the possibly expansive use of online tools for learning, such as open education resources; databases; simulations; probes, cameras, and scanning instruments; tools for writing; mobile devices; virtual reality; spreadsheets; graphing devices; messaging services; planning tools; and crowd sourcing.
*online substitute* (or *online replicant*): use of new information and communication technologies to partially replicate or substitute for classroom learning. Examples include learning management systems, discussion forums, online lectures, and resource sites. This is a new term for the kind of online learning that we see so much of now during the pandemic.
*quasi-academy*: allied institution to the academy, often with a scholarly mandate, but usually not with formal courses and accreditation. Examples include libraries, museums, research institutes, archives, field stations, summer institutes, Americorps, hospitals, community centers, boys and girls clubs, prisons, and many more.
*school as a social center*: the school as the active and organized promotion of the latent richness of the surrounding community, including the intangible things of art, science, and other modes of social intercourse.
*social justice youth development model*: a methodology in which self-awareness, social awareness, and global awareness guide growth.
*third mission*: adding to the usual missions of teaching and research, the third mission is usually conceived as service, community, or public engagement.
*transaction mode of communication*: a model of communication that emphasizes the co-construction of meaning, often in situations where there is no a priori message to send. The use in this book refers to a communicative action or activity involving two parties that reciprocally affect or influence one another through the co-construction of meaning.
*transaction pedagogy*: teaching and learning conceived in terms of co-construction of meaning.
*transmission mode of communication*: a model of communication that emphasizes the construction and sending of a message in a possibly noisy environment.
*transmission pedagogy*: teaching and learning conceived in terms of the teacher sending knowledge into the student's mind; what Freire calls the banking model.

## NOTES

1. Anthony P. Cohen, *The Symbolic Construction of Community* (New York: Routledge, 1985).
2. Martin J. Blank, Reuben Jacobson, and Atelia Melaville, "Achieving Results Through Community School Partnerships," Center for American Progress, January 2012: 1.

# Index

Bold numbers indicate the page defining a term.

4-H, 41, 43n19

academy, 183; place-based. *See* learning, classroom
accountability, xi, 51–54
Addams, Jane, xxix, 10, 95, 113–15, 138–39, 151, 160, 175
agriculture, 24, 149–55, 168–71
Alaska, xv–xvi, 64
Alternative Schools Network (ASN), 172
Arthurdale School, 115–18

Berea College, 136–37
*The Brothers Karamazov*, 34–36

Çaba-Çam, 109–10, 122–23
Cambridge, Massachusetts, x, 86
Canada, 96, 100–101
Çanakkale, Turkey, 122–23
caring, xxviii, 122, 136–39, 165, 167, 175
Chicago, Illinois, xvi, 51, 104, 113–14, 159–61, 164–72
civic intelligence, xvi, 26, 136
Clapp, Elsie Ripley, 115–18
climate, xxx–xxxi, 48, 82

clinical training, 25, 65–68, **183**
colonialism, xv, 166
communication, models of: interaction, 6–16, 25, 78, 84, 95–96, 125, **184**; transaction, xi, xxxi, 9–16, 25–27, 35, 76, 78, 84, 127, **185**; transmission, xi, 4–16, 25, 78, 84, 95, 125, **185**
community: as curriculum, xvi, 16, 37, 125, 153–62, **173**; modes of. *See* communication, models of
community college, 95, 127, 160, 170
community engagement, 14–16, 93–98, 103, 123, 128, 137–50
community school, xxv, 53, 105–16, 127, 158, **173**
communiversity, 81–82, 96, 99, 113, 123–31, 134–37, 147, 160, 170, **174**
constructivism, 38, 103, 185
conversation, 5–7, 13–14, 101, 122, 152
credential, 65–70, 104, **184**
critical, socially engaged intelligence, 45, 148, 163, 177, 181
critical thinking. *See* critical, socially engaged intelligence

Dewey, John, xi, xxi–xxvi, 3, 37–39, 47, 109, 115, 132
dialogue, xxix–xxxi, 1, 9, 11, 15, 19, 34, 76, 86–88, 128, 172
*doxa*, 66, **184**

ecosystem, xxx, 42, 109
education: banking model of, 156, **185**; bricks model of, 3, 24–25; crisis in, 45–59, 63–75; de-colonizing, 156–57; democratic, 46, 72–73, 114, 132–33, 177, 180–81; deschooling, 175; kindling fire model of, 33–34, 83–84; one-room schools, 111–13; progressive, x, xvi, 39, 178; small schools, 121–22; transmission, 24–26, 36, 78, 177, **185**; webs, 92, 175–79
Egypt, 49
Eight-Year Study, x, 178
ethical knowing, xxix–xxxi, 87
eudaimonia, xxvii–xxviii, 168–69, **184**
experiment, x, xvi, 11, 31, 115, 144, 178

field station, 134–35
finance, 54–56
Frames Film Project, 97n2, 100–101
Freire, Paulo, 160, 163–72, 177

Gandhi, Mahatma, 41–42
Gary, Indiana, 26
grading, ix–x, 24–25, 178
guild, 23, 66, **184**

Heidegger, Martin, 151–52
Highlander School, 119–21
Homestead Act, 111–13, 124n2
homestead assistance project, 117–18
Hull-House, 113–14

Illich, Ivan, 92, 175–79
*iNaturalist*, 83, 91–92
India, 22, 41, 147
indigenous, xv, 24, 86, 120

inequality, 47–48, 74n12, 176
information spaces, 32n3
inquiry cycle, 168–69, **184**
Integrated Course, xvi, 149–56
internship, 65, 101–2, 119–20, 134, 179

King's College, Nepal, 103, 145–46, 149–56, 180

LAB Studio, 39, 102–3
land-grant insititutions, 24, 64, 107, 138, 181
learning: classroom, xiv, xxii, 25, 58, 65–73, 78–79, 81, 128, 136–39, 172, **183**; expeditionary, **39**; experiential, 33, 39–40, **184**; hard knocks, xxii–xxv; mobile, 76, 84, 91; online, 37, 49, 65–92, **185**; problem-based, 102–3, 132–33, 149–56; project-based, 149–56; rhizomatic, 163; in the wild, 75–76, 87–92
LEEP online master's program, 69–70
liberal arts colleges, xxvi, 54, 63–64, 73, 136–37
library, xviin3, 23, 29–31, 45, 89–91, 115, 121, 159–61

madrasa, 22
makerspace, xvi
Mann, Horace, 45, 181
Metropolitan Council for Educational Opportunity (Metco), 57–59
museum, xiii, 23, 25, 38, 58, 164, 168–69
mutually transforming relationships, xvi, xxix, 10, 168, 179

Nepal, xvi–xvii, 105n12, 145–57
New American Baccalaureate Project, **137**

Oakland, California, 121–22

Parkland Community College, 128–29
Paseo Boricua, xvi, 159–72

Pedro Albizu Campos High School (PACHS), 159–72
Physics Van, 133–35
planetarium, 82, 128, 177
Plutarch, 33–35
problem solving. *See* learning, problem-based
Progressive Education Association, x, 178–79
psychiatry, xxvii
Puerto Rican Cultural Center. *See* Paseo Boricua

Quill, xv–xvii

racism, xiii, xxix, 46, 73, 109–10, 164, 176, 179, 181
Romania, 30–32

school as social center, 40, 117, 168, 179, **185**
social justice, 40, 109, 120, 132, 165–66
social justice youth development model, 165–66, **185**
social network, 77, 87–91, 164
Sophist, 20
South Africa, 41, 143, 147
STEM, 30, 37, 50

talking to, 4, 175–81
*Teacher's Pet*, xxii–xxvi, 4–11, 19–20, 25, 175
Technology Competencies Database (TCD), 68
telehealth, 86–87
third mission, 107–8, 132–37, **185**
tools for learning, xviin3, 56, 87–91, 137, 185
transaction. *See* communication, models of, transaction
transactive. *See* communication, models of, transaction

University of Pennsylvania, 132–33

walking beside, 9, 175–81
*West Side Story*, 50
West Valley College, 101–2
*Whole Earth Catalog*, 56
whole person, 41–42
Wikipedia, 78, 89–90
work, 95–97
writing to learn, ix, 89–91

Youth Community Inquiry (YCI), xvi, 96

# About the Author

**Bertram C. Bruce**'s recent books include *Thinking with Maps: Understanding the World through Spatialization* (2021), *Education's Ecosystems: Learning through Life* (2020), *Démocratie et éthique sociale* (2019), *Progressive Education in Nepal: The Community is the Curriculum* (2018), *International Handbook of Progressive Education* (2015), and *Youth Community Inquiry: New Media for Community and Personal Growth* (2014).

His writing contributes to a tradition of democratic education. It asks "How can we guide the educational enterprise by an ethical vision, not simply a technocratic one of transmitting isolated facts and skills?" It applies a philosophical perspective to direct work with communities in many countries throughout the world. He is currently a professor emeritus in Information Sciences at the University of Illinois. He holds a PhD in Computer Science (1971) from the University of Texas at Austin and a BA in Biology (1968) from Rice University.

www.ingramcontent.com/pod-product-compliance
Lightning Source LLC
Chambersburg PA
CBHW022012300426
44117CB00005B/145